GANGSTERS VS NAZIS

HOW JEWISH MOBSTERS BATTLED NAZIS IN WARTIME AMERICA

MICHAEL BENSON

CITADEL PRESS
Kensington Publishing Corp.
www.kensingtonbooks.com

CITADEL PRESS BOOKS are published by

Kensington Publishing Corp.
900 Third Avenue
New York, NY 10022

All Kensington titles, imprints, and distributed lines are available at special quantity discounts for bulk purchases for sales promotions, premiums, fund-raising, educational, or institutional use.

Special book excerpts or customized printings can also be created to fit specific needs. For details, write or phone the office of the Kensington sales manager: Kensington Publishing Corp., 900 Third Avenue, New York, NY 10022, attn: Sales Department; phone 1-800-221-2647.

CITADEL PRESS and the Citadel logo are Reg. U.S. Pat. & TM Off.

First Citadel hardcover printing: May 2022

ISBN: 978-0-8065-4180-8
First trade paperback printing: August 2024

ISBN: 978-0-8065-4181-5 (e-book)

10 9 8 7 6 5 4 3 2 1

Printed in the United States of America

For Keith Brenner

AUTHOR'S NOTE

This book is a work of nonfiction. It depicts actual events as truthfully as can be verified by research. Dialogue and actions consistent with these historical figures have been supplemented, and chronology has been adjusted in some instances to smooth the narrative flow.

CONTENTS

INTRODUCTION
The Sock on the Jaw

*So we raided the joint. We went over there
and grabbed everything in sight, all their
bullshit signs, and smacked the shit out of
them, broke them up the best we could.
Nobody could pay me for this work. It was
my patriotic duty.*
—MICKEY COHEN, 1938

I've been a comic-book fan since the days when they cost only twelve cents apiece, which would be the midsixties. Back then, six empty Coke bottles for a comic book was an even trade at the corner store. I've collected them, studied their history, and marveled at their adaptations into blockbuster summer movies.

So, I can state with confidence that the greatest comic-book cover in the history of the art form is *Captain America Comics* #1 drawn by Joe Simon and Jack Kirby. The comic was a product of Timely Comics, which would later change its name to Marvel.

Cover dated March 1941, *CAC* #1 hit newsstands a week before Christmas 1940. The date is important because it is close to a year *before* Pearl Harbor and the United States' forced entry into the Second World War. In 1940, Adolf Hitler had just about conquered Europe and was bombing military and civilian targets in Great Britain. Jews were being brutalized and killed. Hitler's Italian allies had military control of the northern portion of Africa, and the Japanese had conquered large chunks of Asia and the islands of the Pacific. But there were still many in America who felt the country had no dog in the fight. American fascists argued that Hitler had the right idea because "Jewish bankers" and "Jewish communists" were behind the Great Depression that had painted 1930s America a dingy gray.

The bright red, white, and blue Captain America, as it turned out, was having none of that. Cap was the formerly puny Steve Rogers of Brooklyn, New York, who had been transformed by scientists wielding hypodermic needles into a supersoldier, a human being single-handedly capable of giving the Axis powers shaky knees.

The cover of *CAC* #1 was Cap's introduction to the youth of America. It showed him bursting into Hitler's inner sanctum, coolly deflecting Nazi bullets from several guards with his star-spangled shield and planting a devastating right cross onto Hitler's jaw.

The meaning was clear. The evil Nazis needed gats, but even armed, they were no match for a knuckle sandwich dished out by a red-blooded American boy.

Of course, it was a dreamland, a pleasant fantasy for boys who might one day see action in the service of their country. But in some cities in America during the 1930s and the Great Depression, punching Nazis was a reality. And though none of the punchers wore a star-spangled costume and some of the punchers might not have seemed the type, they were all superheroes.

Since the end of World War II and the reveal of the Holocaust's horrors, the predominant images of Jews versus Nazis were photographs of the liberation of the concentration camps, the starved Jewish men and women and children who'd survived—and the dead, the uncountable dead.

Though we must never forget that nightmare, lest it happen again, I submit this additional volume to the Jews versus Nazis story, a volume in which tough American gangsters—like Meyer Lansky, Longie Zwillman, Sparky Rubenstein, Mickey Cohen, Abraham "Kid Twist" Reles, Buggsy Goldstein, and Harry "Pittsburgh Phil" Strauss—along with journalists like Herb Brin and prizefighters Barney Ross, Nat Arno, Abie Bain, and Puddy Hinkes saw the evil of the Nazi menace during the late 1930s and, as would Captain America, socked it on the jaw.

This is the story of those epic fights between Hitler's American armies—one known as the Amerikadeutscher Volksbund, or the German American Bund, and another as the Silver Legion—and those who took on those uniformed storm troopers in fisticuffs and battle royal brawls, an army of patriots composed of Jewish-Americans, demonstrating from coast to coast that a Nazi, too, could have problems.

While most Americans did not know the extent of Hitler's systemic genocide until after World War II, America's Jewish communities knew that large-scale bad things were happening. In America, Jewish communities received letters from their European relatives that described the rounding up of Jews, with no one returning home.

So when a Jewish man heard the anti-Semitic slanders of the Nazi sympathizers, he knew where that hate speech was headed. Responding with violence didn't bother his conscience.

Make no mistake. The gangsters in this book are the good guys. To help explain why, we turn to Myron Sugerman, the son of Barney Sugerman, who fought Nazis on the mean streets of Newark, New Jersey. Myron grew up with these guys, and in 2016, he told Robert Wiener of *New Jersey Jewish News* about the Nazi wars during the Depression. For him, the stories of hoods busting Nazi noses were bedtime stories.

Myron rejected the notion that his father or any of the others could be considered a villain in any way. *Gangsters*. It was just a word. The word should have been *survivors*.

"If a Palestinian Jew was born in Newark, he'd be a gangster," Myron said matter-of-factly.

The Jewish mob has done the world a hell of a lot of good. It was instrumental in the creation of Israel. If there'd been a Jewish mob in Germany in 1923 during the Beer Hall Putsch, "They'd've shot Hitler, and history would have been a hell of a lot different."

For the ghetto of Newark, the Jewish mob was like the police. If the *goyim* came in looking to pick on Jews, the real police weren't going to do anything about it. The gangsters were the protectors.

"They beat up the Nazis and eventually got rid of them," Myron recalled.

PREAMBLE
Fade In

It is important to non-Jews as well as to Jews. Any nation which permits a minority to live in fear of persecution is a nation which invites disaster.
—Professor L. B. Namier

Fade in.

Time: July 1938, 9:00 P.M.

Exterior: An assembly hall in Depression-era America. From inside, we hear the muffled sounds of laughter and shouting. A party. Perhaps a celebration. For an instant, we see a small cluster of men outside the hall, faces darkened with burnt cork, maybe a dozen of them, dressed in dark clothes and clinging to the shadows. They move with silent steps. A tracking shot takes us through a side window for a peek inside the hall, where we see what has to be eight hundred Nazis, with their Hitler haircuts and Hitler uniforms, crammed in like riders on a rush-hour subway car, sweating through their brown shirts in the stifling heat. Though perspiring plentifully, they remain kempt to the extreme. We see a close-up of a swastika pin on one man's brown lapel.

Interior: We see the Nazis in greater detail now, a montage of faces, ruddy and dim. The men speak in guttural voices, loud with inebriation and emboldened by

their numbers. Some wave around copies of <u>Mein Kampf</u>
as if they are magic swords.

Along the rear wall, behind the podium, hangs a red
banner with a black swastika on it. Beside it,
slightly smaller and hung lower, is Old Glory, the
Stars and Stripes of the United States of America.

A uniformed man stands at a lectern, trying in vain
to call the boisterous meeting to order. Behind him
are two framed portraits, one of Adolf Hitler, the
other—slightly smaller—of George Washington.

Pan to the lobby, just inside the front doors, one
side of which is a bar where German lager is pouring
freely, quaffed in giant gulps. The backs of soft,
pink hands wipe foam from truncated mustaches.

The lights dim for a moment, letting those at the
bar know that the meeting is about to begin. There is
a move to enter the meeting room, but gridlock stops
the men. Many will have to listen from the lobby.

Exterior: We see the cluster of shadowy men more
clearly now. There are more than we thought before,
perhaps three dozen, breaking up into groups, one in
front of the hall, one on either side, covering all
three exits.

Their pockets bulge ominously. Some are holding
weapons in their hands: sawed-off pool cues, blackjacks, baseball bats. If there was one thing an
American Jew is bound to learn, whether or not he
makes it out of grammar school, it is how to swing a
baseball bat.

We see a close-up of one man putting brass knuckles
onto the fingers of his right hand.

Look closely and you can see that some of those
tough guys have had their pictures in the paper—a
strike force of underworld soldiers, bosses, and
well-known prizefighters. Look, there's the former
bootleg king himself, air boxing in anticipation.

The three groups enter the hall simultaneously. They don't get far inside before they hit the gridlock, and the action commences suddenly, like a fizzy chemical reaction. The crowd loosens as frightened Nazis flee out the front and side exits.

The scene instantly transforms into a seething turmoil of angry, fighting men. Teeth shatter, jaws dislocate, bruises and welts rise like sudden volcanoes.

The Nazis are getting by far the worst of it. Crimson stains blotch crisp brown shirts. Folding chairs fly through the air.

In a side hallway running alongside the main room is a glass display case filled with group photographs and trophies in commemoration of long-forgotten achievements, a display case that abruptly acquires a spiderweb of cracks when struck by a Nazi's sloping forehead. Half-crazed with pain and fear, blood now streaming down his face, the Nazi stumbles and falls.

As the savagery escalates, a man at the podium yells into a microphone, "Halt! Halt!"

Through broken lips, a German American asks, "Who are these invaders? Who has ruined us?"

"Call us the true Americans!" a man with a rubber truncheon says with a toothy grin.

"Whenever you Jew-haters get together," says another, examining his bloody knuckles, "we will be on the scene in a flash and send you to the hospital!" With that, he socks a Nazi across the jaw with a devastating right hand, sending his foe to the floor in a heap.

The Nazi at the podium is shoved aside, and a gangster takes the microphone. "Look, look! This is what we do to Hitler's clowns!"

PART ONE The Cloven Hoof

Once evil is invited in, tremendous effort is required to show it to the door and kick its cloven hoof off the threshold.
—E. A. BUCCHIANERI

CHAPTER ONE
Jewish Gangsters

The Jewish migration to the United States began in the nineteenth century, largely from central Europe. Jews arrived alone or in families, speaking a variety of languages (German, Yiddish, Polish, Romanian, Hungarian, etc.), dressing in the Old World style and retaining their Orthodox piety.

The largest number came from Russia, where they had grown increasingly unwelcomed in their own villages, in their own homes. In 1881, laws were passed that limited the Jewish population's access to rural areas, forcing them into overcrowded villages in the western provinces. Even then, they fled the *shtetls* as government-stimulated pogroms (the Russian word for "devastation") flattened their homes and turned their eyes to the New World.

In 1882, there were about a quarter of a million Jews in the United States. By 1924, that number had grown to four million.

With each generation, Jews in the New World modernized and Americanized, both in dress and style of worship, until the fourth decade of the twentieth century, when they were as much in search of the American Dream as were the blue bloods that could trace their roots back to Plymouth Rock. That dream was most in focus when it was projected onto silver screens inside palace theaters built by Jewish moguls like Marcus Loew and Adolf Zukor.

As a centerpiece of Jewish communities, however, the cinema remained for most Jews only a distant second to the synagogue. Temple was the primary gathering place, providing both spiritual and social services.

For most Jews. But not all.

While some Jews' lives were dominated by Old World religious practices—services twice a day, strict dietary laws, separation by gender, abstinence from labor on the Sabbath, Hebrew classes for the men, ritual baths for the women, and such—there were also teenaged boys of the 1920s who sought to avoid a life of shopkeeping or factory drudgery and planned to go into other fields—like crime. They caused their fathers to pray for their lost souls and broke their mothers' hearts.

They ran wild, became rebellious to the bone, played hooky, and snuck into the movies. They formed gangs and fought over turf sometimes as small as a lone street corner.

They rebelled for a reason. They were observant and saw how things were. Jews in America were not free to pursue happiness to anywhere near the extent that gentiles enjoyed. Christians blocked many pathways to prosperity, so Jews became shopkeepers, butchers, tailors, and so on, for the simple reason that these were the jobs they were allowed to have. They worked hard and they remained poor.

Rebellious young men decided not to follow in their fathers' footsteps and rather took up career paths via which a Jew could become rich: show business, boxing, and, of course, the rackets. Teenaged Jewish gang members graduated into organized crime. During the 1920s, that meant bootlegging. When Prohibition was repealed, they moved into other rackets: policy banking (also known as "the numbers," an illegal lottery), extortion, murder— sometimes losing their Jewish accents in favor of a cheap imitation of movie gangsters like Jimmy Cagney and Edward G. Robinson.

Like all boys, they kept their heroes close to their hearts: baseball players, fighters, but especially Jewish gangsters. To borrow a phrase from historian Rich Cohen, Jewish boys had "a favorite gangster the way Catholics have patron saints." They imagined the Jewish hoods to be just as cool as the Hollywood actors who portrayed them, and they were often right. Jewish gangsters did not cower from danger; they were the danger.

The prototypical Jewish gangster was Edward Osterman, whose cowlicks rendered his hair comb-resistant, sticking up in the back like Alfalfa's no matter how many glops of Murray's Superior Pomade he applied. His cratered face was an homage to the smallpox he'd survived.

Even as a young man, Osterman was jowly, with thick lips pulled into a perpetual sneer. His nose was flat, or had been flattened so it was difficult to see in profile. He was known on the street as Monk Eastman, born in Williamsburg, Brooklyn, son of a restaurant owner.

His dad had tried to set up Monk in business, but Monk had other ideas and took a bouncer job at New Irving Hall. The establishment would later clean up its act and become known as the Yiddish Art Theater, but when Monk worked there, it was a rough joint, and he made a name for himself by wading into fights and tossing the combatants on their ears into the bricked street out front.

Tough guys tried to take him on, bigger men, but Monk had fists of lightning, threw short and accurate punches to damaging effect. He was so tough that, despite his unruly hair and pocked face, women loved him one-two-three.

Ah, but even the toughest men are not bulletproof. Monk mixed with ambitious criminals and didn't live to be old, shot five times, and killed in front of a Fourteenth Street café on December 26, 1920.

The next famous superstar Jewish gangster to come down the pike was Arnold "the Brain" Rothstein, who grew up rich on the Upper East Side of Manhattan. His father, Abe, was a successful businessman known for his kindness and called by his neighbors "Abe the Just." That kindness didn't wear off on his son. Arnold had cold, dark eyes that made all in his company feel inferior, insignificant perhaps. He had I'd-rather-kill-you-than-look-at-you eyes, flanking a hawk's nose, downward pointing and sharp. He wasn't much of a smiler, but when he did smile, he grinned as if appreciating his own sadistic joke.

Rothstein could have been a lazy pretty boy but instead became a lone wolf seeking adventure and profit, slumming as much as he could, hanging with the tough-guy Jewish boys of the ghetto.

In 1909, he married a *shiksa*, a cooperative actress named Carolyn Greene. His wealthy dad disowned him—freed him, in essence—and Arnold never looked back. He became a professional gambler, opened a series of backroom gambling parlors. Eventually, he opened a palace casino on Forty-sixth Street in midtown Manhattan, ornate in the same fashion as the Loew's State and Paramount Theaters in nearby Times Square. Opulence was very hip back then. Customers were more apt to empty their wallets if their very surroundings made them feel rich.

When Rothstein had sufficient funds, he became the underworld's number one financier, offering loans with an outrageously large vig, making him the most powerful Jew in America.

One of the ways he made so much cabbage was fixing games—small games like roulette and big games like baseball. He fixed the 1919 World Series in what came to be known as the Black Sox Scandal. Rothstein was already flying pretty high when the Volstead Act tried to dry America out, and he was quick to hop the bootleg whiskey train.

When it came to running and enforcing his empire, Rothstein proved to be a remarkable judge of criminal talent and recruited a veritable future mob hall of fame—Jewish gangsters and their Italian cousins, too. Rothstein hired on Meyer Lansky, Bugsy Siegel, and Lepke Buchalter, men who will be among the heroes of our story.

Later, when Lansky advised Lucky Luciano as "Looch" designed the Five Family system, not everyone was thrilled with a
Jew having the ear of the *capo di tutti i capi*. Boss Vito Genovese
didn't like it, didn't like to mix. Frank Costello, on the other
hand, looked at Lansky and all he could see were dollar signs.
Lansky recalled the first time he ever locked eyes with Luciano.
They were just kids at the time, face-to-face in Little Italy, a tiny
enclave in Lower Manhattan tucked between Chinatown and the
East Village. Lansky and Luciano both felt it, the shared attitude.
Fuck the world. Fuck the whole fucking universe. They were
gangsters among gangsters. Later, when they worked together in
the casino biz, they were like an old married couple, finishing
each other's sentences, sometimes understanding without speaking at all. It was funny. Other than running the rackets, the two
men had nothing in common.

Rothstein was a powerful man—he was the model for the character Meyer Wolfsheim in F. Scott Fitzgerald's 1925 novel *The
Great Gatsby*—but he still had his private peccadillos and was no
more bulletproof than Monk Eastman. On November 4, 1928,
Rothstein received a phone call at Lindy's restaurant telling him
to come to the Park Central hotel, catty-corner from Carnegie
Hall. Rothstein strode confidently into the hotel okay, but he
came out on a stretcher with a bullet in his guts. (Murder, Inc.'s
Albert Anastasia was shot in the same building a generation later,
dead on the floor of Grasso's Barber Shop off the hotel lobby.)
Rothstein survived for two days before succumbing to his
wounds. He was forty-six and was buried in the Union Field
Cemetery in the Ridgewood section of Queens.

The year after Rothstein was killed, the stock market crashed,
unemployment went sky high, and the Great Depression covered
America like a smoky blanket of despair. In that atmosphere,
more Jewish boys than ever turned to lives of crime.

Jewish gangs ruled their turf and fought rumbles with rival
gangs. In the gangs, many Jewish boys found a brotherhood that
they couldn't find at home or school. In the gangs, boys met oth-

ers who were the same, Jews who were unafraid. They grew to be adult gangsters, who in turn became the idols of the next generation of boys who were tired of being bullied by thick-necked gentiles.

As the fascist menace grew to crisis proportions in New York City, Meyer Lansky became the nation's top Jewish gangster and would be the one to lead the anti-Nazi effort there.

CHAPTER TWO
Rise of Fascism

To put it simply, fascism is the belief that a dictatorial leader is preferable to an elected one because many voters are enemies of the people and need to be oppressed. As a philosophy, it requires a strong leader and a weaker scapegoat. In Germany, Hitler became the dictator and Jews the scapegoat.

Hitler preached of "Aryan supremacy," the notion that healthy White Germans were the only ones who mattered, and certainly the only ones who should be allowed to make decisions.

Fascism always gains popularity during times of economic crisis, so it was no coincidence that its rise in Europe, and in the United States, coincided with the Great Depression, which caused global hardship.

In Germany, there was mass discrimination and violence based on racial, ethnic, sexual, and religious identities. Hatred of Jews, commonly known as anti-Semitism, was a lynchpin of Hitler's version of fascism, which he called Nazism, a contraction of National Socialism.

Hitler's plans didn't stop at stifling and eventually eliminating Jewish people. He wanted to rule the world, and during the 1930s, he stomped over smaller and weaker European nations until only England stood between him and the United States.

The last thing Hitler wanted was to fight the US, whose entry into the First World War had halted German aggression. His plan was to convince Americans that Germany was their friend and Jews were the enemy.

In America, German immigrants were second only to the Irish in number, and they were recruited to organize and form paramilitary groups that would echo the Third Reich's noxious philosophies, first and foremost that Jewish people were behind the world's problems.

And so organizations sprung up. The first was the Friends of the New Germany, created through the auspices of the German consul in New York City, but it suffered from bad press, which proclaimed it un-American.

As if by magic, the Friends transformed into the Amerikadeutscher Volksbund, the German American Bund, under new leadership. Try and call that unpatriotic. Now it said *American* right in its name.

But it was, of course, just a game of semantics. The new Bund had one goal: promote Hitler's agenda. That included spreading hate toward Jews and non-White Christians and keeping American soldiers the hell out of Europe. (Unless they wanted to fight on Hitler's side; that would've been all right.)

The Bund would convince its followers that America's urge to defend Great Britain was the product of a communist/Jewish conspiracy. When the Bund members assembled peacefully, they defended their hateful message by holding up the US Constitution. They had freedom of speech on their side. They had the *right* to assemble.

True, opponents noted, but in this case there was a sharp distinction between legal and *just*.

From the start, the Bund expertly manipulated the minds of its followers. It advertised itself as an "organization of Americans of German stock." The stages at rallies were always neat and precise, with American flags and swastikas side by side.

The initial Bundists looked back as much as forward, regretting the loss of the Great War and calling for Germany's return to greatness. They acted like little soldiers, with uniforms. They recruited children to their German American camps, where pro-Hitler brainwashing accompanied the swimming and playing.

Some German Americans ate it up—but not all. As you read these stories, remember that the great majority of Americans, including those of German heritage, saw through the Bund's message. They recognized hate when they saw it. There were upward of twelve million Germans in the United States during the Depression, and Bund membership represented only 0.2 percent of that number, one in five hundred.

But the believers, that 0.2 percent, were zealous and dangerous. By 1933, there were more than one hundred anti-Semitic groups in the US, functioning openly and in evangelical mode. American Nazis preached that Germany and the US could get along if it weren't for the Jews, who were unthinkably powerful, had all of the money, and were pushing the two countries in the direction of war. They would hoist the swastika flag and *Sieg heil* to their hearts' delight. They had parades, practiced their goose-stepping, and published magazines filled to the margins with disinformation—Jews had horns and belonged in hell—fake news before the term existed. The Bund communicated with its fifty thousand members via a weekly newspaper known as the *Deutscher Weckruf und Beobachter* (The German wake-up call and observer).

The message appealed to some non–German Americans as well. Among these were isolationists who felt the US should never fight someone else's battle, largely the same group that kept the US out of the First World War until the very end. The message also resonated with the Christian Right groups like Defenders of the Christian Faith, which was already suspicious of anyone belonging to a non-Jesus religion, and to capitalists who liked the idea that no one hated communism more than a fascist.

Americans Jews suffered in the Depression, too, of course. That "unthinkably powerful" stuff must have seemed like a cruel joke to the Jewish ragman in Brooklyn whose sick horse didn't want to pull the cart that morning. Reality had nothing to do with it. The stereotype that Jews were money-grubbers fueled the hatred.

In those days, anti-Semitic propaganda was shockingly mainstream. (For that matter, all types of racism were mainstream.) Today, we forget that a leading American industrialist, auto manufacturer Henry Ford, was also a virulent Jew hater who published and sold a book of anti-Semitic claptrap titled *The Protocols of the Elders of Zion*, a Russian book that pretended to be the minutes of a meeting of Jews plotting to control the world. Ford offered free copies of the book in dealerships with the purchase of every Model T. He also bought a newspaper, the *Dearborn Independent*, which became Ford's outlet for anti-Semitic filth. For generations, Jews refused to buy Ford cars, long after Henry Ford was dead and World War II was over, much in the way Jews refused to buy German cars.

National hero and aviator Charles Lindbergh, the first man to fly solo across the Atlantic Ocean, was a Nazi sympathizer. History hates nuance and thus keeps many dirty secrets.

In addition to the Bund, other similar groups, each with their own take on anti-Semitism, were active during the 1930s from New York to California. Not all of them were German, but all of them were hateful.

There were the Silver Shirts, a glittering fraternal lodge of fascist thought; the Christian Front, with their goody two-shoes noses in everybody's business; and the Knights of the White Camellia, oldest of the bunch, around in Louisiana since 1867, just two years after the emancipation of the slaves, founded on the premise of White supremacy and the ruination of mixing blood.

The White Camellias were a lot like the Ku Klux Klan, but their members were exclusively landowners. The KKK riders were the guys in the saloon on a Tuesday morning. The White Camellias were doctors and lawyers, newspaper publishers, community leaders, all dedicated to keeping the White race pure.

During the Depression, the national commander of the White Camellias was George Edward Deatherage of Charleston, West Virginia, an architectural engineer. He was a man who often wore sunglasses in public to hide the fact that he had sneaky little eyes set too close together. At other times, he hid his entire head with a white hood.

Deatherage first made a name for himself by writing books about construction, but it was his politics that he would be best known for. He became a popular and well-spoken purveyor of anti-Semitism. When he testified before a congressional committee investigating un-American activities in the late 1930s, he switched up his mustache from a Hitler-esque toothbrush to something so thin it looked penciled on.

He once claimed that he was investigating the wives of some of the members of President Franklin Delano Roosevelt's cabinet to determine if they had "Jewish blood in their veins." He'd been taught that nothing splits a country in two like the creation of an "enemy within," hence anti-Semitism in America was vital to White Camellia plans. Deatherage's political being was dedicated to convincing farmers and the lower middle class that America was run by evil Jewish bankers and that they alone were responsible for the Great Depression.

The fascist organization that we'll be focusing on most in this book is the German American Bund. They were by far the largest, with branches from coast to coast. They recruited young people aggressively, for a variety of reasons. And the foundation of their message was that Jews were evil and had to go. The Bund took over an entire town on Long Island.

As might be expected, the growing anti-Semitic movement in Depression-era America scared the already nervous American Jews, who now felt like their people had targets on their backs on both sides of the Atlantic.

In this book, we will tend to generalize, but the Jews' fight here in America was far more complicated than just punching Nazis. During the 1930s, *Fortune* magazine—a magazine basically about money—revealed that about one in ten Americans wanted all Jews to be deported.

For years, the American Nazis did their thing unopposed. Despite efforts by journalists such as John C. Metcalfe, who wrote a series of exposés about the Bund menace (see chapter 3), White Anglo-Saxon Protestant America still urged neutrality in the European fight. Outside the major cities, most folks knew no Jewish people, and it was too early for Americans to care one way or the other about Hitler.

The leaders in American Jewish communities largely kept their mouths shut, afraid that anything that remotely resembled retaliation would result in escalation. But eventually, one group did step up. The goose-steppers of the German-American Bund and the Silver Legion finally met their match from an unexpected source: Jewish gangsters.

In New York City, Newark, Minneapolis, and Los Angeles, Nazi rallies terrified Jews, but what could they do? The rallies, where Hitler wannabes worked the troops into a Jew-hating frenzy, were not illegal. That was what made the Jewish gangsters the perfect warriors for the cause. They hurt and killed people for a living and didn't particularly care about the law.

CHAPTER THREE
Fritz Kuhn

The leader of the German-American Bund (i.e., the Bundesführer) was Fritz Julius Kuhn, a popinjay with a protruding jaw
and a low brow. He maintained a grim countenance, like a general who dreaded slaughtering his enemy but, alas, it needed to be
done. When he spoke in public, that jaw pointed upward, a picture of arrogance and defiance.

Kuhn was born in Munich in 1896 and fought in the First
World War as a German infantry officer. He was a big man, well
over six feet, 240 pounds. After the war, he earned a degree in
chemical engineering at the Technical University of Munich.

Among Kuhn's uncorroborated boasts were that he'd been a
charter member of the Nazi party and had fought beside Hitler at
the 1923 Beer Hall Putsch. His Nazi heroics aside, he was a loner,
a womanizer, an alcoholic, and a man of poor character whose
foibles leaped up and bit him on a regular basis. As a young man,
he'd been arrested repeatedly for petty theft and had probably left
Germany to avoid jail time.

He came to the US in 1928, lived in Detroit, and worked on
America's first assembly line for America's number one fascist,
Henry Ford. There, he helped build Model A's.

Kuhn became a naturalized citizen in 1934 for public relations
purposes and worked at the Henry Ford Hospital—no Jews al-

lowed. He was always in trouble, usually for attempting to dally with the nurses.

He was also a con artist, frequently passing himself off as a physician even though he was merely an x-ray technician. The last straw came when he annoyed coworkers by practicing his Hitler impression at the top of his lungs in the hospital's darkroom.

Out of work, Kuhn joined the Friends of the New Germany and, because of his ambition, size, and booming voice, became a leader of its Midwestern division, headquartered in Detroit.

He put that Hitler impression to work and gave rousing speeches. He spoke of the necessity for unity between Germany and the United States. What German Americans needed, he ranted, was a new organization, one that would result in Hitler's agenda working in the US.

Hitler's movement, he explained, may have seemed un-American to the Jews and liberals who'd taken over the US, but it was actually parallel to American principles as expressed by the Founding Fathers.

"I am sick of Germans being treated as guests in America," he railed. A new Nazi party, he insisted, could grow from within America. A ruling-class hero was something to be. All German Americans had to do was follow him.

In October 1936, Kuhn informed the Bund that it was to vote as a unit for Republican Alf M. Landon, as Landon was the presidential candidate "most sympathetic toward Chancellor Hitler's Germany." Kuhn wrote that FDR's leadership and the government's movement to the left distressed him. If FDR were allowed to remain in power, Kuhn argued, the United States would be led into a "united Communist front and subsequent chaos. We hope with the election of Landon to create a friendly understanding between our adopted country and Germany, our native land." He added that he also hoped that one day a "member of our own race," that is, a German, would sit in the White House.

There were not enough Bundists to affect the presidential election, and Landon finished a distant second to the wildly popular FDR. But Kuhn did get the Bund thinking in terms of voting as one, so when it came time to elect a Bundesführer, Kuhn ran for reelection unopposed and—in true fascist form—was elected unanimously.

Kuhn told his followers that he had recently returned from Germany, where he'd been granted an audience with the great Hitler, who emphasized to Kuhn that Bund membership must remain *pure*. That is, all members must be Christian Caucasians who were naturalized or native-born Americans and sympathized with the Nazi cause. As proof of the meeting, he offered up a photo of himself and Hitler standing side by side, although it might have been the thousandth photo of the day for Hitler.

The Roosevelt administration was wary of the Bund, and orders came down from the president's home in Hyde Park, New York, to make the American Nazis uncomfortable whenever possible. If the Bund failed to file the proper paperwork before a gathering or if there was an undotted *i* or an uncrossed *t*, officials swooped in to deny the Bund of whatever it hoped to do. For example, a Bund rally in 1937 was repeatedly delayed because Kuhn had "failed to file a statement of the purposes of his organization with the Secretary of State."

Despite the clerical harassment, the Bund grew larger and bolder, adept at making a show in places where it would be difficult for opponents to criticize or disrupt. In March 1937, a nine-year-old German American girl living in New York City, little Einer Sporrer, was murdered by sex maniac Salvatore Ossido, a barber by trade. At the poor victim's funeral, an event that attracted more than five thousand spectators, as the tiny white casket was borne out of St. Barbara Church at the corner of Bleecker Street and Central Avenue in the largely German Bushwick section of Brooklyn, the Bund was there in full force, with a Bund band playing the dirge and spectators raising their arms in the Nazi salute.

* * *

Only days after Einer's Nazi funeral, a US House of Representatives Committee on Naturalization and Immigration discussed the American Nazi problem. The committee—chaired by Samuel Dickstein, a Democrat representing the Lower East Side of Manhattan—investigated the use of propaganda against democracy. Dickstein would go on to become a leader of the legitimate anti-Nazi movement. He was born in Lithuania in 1885, son of a rabbi and his wife. When he was two, he crossed the ocean with his parents and lived on New York's Lower East Side. He attended City College and earned a law degree at New York University. His face seemed divided into two parts, a strong, wide forehead with keenly intelligent eyes at the top and below that, small, pursed lips and a chin that didn't look like it could take much of a punch.

Dickstein told his committee that Kuhn ran the Bund and claimed two hundred thousand members (a greatly inflated but frightening number), all of whom had taken an oath of fidelity to "their leader," Adolf Hitler. Dickstein referred to Kuhn as "enemy number-one on my list."

According to Dickstein, the Bund oath read as follows (note that it came with its own legal disclaimer): "I solemnly swear fidelity to my leader, Adolf Hitler. I promise Adolf Hitler and everybody designated by him known to me or to be known to me, through his credentials, the respect and absolute obedience and give allegiance herewith to fulfill all orders without restrictions, and with my entire will, because I know my leader does not demand from me anything illegally."

Dickstein told the committee that the best way to combat written Nazi propaganda was to close the mails to it. The dissemination of propaganda would be severely hindered if the Nazis could no longer simply put a stamp on their stuff and drop it in a mailbox. The modern equivalent would be getting kicked off social media platforms like Facebook, Twitter, and Parler.

Even as Dickstein was busy in Washington, DC, Kuhn—whom the papers had taken to calling the "vest-pocket Hitler"—was in New York verbally blasting one of his favorite targets, Mayor

Fiorello LaGuardia of New York City. Kuhn called LaGuardia, Dickstein, and anti-fascist activist Samuel Untermyer a "three-horse team" of communists who were responsible for the "sit-down and handout system" of dealing with the workingman.

Kuhn was giving his remarks when he was informed of Dickstein's statements regarding the Bund's oath. He grinned and claimed that Dickstein's "oath" was a fabrication. He pulled out a Bund application form and read aloud, "'I hereby apply for admission in the German-American Bund, the purposes and aims of which are known to me, and I obligate myself to support them to the best of my ability. I recognize the leadership principle, in accordance with which the Bund is being directed. I am of Aryan origin, free from Jewish or colored blood.'" He slapped the paper against his hand. "*That* is a bona fide membership card."

Kuhn said that he would not give up until he had Nazi-fied America, until the Bund was part of America's fabric, a thing that would, like the Third Reich itself, live for a thousand years. He would create a "new generation" of Nazis, and to do that he would need to transform the minds of America's children.

The war of words between Dickstein and Kuhn continued. Dickstein placed on the Congressional Record the names of forty-six people who were "Nazi propagandists, agents, stool pigeons, and spies." He demanded that "Congress halt this smuggling in of arms, propaganda, and uniforms—and all of this goose stepping and parading with the swastika flag."

Dickstein pointed out that Kuhn had placed several Nazi headquarters close to "the largest ammunition factories of this government." The problem, he said, was getting worse every day.

Kuhn managed to deflect all of this frightening rhetoric by refusing to play the part of an enemy of the people. He was a savior, and Hitler *the* Savior. Kuhn told his people he was here to *save* America, not ruin it.

During the autumn of 1937, Kuhn allowed an American journalist into his inner sanctum in Manhattan. John C. Metcalfe, investigating reporter, sat and watched as Kuhn athletically worked over his correspondence, signing letters, sealing and stamping envelopes, all while letting loose with a steady stream of patter.

Metcalfe was fearless and an excellent actor, requisite skills to break a big story from the inside. He could flatter and cajole, agree and stroke, with the best of them. In a remarkably short time, Kuhn's defenses dropped and he was sharing his secrets with Metcalfe. They became sort of confidants, which was why Metcalfe's eventual series of exposés on the Bund were such game changers. Before Metcalfe, the Bund was thought to be composed of nostalgic German immigrants, homesick for the fatherland. After, everyone knew them as Nazis.

Metcalfe told Kuhn that he had just visited a Bund meeting in California. It wasn't impressive.

"The Germans in California are more spread out than here in New York, harder to organize, but they have money," Kuhn said.

"When I was there, they were complaining that their Bund uniforms still hadn't showed up," Metcalfe replied.

Kuhn exploded with fury. "I told them many times, send money first, then I send uniforms."

Metcalfe looked around the office. Both the Nazi and American flags were prominently displayed. The Nazi flag was mounted on the wall, considerably higher, the dominant flag.

"I will have to go to California and speak with the troops," Kuhn said, calmer but suddenly dejected.

"You do not like California?" Metcalfe asked.

"Not that. Last time, I drove by myself and took a tour of all the outposts. I drove seventeen thousand miles in three weeks. Once I woke up with my car hanging over the edge of a bridge. Another time I woke up in a ditch. If I go back to California, I'm going to have to bring a relief driver."

Metcalfe learned that Kuhn's staff worried about him. In addition to being a driver who drank daily and sometimes fell asleep at the wheel, he was a loner to a peculiar degree, with no sense of personal security. He didn't realize that he had enemies and that it wasn't a good idea to, alone and unannounced, drop in on places all over the country. It was dangerous, an unbelievable opportunity for a "Jew communist fanatic" to take him out. But Kuhn wasn't worried. He was on a mission. He needed the world to understand the Jewish conspiracy and how Jews were using communism to achieve their goals.

One of the most sensational parts of Metcalfe's exposés was that many Bund members were German citizens and had no intention of becoming American citizens. In public, they would always say that the Bund was primarily an American organization, but that was balderdash. In private, they said they could never have allegiance to two countries. They were *Germans*.

In 1938, the year during which the great bulk of our story takes place, Metcalfe became an investigator for the House Un-American Activities Committee (HUAC), a body founded by Representative Martin Dies Jr., a Texas Democrat who was first elected to the US House of Representatives in 1931. Dies was blond-haired and blue-eyed with a wide, friendly mouth that smiled easily and a cleft chin. He was tall and had a firm handshake, attributes that were obligatory if one wanted to be elected to public office in the Lone Star State.

His committee was designed to root out subversives in and out of the federal government. It was designed to expose both communism and fascism, and Dies was its chairman from 1938 until 1944.

Metcalfe reported to the HUAC that the Bund was anything but a grassroots organization. In fact, he'd found evidence that Kuhn's army was funded largely by a handful of "high American industrialists." Kuhn had told him that Hans Luther, the longtime German ambassador to the United States, had been fired because he had failed to cooperate completely with Bund activities.

"I have secret relations with Germany whereby I can get anything I want," Kuhn told Metcalfe.

Talking about the Bund's funding, Metcalfe said that, should his investigation be given more time and money, "We would be able to get definite and tangible proof that something of this sort exists and who these people are. The evidence I have gathered so far shows them to be very influential and powerful fascist-minded industrialists."

Metcalfe reported that the Bund had laid the groundwork in the US for a "sabotage machine and spy ring" staffed with Bund storm troopers who would go into action should the US and Germany go to war.

Most of these storm troopers were in New York, Los Angeles, and Milwaukee. American Nazis had worked their way into the system, sleeper agents, ready to go into action should there be war, including some who were working in the US Navy yards, in positions privy to secret plans for building state-of-the-art US Navy battleships.

Metcalfe testified that, in addition to his Bund investigation, he'd investigated the Silver Legion as well. He had been invited to and attended a meeting of the Chicago Silver Lodge. There, Field Marshal Roy Zachary had urged members to "get guns and ammunition to crush the coming communist revolution."

Chairman Dies asked Metcalfe how many supporters or sympathizers Hitler had here in the US. The witness said he thought it was somewhere in the neighborhood of half a million. There was a gasp in the room.

Following Metcalfe's testimony, the committee called to the witness stand his brother, James J. Metcalfe, who was also an investigator, in this case working for the Department of Justice. James's claim to fame was that he had been among the feds to trail the bank robber John Dillinger, before Dillinger was shot down by trigger-happy G-men outside Chicago's Biograph Theater while accompanied by a mysterious "lady in red."

James said that the Bund was already building youth camps across the nation to indoctrinate the young and that there were plans to build rifle ranges and to train young men in the operation of military-grade weapons. There was even talk of purchasing aircraft and training pilots to form a Nazi air force inside the US. They wanted to take over, and they were willing to do it by force.

In public, the Bund leaders said that they were a wholesome

American organization with no connection to Nazi Germany, but in private, they said the opposite, that the youth camps and the Bund were Hitler's domain inside America. The distinction was legal as well as moral. The instant that the Bund admitted to representing a foreign power, it would lose the protections of the US Constitution.

"They say they are dissatisfied with the American form of government and want to replace it with the National Socialist system, under one leader, as much like Hitler as possible. Their entire loyalty is to Germany, and they openly professed this," James Metcalfe told the committee

Kuhn and his Bund planned a national tour, holding rallies from New York to California. If there was pushback from a community, they screamed about their rights under the US Constitution. When a Polish American hall in Schenectady, New York, told the Bund they couldn't hold a rally there, the president of the Schenectady branch of the Bund, Willi Latterman, protested. "Sooner or later, Fritz Kuhn will speak in this city," he said. "They speak so proudly of freedom of speech, but where is ours?"

Much was written about Germany's influence on German Americans, much less so about America's influence on Hitler and the policies of the Nazi Party. Hitler, it seemed, was a student of US history, and he took note when reading about the New World and its centuries of race slavery. Slavery not only provided the Southern economy with free labor, but, it has been argued, it also kept White people from admitting the apparent inequalities among their own ranks. Before the Civil War, US Vice President John C. Calhoun said that keeping a racial minority down was the simplest way of guaranteeing equality among Whites. In the 1930s, the Southern states still maintained Jim Crow laws that kept Black people separate and unequal in the eyes of the law. Hitler disagreed with America's insistence that "Jews were White" but otherwise liked the strategy.

Hitler also liked the idea that once they were united against a common enemy, Jews in this case, Americans would feel morally right, even if they committed acts that broke US laws. America, Hitler figured, was bound to understand the mistreatment of Jews in Germany because of America's own history of lynching.

In 1934, there had been a meeting of Nazi Germany's leading lawyers, a meeting that would result in anti-Jewish legislation. During the meeting, they discussed the race laws of the US in detail, as Hitler had urged them to do.

The other topic at that meeting that had been lifted from US history was the notion of manifest destiny, the unwritten law that allowed White men in good conscience to wipe out millions of Native Americans because of the belief that it was manifest destiny that the White man would control North America from coast to coast. Hitler told his followers that the "Americans had gunned down millions of Redskins to a few hundred thousands and now kept the modest remnant under observation in a cage."

America's actions emboldened Hitler, as he had genocide of his own in mind.

It is one of the most enduring, iconic images of the twentieth century. The crash of the German passenger airship LZ 129 *Hindenberg* in 1937, at the Front Gate Naval Air Engineering Station in Lakehurst, Manchester Township, New Jersey, about fifty miles south of New York City. That image even graced the cover of the first Led Zeppelin record.

Close your eyes and you can see the incredible rate at which the huge airship became enveloped in flames, listen and you can hear the stunned radio reporter Herbert Morrison crying out, "Oh, the humanity!"

It was not just a visual spectacle but a tremendous tragedy as well. Thirty-six passengers and crew, and another person on the ground, were killed in the accident. But what has largely been forgotten is that the *Hindenberg* was a Nazi aircraft.

Six days after the crash, twenty-eight of the dead, all Germans, were memorialized in a ceremony on the pier of the North German Lloyd steamship line at the Forty-second Street pier on the West Side of Manhattan, near the current site of the *Intrepid* Museum. The twenty-eight caskets were laid in state in a neat row on a black-draped, flower-banked gangplank stairway, each covered with the Swastika flag.

An estimated five thousand men in black ties and women dabbing at their eyes with lacy handkerchiefs filed past with heads bowed. Some mourners showed their respect by offering up the Nazi salute. After the ceremony, the caskets were to be loaded onto the ocean liner *Hamburg* for a midnight departure back to Germany.

During the ceremony, the US Navy sailed a blimp of its own (the *G-1*) overhead, its droning engines causing everyone below to speak a little louder than they wanted to. After the ceremony, the blimp flew a circle around Manhattan and dipped its nose over the Hudson as a farewell to all of that humanity.

At the head of each casket, Bund-leader Kuhn stationed a "soldier" in a full uniform designed and tailored to resemble as much as possible those of German storm troopers.

That was the sort of thing that was making the Jewish communities in New York and New Jersey very nervous. That, and the Nazis' insistence that no German Americans were too young to be indoctrinated into the Bund's anti-Semitic ways.

CHAPTER FOUR
Nazi Youth Camps

In Suffolk County, Long Island, in the township of Brookhaven, there is the bucolic village of Yaphank, home of the US Army's Camp Upton, where eighteen thousand soldiers at a time were housed in box-like barracks and trained over 1,600 acres. The camp was used in 1918 as a point of embarkation for soldiers who'd completed training and were ready for the trenches. Among the units sent eastward to finish up the First World War were the 325th and the 327th Infantry Regiments and the 27th Infantry Division's 53rd Brigade.

One of the most famous soldiers trained at Camp Upton was composer Irving Berlin (born Israel Baline and composer of "God Bless America" and "White Christmas"), who wrote the musical revue *Yip Yip Yaphank* (featuring the classic soldier's song "Oh, How I Hate to Get Up in the Morning") while stationed in Yaphank.

Immediately after the war, the camp was transformed into a school where enlistees—immigrants and country boys, most of them—were taught to read and write in English. But by the Great Depression, the US Army had abandoned the camp and the German American Bund had moved in.

The camp shared a border with a 3,700-acre haven for wildlife, where more than two thousand quail and two hundred pheasant and grouse were theoretically safe. The rest of the area had its share of fowl as well, being made up of "duck ranches" where millions of ducks blanketed the lush landscape in an innocent white.

The Bund changed the camp's name to Camp Siegfried, and the facility was transformed into a youth camp where youngsters of German heritage could breathe the clean country air, swim and play, and learn to love Hitler.

The main drag down the center of the camp was now called Adolf Hitler Strasse (Adolf Hitler Street). Boys and girls from ages six through ten were trained at the site, at a cost to parents of four dollars a week.

The camp's appearance and the uniforms worn by the children greatly resembled those of the Hitler youth camps back in the fatherland. As they laughed and played volleyball, the kids wore swastika armbands and Sam Brown belts, which were part belt, part suspenders, with a strap that went from the front of the belt to the rear diagonally across the chest and over the right shoulder.

The children rose in military fashion to a bugle at 6:30 A.M., spent the day both playing and engaging in military drills. They were read evening bedtime stories taken from German history (and American history in which Germans played a part).

On Sundays after church, German Americans of all ages in the New York City area would don their traditional garb and hop on the Long Island Rail Road aboard the "Yaphank Special" express: next stop, Nazi-land—for the weekly Bund festivities.

Siegfried was the first of many Nazi youth camps in the United States. There were eventually twenty-one of them stretching from coast to coast, in locations chosen strategically to take advantage of nearby clusters of fascist activity. Camp Siegfried, for example, was convenient to Lindenhurst, a Suffolk County community that had its own Nazi group, known as the Black Shirts. They attended all of the Sunday rallies in Yaphank and lent hard-edged pro-Hitler zeal to the festivities.

The great bulk of the people in Suffolk County, even among

the German Americans, were not Nazis, and those people expressed concerns about impressionable minds being exposed to
hate talk. Although, to be fair, they complained equally about the
traffic problems the camp caused and how the rally-goers' exces-
sive drinking caused Sunday-night car accidents.

The Sunday events were drunken, all right, but also purposeful, and no one got away without listening to a few speeches
about rising up and fighting the enemy, namely Jewish communists. Speakers railed against the powers that be in New York
City and New York State, in particular Mayor LaGuardia and the
German-born Governor Herbert H. Lehman. These men, the
theme went, hated Germans and should be stripped of power. One
speaker bragged of the number of young German Americans who
had attended the camp and been indoctrinated to the cause: "We
are training these beautiful young people to fight the Jews because the Jews are the originators of communism."

But the words were seemingly secondary to the pageantry.
There was a marching band that blasted out martial tunes as a
thousand people—men, women, and children—goose-stepped past
a reviewing stand where German American dignitaries, including
Bund Secretary Walter Happe, nodded their approval and offered
up hardy applause. The parade continued with the elders, who
rode in cars and waved royally to the spectators, the cars embla-
zoned with slogans such as "GENTILES, AWAKE!"

The scene was repeated in the other Nazi camps. For residents
of the Bronx, the only one of New York's five boroughs that
was on the mainland, the Bund built a camp in Windham, New
York, in the Catskill Mountains, and called it Camp Highland.

Of all of the placements of the Nazi youth camps, Highland
was the scariest, as the Catskills were known for their Jewish
summer vacation resorts, the so-called Borscht Belt. It was a
place in America where prosperous Jews went to have fun. To
build a Nazi youth camp there seemed like an attack—which, of
course, is exactly what it was.

At Camp Highland, the Nazis filmed a twenty-five-minute pro-motional movie that was shown in German-language theaters. It convinced parents to send their precious small fry to Nazi camp. The film began with a flag-raising ceremony. As children gave the Nazi salute, the American flag and the Nazi flag were raised side by side. The film boasted that the camp would teach kids how to use weapons. Precision drilling with wooden rifles was shown. The film showed kids having fun, getting muddy, boxing and wrestling, playing checkers, and learning about their glorious heritage.

As much as any other law enforcement agency, the New York Police Department was concerned about the camps. The camps themselves were not in their jurisdiction, but many among the clientele were. With varying amounts of cooperation from neigh-boring police forces, as well as state troopers, the NYPD orga-nized a spy system to learn what was actually going on inside those camps. Sons of cops, as Irish as four-leafed clovers, infil-trated the camps and reported back to their dads what was going on. Some of the treatment was harsh. To "toughen up" the campers, they were sometimes awoken in the middle of the night and forced to go on twenty-mile hikes through woods and up mountains. When the children were fatigued to numbness, they were forced to build a campfire, sit around it, and sing "Deutsch-land, Deutschland Uber Alles".

A list was made of the adults working at the camps, and it was a good thing. One camp supervisor, Gustav Wilhelm Kaercher, went on to work as a power plant designer for a utility company and was arrested by the feds in 1942 as a foreign spy.

We switch our sights now to the 150-acre Camp Nordland on Lake Iliff in the Sussex County hills of New Jersey. As was true at Camp Siegfried, to outsiders the camp appeared to be predom-inantly fun, traditional, and innocent. The wooden barracks were painted white.

There were many happy things going on: music, singing, beer.

Beefy men and women swayed to oompah-pah bands, with the tuba playing the background ostinato: alternating root, fifth, root, fifth. The bands were usually a quartet, musicians dressed in old-world fashion with long-sleeved white shirts, lederhosen, patterned suspenders, knee-length white socks, and a jaunty Tyrolean hat garnished with an aggressive feather. A trombone, accordion, and clarinet accompanied the tuba.

Waitresses—beer wenches, they were called—demonstrated expert breast presentation with a corset-style blouse and apron with white stockings. The sausage sandwiches were out of this world. You could buy them there, but many families brought picnic baskets with them. This was the Depression, after all.

On one hot summer Sunday afternoon in 1937, spies kept an eye on Camp Nordland inside and out as the Sunday fest filled the air with laughter. Sure there was fun, but the Nazis were using that "fun" as a lure, drawing innocents into their mind-control program. Along with the oompah-pah and thigh-slap dancing, the camp's focal point was a meeting hall, with a foyer that displayed a large black swastika mounted on the ceiling.

On this day, there was an exceptionally large crowd because Fritz Kuhn, America's number one Nazi, was going to be there to address the crowd. Some families arrived in cars, others by chartered bus.

Many men brought their own steins—ornate, glazed, and fired receptacles. Like the size of a man's car, you could tell a lot by his earthenware vessel. To keep the beer fresh and foamy, steins were capped with a bell-shaped silver-colored lid, opened by a handle that you hooked with your thumb. Made of pewter, there was usually a quaint painting on it, a small German village in the background and a busty beer wench in the foreground, seemingly serving beer *und Titten* simultaneously. You handed the stein to the man at the tap, often a fellow with a large foamy mustache. He filled it and handed it back.

Girls and women had to beware. Later in the day, there would be much *Arsch kneifen*.

A parade initiated the festivities with four hundred uniformed

Bund soldiers goose-stepping, carrying swastika banners, and *Sieg heil*-ing. On this Sunday, one squad of marchers was made up of Italian fascists, there to demonstrate their unity with the Nazis. Among the honored guests sitting with Kuhn at a review stand was State Senator William A. Dolan of Sussex.

Dolan said he "welcomed" the members of the Bund "as representatives of a foreign government." (New Jersey Governor Harold G. Hoffman was invited to the parade but sent his regrets.)

After the parade, there were speeches. Rudolph Markman, the Bund's "leader of the Eastern District," stood on the platform set at the base of a hill. He systematically accused US governmental leaders with being part of a vast communist plot.

Another preliminary speaker was Salvadore Caridi, the Union City, New Jersey, leader of Italian War Veterans. Caridi was billed in the program as Dr. Caridi, but it was unclear what his degree was in. He praised the swastika, Hitler, and Mussolini, and proclaimed Germany and Italy the two greatest countries in the world. He didn't mention the United States.

The last speaker was Kuhn himself, who lauded the clean, fresh whiteness of his audience and reminded everyone that the reason there was no money was that *schweinehund* Jewish communists had taken it all.

He sought a world that was *dreckjudenrein*, cleansed of dirty Jews. That was the road to prosperity. So it was in Germany, and so it should be in America.

The horror of these words was lost on the sunburned and drunken audience.

Later, after many of the families had left, weaving their way home, men with Hitler haircuts and perfect posture sat in the Camp Nordland meeting hall and discussed insidious ways to better spread their hateful message.

The event drew eight thousand people. When the spies returned and reported what they'd seen, many were angered. But what to do about it? The Nazis had a right to assemble, a right to speak their minds. Still, it was just so disgusting. Men who'd fought the Germans in the First World War were particularly ticked off.

Commander Harry Striner of the General Joseph Wheeler Post of the Veterans of the Foreign Wars in Jersey City said that their motto was "One Flag, One Country, and One Language" and that the idea of Americans saluting a swastika was abhorrent. Striner said that his unit planned to attend future Bund meetings. Uh-oh.

"We want to observe and make sure only the American system of government is upheld," the commander said.

When newspaper editorials criticized the camp and its activities, the camp's director, August Klapprott, answered, "The assertion that American Nazis are preparing to seize control of the United States is a lot of hooey. We have nothing to fear, nothing to hide."

The newspaper stories got the attention of US Representative Mary Norton, a Jersey Democrat, and she took up the cause, protesting that the youth camps were "fostering an alien allegiance."

Norton said, "I would be interested in learning where the Bund gets its money."

She noted that the camp was a brainwashing device, practically injecting Nazi allegiance into the veins of German Americans. She objected to the fact that there were times when the kids were required to speak "only German" while at the camp and condemned State Senator Dolan for being a part of the Nazi program.

By today's standards, the Bund's public relations campaign is laughably racist, but back then their message was intended to soothe the anti-Nazi anxiety many segments of society were feeling.

"We are not a Nazi camp. Everyone at the camp is an American citizen. Although we do sympathize with the Hitler national socialist government in Germany." The man saying those words was the Bund's PR director and a featured speaker at many Bund events, Wilhelm "William" Kunze of Philadelphia. Kunze was Kuhn's second in command. When Kuhn spoke at the podium, Kunze took up a position to his left and rear, inevitably standing in front of the swastika banner so that photographs show him wearing the black symbol like an evil halo. Kunze reassured America that Camp Nordland was nothing to worry about, as it was a "white man's camp."

A New Jersey reporter chased down Dolan about his Camp Nordland visit. Dolan defended his presence.

"I thought it was a very well-conducted function, and I saw nothing whatever anti-American through the whole day. I saw nothing to criticize," Dolan said.

Other Nazi camps included Camp Will and Might in Griggstown, Somerset County, New Jersey; Camp Hindenberg in Grafton, Wisconsin; Camp Deutsch Host in Sellersville, Pennsylvania; and Camp Sutter, near Los Angeles, California. There would have been more, but not every community welcomed them.

An attempt to build one in Southbury, Connecticut, was instantly and prohibitively controversial. Protesters took to the streets carrying signs that read "Old Glory Is Our Flag," "Southbury Wants No Swastikas," "United Americans Show the Way," and "No Nazi Camps."

For the most part, the Bund grew unimpeded. That was, until a judge in New York City came up with a brilliant plan.

PART TWO New York City

They should know that being a Nazi is dangerous.
—JUDGE NATHAN D. PERLMAN

*The stage was decorated with a swastika and a picture of Hitler.
There weren't that many of us, but we went into action hard. We
threw some of them out the windows. We wanted to show them
that Jews do not always sit back and accept insults.*
—MEYER LANSKY

CHAPTER FIVE
Judge Perlman and Meyer Lansky

The judge who thought outside the box was former US Congressman and now Special Sessions Judge Nathan David Perlman. Born in Prusice, Poland, in 1887, Perlman was four when he and his mother came to the United States and settled in New York City. He was public school educated, and after graduating from high school, he attended the City College of New York in Harlem. He earned his bachelor's degree and was accepted to New York University Law School in 1907. Two years later, he was admitted to the bar and for three years practiced law. As a twenty-five-year old, Perlman was appointed a special deputy New York attorney general, a position he held for three years, then served a three-year stint in the New York State Assembly.

When future New York City Mayor Fiorello LaGuardia resigned from his seat in the US Congress in 1920, Perlman ran for his seat in a special election and won, and he served as a member of Congress from 1920 to 1927. Afterward, he returned to his law practice until 1935, when he began serving as a New York magistrate. He was active in Zionist affairs and was chairman of the American Jewish Congress.

Perlman was a barrel-chested man, bald with comb-over and a double chin. He could appear jolly when he wanted to, then menacing at the drop of a hat. But mostly jolly. He loved people, life,

food, and drink. He was a popular guy who had no trouble winning over friends. All he had to do was mention that he'd helped
repeal Prohibition and everyone wanted to buy him a drink. Because of his career path, he knew people in both high and low
places.

By 1938, Perlman took a good long look at the Nazi problem
in America and saw where it was headed. The Nazis were growing bolder. Just the other day, they'd marched in storm trooper
uniforms to the US Customs house at Bowling Green, at the
southern end of Manhattan. The National Maritime Association
had been holding their memorial services on the steps of the historic building when the Nazis arrived—uninvited and unexpected. American Legion officials refused to send their colors
outside until the Nazis left, but the Germans stood their ground. It
looked like a full-fledged riot might ensue until the ceremonies
were moved inside. Good Americans had been terrified and
forced to hide.

Perlman brooded on the matter over a drink in a Manhattan saloon and then snapped his fingers. "What the Nazis need is a
good ass whipping," he said.

But how?

He needed an army—better yet, a *Jewish* army. He didn't have
one, so he'd have to borrow one. He pondered the matter
overnight, and the next morning in his chambers, he picked up
the phone.

The judge called Meyer Lansky, who was a Jewish organized
crime boss. Lansky was not just a big-time hood, one of the
biggest, but also a human slide rule, a guy who would have a
dream—like a crime syndicate takeover of the world, for example—and he'd turn it into a math problem that could be *solved*.

The boys from the press called him "the Mob's Accountant,"
but that was insulting and greatly undervalued the man. He was a
man of details, a man who could organize the most confusing

chaos. Once he'd formulated a plan, he would whisper in Lucky Luciano's ear and the world would change.

In fact, Lansky should get partial credit for the Five Family system of the New York mob. He also taught the mob bigs like Luciano and Ben "Bugsy" Siegel the value of well-manipulated books and Swiss-based bank accounts. What organized crime needed was consolidation, which turned out to be Luciano's forte. He consolidated by bumping off Joe "the Boss" Masseria and Salvadore Maranzano in 1931. Lansky's power grew exponentially.

Lansky was born Maier Suchowljansky on the Fourth of July 1902. The meaning of July 4 was absent at Lansky's birth, as it took place in Brodno, Bellarus. He came to America (i.e., the Lower East Side of Manhattan) with his parents in 1911.

He'd grown up with Luciano and Siegel as his friends, three kids from New York City who plotted world conquest. And, second maybe only to Dwight Eisenhower, they almost pulled it off.

The Mafia has become a generic name for all mob activity, but in reality that secret society, exclusively Sicilian, made up only a fraction of organized crime in twentieth-century America. There was a Jewish mob and an Irish mob, too, and they all did a pretty good job of sticking to their turf and staying out of each other's hair. The Jews and Italians in particular worked well together.

The thinking at the time was that their perceived skill sets complimented one another, brains and brawn.

Lansky was not just the son of immigrants, he also was an immigrant himself and bore witness to the horrors of rising Nazism in Europe, specifically the burning, raping, and looting pogroms that swept through his home village.

He was initiated into the underworld early on, before Prohibition. As a teenager, he worked briefly at a tool-and-die shop before telling himself that there had to be a better way to make a living.

Lansky was best known for his brains, but he was tough, too. He had two fists, and when the call came for someone to be hurt, Lansky didn't need to farm out the duty. If he was in the mood, he took care of it himself.

The Jewish gangsters all had chips on their shoulders. Jewish kids were bullied, and they believed a Jew needed to be tough and stand up and fight.

Lansky attributed the philosophy to an elder who once told him, "If you are going to die, die fighting."

Lansky, Siegel, and Lepke had watched as Irish, Italian, and Polish gangs beat up *yeshiva bochers*, the good and obedient Jewish boys. They hated the fact that Jews were considered timid and weak. So they formed a gang of their own, the Bugs and Meyer Gang, and they recruited into their fold teenagers and young men who were neither timid nor weak. They dished out a lot more than they took, telling anyone who would listen that "Jews are tough."

They fought to send a message, and they fought to survive.

Lansky got his feet wet in a crime world that was barely organized—only organized in the most hyperlocal way. All you had to do was cross the street and you were dealing with a new and different organization.

The gangs owned street corners and floating crap games. Lansky envisioned a world in which they owned entire industries.

Once the US government made alcohol illegal, the mobs took over alcohol sales. In the Jewish sections of New York City, gangsters became heroes of the streets. It was survival of the fittest out there, and powerful men frequently usurped lesser men, until only a handful of guys ran the NYC rackets.

Lansky became a very rich man during Prohibition, and when the Volstead Act was repealed, he seamlessly moved that fortune into gambling. Again, he was a man of vision. He didn't see smoky back rooms with a poker table, two sad one-armed bandits, and a roulette wheel. He didn't hear the noisy phones ringing in a sweaty bookmaking parlor. What he saw were huge luxury hotels and casinos, where all of man's indulgences could be acquired in oxygen-rich air and under a stimulating bath of neon. He heard the sound of money running down a pipeline into his ravenous coffers, and all he had to do was turn on the tap.

In the parlance of the hoods of that era, he replaced the sawdust-floor dives with "carpet joints." His carpet joints in the US, of course, were illegal. They were built in Saratoga Springs in New York, near the racetrack, in Hallandale, the first suburb north of Miami, and in the crossroads of Council Bluffs outside Omaha. The idea was to put the casinos near population centers but outside the jurisdiction of those centers' law enforcement. Each joint came with its own intricate system of payoffs to police, politicians, and churches, so that it was in just about everybody's interest to look the other way. No one wanted to carefully scrutinize Lansky's new fun houses.

Lansky was married a couple of times. The first wife knew what Lansky did for a living and hated it. He had two sons, the first an invalid and the second strong and tall (who in 1950 was accepted to West Point).

In a world of thieves, Lansky was an honest man. He'd make a deal and then stick to it. The deal might not have been legal, but it was honest. He wouldn't cheat you, and he didn't cut corners. He did what he said he was going to do, a tremendously valuable asset in a world of backstabbing rats. He lived to be old because of that integrity. It was the Pall Malls that ended up killing him.

So it was this man—who was in the process of building and operating a strip of fantastic casinos and clubs in Havana, Cuba, with his millions of dollars in bootlegging money—who answered the phone one day and it was Judge Nathan Perlman on the other end. The judge said he needed a face-to-face meeting. Lansky said sure, and Perlman went to him. He brought Rabbi Stephen Wise with him so he could lay on some guilt if Lansky gave him a hard time.

"These fucking Nazis, they are becoming bolder with their

shenanigans. They march in the street, and they are anti-Semites, and they think we are soft, Meyer," the judge said.

"I hate that, too," Lansky said.

"It is a movement," Perlman said. "Powerful men are openly making anti-Semitic remarks. Some of the newspapers and magazines are backing them up. Nazism is flourishing in the United States."

"It's no good," Lansky agreed.

"You got some boys who might want to punch a Nazi?"

"I do. Judge, Rabbi. Respectfully, you understand we can do better than punch? We could give somebody a deal. Very deterring to the survivors."

"I'm sorry, we cannot condone killing. There must be no killing," the rabbi said. Perlman nodded in agreement.

Meyer saw the wisdom in this and told them so: "It's always better not to shoot, right? But there will be violence, am I correct?"

"Oh, yes, let me rephrase. I want you to do anything *but* kill them. You have the men . . . ?"

"I know just the crew—in Brownsville. The boys in the press call them Murder, Inc."

"Good. I understand you are professionals. I will arrange to have you paid. I . . ."

"I need no pay, Judge. I am a Jew, and I feel for the Jews in Europe who are suffering. They are my brothers."

"Okay," Perlman said. "No money. But if you guys get in trouble, I'll make sure there is legal assistance for you."

"I appreciate that, Judge," Lansky said. Of course, that meant Perlman now owed Lansky a favor. Well, so be it. This was important. When the rabbi stepped out of the room for a moment, Lansky asked, "Pipes okay? Baseball bats?"

"Yes, yes, just don't kill them," Perlman replied. "Broken bones, I would think, are to be encouraged. They should know that being a Nazi is *dangerous*."

Meyer thought the no-kill rule took a little bit of the fun out of it, but leaving a bigmouth Kraut wailing in pain was satisfying, too, so he agreed to the terms.

As the rabbi returned to the room, Lansky had one more request.

"I assume you have some influence with the press, Judge."

"Some."

"The Jewish press?"

"More."

"If we get caught, please, no bad ink," Lansky said. "I don't want anything in the Jewish papers that my wife shouldn't read."

"Deal," Perlman said as the men shook hands. "*Mazel.*"

CHAPTER SIX
Murder, Inc.

The army that Lansky had in mind, the boys from Murder, Inc., were the sort who enjoyed shoving a snub-nosed .38 in a guy's gut or slicing him in half with a rat-a-tat-tat tommy gun. In a fair fight, some of them might not excel.

So Meyer took the boys to a dilapidated abandoned warehouse on Westchester Avenue in the Bronx to take lessons in pugilism from boxer Bobby Gleason so they could handle themselves when they ambushed Nazis. Once word got out that tough guys were needed, Lansky pulled walk-ins, stone-fisted fellows eager to wring a Nazi's neck.

Gleason was certain he was about to be whacked when Lansky and the fellas came into his gym, and he quickly agreed to get the gang in shape to throw combinations free of charge. (Gleason's Gym still exists, although it has moved several times and now makes its home on the waterfront in the DUMBO section of Brooklyn.)

Truth be known, the lessons were mostly an exercise in team building. A hood with a baseball bat or a pipe in his hands didn't need to punch, and those who did punch usually held with their left and pounded away with their right, a maneuver that would get you nowhere in the ring.

* * *

In order to understand Murder, Inc., you have to understand the old Sicilian Mafia concept of a *sette*. Back at the start of the twentieth century, the Mafia often didn't do its own killing. They contracted out. Certain hoods with a killer's skill set were organized into a sette, a secret society in its own right with its own initiations and rituals. That included, of course, the pledge of *omerta*, which says keep your lip zipped or sleep with the fishes. The American version of the mob got away from the sette concept for a while. Crews did their own killing, and the result was everybody killed everybody until it was a mess. Civil wars were terrible for business.

Along with setting up the Five Family system in New York City, Luciano and Lansky reinstituted the traditional sette. Now, if someone couldn't pay back the loan or was skimming the profits and needed to be taken off the board, the guy with the actual beef stood down. All hits needed to be approved from above. If someone needed to be whacked, you told the boss, and the sette took care of it.

The sette didn't care who it whacked. They were pros. Personal feelings had nothing to do with it. In the long run, the sette system prevented internal problems from affecting business. Luciano set up his sette, Murder, Inc., both outside the Five Family structure and outside the Italian mob structure as well. Both Italians and Jews were recruited. For Jewish killers, Luciano went to Louis "Lepke" Buchalter, who ran a gang of killers that he'd himself gotten from Abraham "Kid Twist" Reles, another son of an immigrant from Brownsville, Brooklyn, with forty-nine arrests on his record.

Lepke Buchalter was another of Lansky's childhood buddies. Lepke, which is Yiddish (Lepkeleh) for "Little Louis," was born in the Williamsburg section of Brooklyn in 1897, son of Russian-born Jews. He was one of thirteen kids, so it was easy for him to slip away and hang out on the streets. It could take his parents days before they took a head count and discovered he wasn't home. Any discipline he might have been receiving evaporated when he was still a child. His dad died and his mom ran off. After that, Lepke became a king on the streets. He teamed up with another delinquent, Jacob Shapiro, and they worked as a team, stealing and extorting. Lepke's specialties were mugging and pickpocketing. He was first arrested at age fifteen for stealing a door-to-door salesman's sample case. A judge thought some fresh air might do the kid some good, so he was sent to live with a cousin in Connecticut, but he robbed stores there, too, and ended up in a reform school in Cheshire.

As a teenager Lepke had a gang called the Gorilla Boys. It was said that he had extortion on his breath and always had plenty of craps money by levying tribute from pushcart peddlers. He developed a nice eclectic resumé, with crimes involving furs, garments, baking, trucking, drug smuggling—and murder. Back in New York, a second bust at age twenty-one sent him to the Big House in Ossining. After prison, he was a grown man, wearing the formal attire of a businessman. He was recruited by Arnold Rothstein, and his stock went up. Lepke liked to stay in the background and for many years wielded great power without publicity. He ran Brownsville.

Among Lepke's contributions to Western Civilization was his coining of the word *hit* to mean a contract murder.

Outside of being a thief and a homicidal maniac, Lepke wasn't a guy you'd figure to be a criminal. He was happily married to Betty Arbeiter Wasserman, a divorcée with a son. It was by all accounts true love. Lepke didn't fool around with women and wore conservative suits. He had a downright cheerful countenance and a nonchalance best symbolized by the way he wore his fedora perched atop the crown of his head.

What Lepke did when he went to work was another matter. At work, he was best known for his sadism.

Lepke might not have wanted to look like a gangster, but he sure knew how to act like one. On October 15, 1927, he proved that he could kill without emotion as he whacked his old friend Jacob "Little Augie" Orgen—not to be confused with Anthony "Little Augie" Carfano, who wasn't whacked until 1959—at the corner of Norfolk Street and Delancey. Orgen was a pedestrian. Lepke hopped out of a car, shot him four times in the guts, and got back in the car. Lepke went on to become a hero to Jewish kids across New York City, a guy who didn't take shit from anyone, a Jew who fought back.

By all accounts, Lepke didn't have a temper. He maintained an even strain even as he dispatched his latest victim. It was that chilliness, that cold blood, that scared everyone, even his closest friends. He could turn on them at any moment, and he could do it without raising his blood pressure.

To operate the sette, Luciano named his longtime right-hand man, Albert "Lord High Executioner" Anastasia, who ran the Red Hook piers in Brooklyn and would one day be boss of his own crime family (now known as the Gambinos).

Anastasia and Lepke worked together well at first, and their crews lived together as one. Ofttimes, they played a group game of *Strangers on a Train* and traded their assignments. Lepke would send guys to fix waterfront issues, and Anastasia would use his men to police Lepke's garment industry in Brownsville. Police saw a pattern in which Jewish guns killed Italian thugs, and vice versa, and they couldn't make any sense out of it. It looked like the Jews and Italians were at war.

According to Lansky, Lucky Luciano said that all members of the sette, Italians included, were available for the Nazi-busting fun, but Lansky said no, thanks.

"It was a matter of pride," Lansky said. "It was a job for Jews."

There may have been a matter of trust involved, too. The Italian mobsters as a rule hated Mussolini because he was anti-Mafia, but Italy and Germany were on the same side, and it only took one rat to ruin a surprise attack.

And so Meyer Lansky fought Nazis with an all-Jewish roster. They were:

Emanuel "Mendy" Weiss, a big man born in New York in 1906 who could handle himself in a bar fight. He killed with his hands and brutally overpowered his victims. If you asked

him what he did for a living, he'd say he had a dual voca-
tion: "I'm a kidnapper and a choker." He was a psycho
among psychos, capable of robbing a woman while holding
a gun on her baby.

Abraham "Kid Twist" Reles, whose nickname was passed
down from Max "Kid Twist" Zwerbach, a turn-of-the-century
torpedo. Reles earned the name because he looked younger
than he was and, before switching to the ice pick, his favorite way of killing was wringing a man's neck like a barn-
yard chicken's.

Twist was born in Brownsville, only a few blocks from
Murder, Inc.'s headquarters, the son of a garment worker.
He stayed in school through the eighth grade before taking
to the streets and hanging out with his childhood pals Buggsy and Pep, who we'll soon meet. During Prohibition, he
made a living moving hooch but was smart enough to never
touch the stuff.

Twist always had an expression of desperation on his
oval-shaped face, like a werewolf who's just noticed the full
moon. He had large features with big dark eyes, thick eye-
brows, and slightly blubbery lips. His hair was thick, black,
and wavy. His cigars were well chewed and wet.

Twist became a maestro of the ice pick. It was said he
could dispatch a man so neatly that the same coroner who
puked when he saw Pep's handiwork would mistake the
cause of death in a Twist murder for cerebral hemorrhage.
He was a sucker puncher, both literally and metaphorically.
No matter what the scenario, he believed in the sneak attack.

Martin "Buggsy" Goldstein, class clown, always cracking a
stupid joke, even as he was icing some poor slob. "I know, I
know, you need me like a hole in the head," he'd laugh as he
held a .38 to a sweaty man's temple. And then he'd pull the
trigger. Goldstein grew up on the same block as Kid Twist.
The nickname meant nuts, off his rocker, and in this case, it
was well earned. Goldstein came off as shy and gentle until

it was killing time. Then he'd get the job done efficiently and effortlessly, same as if he were swatting a fly.

He'd been with Kid Twist for as long as anyone could remember. Even in grade school, they were having criminal competitions, seeing who could steal the most stuff. They went full-time truancy, and both got popped for sticky fingers. They were active enough to attract the attention of the grown-up hoods and joined the farm system for Brownsville's lucrative rackets as an entry. There were other guys in Twist's gang back then, charter members—Big Head, Fatty—but who knew where they ended up? Buggsy stuck.

Buggsy was a guy of whom you did not want to be on the wrong side. Even if you were on the right side of him, there was reason to steer clear. At least twice, Buggsy and his partner-in-crime Seymour "Blue Jaw" Magoon—nicknamed because of his cobalt-colored five-o'clock shadow—were sent out to whack one guy and instead whacked another by mistake. Simultaneous to Buggsy and Blue Jaw's participation in anti-Nazi activities, they went out to shoot a recent parolee named Matthew Kane and ended up killing a financial district investigator named O'Hara. Call that "the Big Oops." The only one who didn't call Goldstein Buggsy was his long-suffering mother, who called him Mot'l.

Harry Strauss, also known as "Pep" Strauss, "Big Harry," and "Pittsburgh Phil," although he'd never actually been to Pittsburgh. Strauss had a face chiseled from stone, and he rarely changed expression, that expression being one of impatience. He was big, strong, and ruthless. He wasn't much for arithmetic.

"How many guys you killed, Pep?" someone might ask.

"Do you ask the baker how many black-and-whites?" Strauss would reply with a glare.

Later, it was said he'd killed upward of a hundred men. The number could easily have been twice that.

Strauss was a homicide artist with a variety of styles. It

depended on his mood. He experimented with a rope, knife, gun, ice pick, bare hands, disemboweling. He was an interesting guy, with an iron stomach.

Buggsy Goldstein used to joke, "You could make a coroner puke, Pep."

Strauss was a guy who had formulated a strict moral code, the breaking of which meant instant justice, with him as the judge, jury, and executioner. As historian Rich Cohen first observed, Strauss's behavior was intrinsically Jewish. He seemed to be emulating the God of the Old Testament.

Albert "Tic Toc" Tannenbaum was in. Born in a small town in Pennsylvania, Tannenbaum moved with his family to New York's Lower East Side when he was three. They moved again to Brownsville, where Tic Toc did the bulk of his growing up. He was different from his Murder, Inc. comrades in that he hadn't been a street kid. He'd finished school, worked in the garment district, and then at a country club owned by his father. He didn't know from the rackets until he was twenty-five years old and began hanging out with Lepke's crew. He might not have been a born killer, but he took to it quickly and became a trusted member of Murder, Inc. right up until the day he turned blabbermouth.

Charles "Bug" Workman had a screw loose, as his nickname would imply. He was short, with curly hair, and claimed twenty notches on his gun, every victim a gangster. With him, there was no collateral damage. He grew up on the Lower East Side of Manhattan in a small apartment crawling with siblings. He quit school before high school and took to the streets, just for the fresh air. He was popped for the first time at age eighteen for stealing twelve bucks worth of cotton off the back of a truck.

"It fell off!" he complained.

Bug was in his early twenties when he met Lepke, and he made a living busting up picket lines. His biggest claim to fame was being in on the Dutch Shultz hit on October 23,

1935, at the Palace Chop House on East Park Street in Newark. Schultz was at the urinal in the men's room when Bug shot him in the back. Bug was in and out of jail during the 1930s, but never for anything close to murder. His biggest bust was for breaking the nose of a cop who'd just given him a speeding ticket. He claimed that base pay for Murder, Inc. guys was $125 a week, with bonuses. He was out of jail just in time to fight Nazis.

Jacob Drucker was another ice pick man. His most famous kill came during the summer of 1937, when Anastasia sent Drucker and Irving "Big Gangi" Cohen to the Catskills to burn Walter Sage, a former Twist gunman turned gambler. They took Sage for a ride, stabbed him thirty-two times with an ice pick, then tied his body to a slot machine and a rock and dumped him into Swan Lake near the town of Liberty, New York. The weight failed to keep the body from bobbing to the surface, and it was found on July 31. The police had no trouble identifying Sage's body because his fingerprints were on file from when he was twice arrested for murder in Brooklyn a few years earlier.

The killers kept their mouths shut, even after they were caught in 1940 (well after the anti-Nazi campaign) and put on trial. Cohen was acquitted, but Drucker drew twenty-five years and died in Attica in 1962.

There were dozens of others in the Brownsville sette, killers whom time has forgotten. Guys who killed and were killed, the bodies lost in Jamaica Bay or in a landfill. Only a couple of them lived to be old.

They didn't call themselves Murder, Inc., at least at first. That was something that came out of the newspapers. But they earned their name—and their money. They were nothing if not prolific, and guys who'd failed in some way to do the right thing were being disappeared on a nightly basis.

Headquarters for the sette was the back room of the Midnight

Rose Candy Store in Brownsville, an ordinary-looking storefront at the corner of Livonia and Saratoga Avenues, underneath the elevated portion of the Number 3 subway train. There was a window in the front so neighborhood kids could buy the penny candy without going inside the store. Most customers didn't go in. Cigarettes, newspapers, they went through the window, too. The ones who did go inside tended to slink like coyotes. There was a movie theater on one side and a shoe repair shop on the other, ten paces from the Saratoga Avenue subway stop. Also on the block were a Jewish deli, hosiery dealer, barbershop, and a pharmacy where the backroom potions of cocaine and codeine guaranteed regular customers.

One function the store served for the community was that it had a phone, at a time when most people didn't. Making or receiving a call cost a nickel. For a piece of candy, some kid would run and tell so-and-so that they had a call down at Rose's.

"Midnight Rose" was a hit song from 1923, then a Broadway musical five years later, but in this case the name referred to Mrs. Rose Gold, proprietor, who earned her nickname by keeping her store open at all hours, making it the only thing open on Saratoga Avenue after midnight.

Rose was illiterate but a racketeer in her own right—numbers, girls upstairs—and she knew how to keep her foul mouth shut. She had an adult son named Samuel Siegel, who operated the Brownsville shylock racket. Asked to testify regarding the goings-on in her back room, she said she had no idea what her boys were up to. That was their business.

One of Rose's favorite scams involved rich housewives who liked to play cards. When a woman would get in debt, she'd get money from a shylock. If she couldn't pay it back, she was tricked out. If she wasn't a desirable trick, she'd be given an opportunity to rat out rich-blooded card games that the thugs could then raid, rob, and/or skim. If Rose needed to teach someone a lesson, there were always eight to ten lesson teachers in her back room, usually itching for something to do.

By 1938, Murder, Inc. was no longer at its strongest. As with any endeavor that dangerous, there had been attrition. By the time Judge Perlman was recruiting Jewish toughs to *shlom* Germans, the Law had already taken Lepke off the board. The man who ran the Brownsville rackets began having troubles that wouldn't quit in 1936. Looking back at it, Lepke couldn't figure out what he could've done differently. He ordered his boys to whack a guy named Rosen, which they did, but when the police leaned on the local hoods, someone spilled and said Lepke ordered the hit because Lepke thought Rosen was a rat. And for that, Lepke was a wanted man. He went on the lam. It was during this period that the battles with the German American Bund took place, and it is unlikely that Lepke came out into the open air long enough to take part.

It is believed that only Anastasia knew where Lepke was. Lepke might have been hiding, but he wasn't suffering. He was living above Louis (no relation) Capone's Oriental Danceland banquet hall on Stillwell Avenue in Coney Island, growing a large mustache, going out every day and walking the beach, gaining twenty pounds on Nathan's hot dogs.

During the time Lepke was on the lam, Murder, Inc. had been busy. It is estimated that between sixty and eighty men who knew a guy who knew a guy who might've testified against Lepke were eliminated during that stretch—strangled, ice-picked, shot, stabbed, buried in shallow graves, and covered in quicklime.

But even as the witnesses disappeared or floated ashore, the heat on Lepke's friends grew. The NYPD distributed wanted posters for Lepke, with his photo front and side and this description: "Eyes, piercing and shifting; nose, large, somewhat blunt at nostrils; ears, prominent and close to the head; mouth, large, slight dimple left side; right-handed; frequents baseball games."

Cops were everywhere, leaning on guys: "Where's Lepke? Tell me where Lepke is and everything goes back to nice."

The boys at Midnight Rose's could feel the heat at the backs of their necks, so Anastasia convinced Lepke to give himself up, promising that the legal business would be quick and painless and that he'd be back on the street with a snap of the fingers. The fix was in, Anastasia assured him. Lepke agreed, and Anastasia did nothing but cross his arms as Lepke was convicted of first-degree murder and sizzled in Ol' Sparky at Sing Sing, the richest man to ever be executed in the United States.

Like many big-time gangsters, Lepke tried to keep his criminality a secret from his wife and son, but the best bet is that at some point before the executioner flicked the big switch and sparked Lepke into eternity, they figured it out.

Of the boys Lansky chose to fight Nazis, a surprising number had been Bar Mitzvah-ed. Even those who never made it out of grammar school had gone through the ritual of becoming a man, being tutored in Hebrew, "reading" (phonetically but without understanding the meaning of the words) a section of the Torah in the synagogue, and acting happy when he received the requisite fountain pen at the reception after.

Buggsy Goldstein claimed his mom's curvaceous cousin had given him a blow job after his Bar Mitzvah, but nobody believed him.

Tannenbaum said he had placed his first bet after receiving five dollars at his Bar Mitzvah. "I took it to Lukey Litsky"—the well-known Brownsville bookie—"and blew it on a horse," Tic Toc said with nostalgia in his eyes. That one everybody believed.

CHAPTER SEVEN
The List

Judd Teller, a reporter for a New York Jewish daily, had had his earnest eyes on Europe ever since the name Adolf Hitler had first appeared in American newspapers in 1923. (Hitler's first attempted power grab, the Beer Hall Putsch, came in November 1923 when Hitler and his associates got themselves a belly full of beer at the Bürgerbräukeller and marched in Munich against Germany's Weimar Republic government. A riot ensued in which sixteen protesters and four police officers were killed. Hitler was injured in the fight, a dislocated shoulder, and was arrested and charged with treason, but the incident made splash headlines and put Hitler on the map. Beer and revolution went hand in hand in the Nazi myth.)

Teller was one of the first American journalists to note that Hitler was using Jews in Europe as scapegoats to launch a revolution, one that grew from a local revolution to a national one and an attempt at a global one.

Journalism was Teller's day job. At night, he wrote poetry about anti-Semitism. He was born in Ternopol in the Ukraine in 1912 and came to America when he was nine. In the meantime, he had survived the First World War, during which he witnessed horrible things that showed up in analogous form in his verse.

He earned his bachelor's degree at City College of New York

and then studied psychology at Columbia. He published his first book of poetry at age eighteen and was still a young man in his twenties when Judge Perlman and Meyer Lansky went to war against the Nazis.

Teller had returned to Europe a few times to cover stories, witnessing the aftermath of the pogrom at Brisk, which triggered in him post-traumatic stress. He twice interviewed Sigmund Freud. For the Jewish community, Teller became a vivid new voice—describing anti-Semitism, anti-Semitic violence, and the psychology of being scapegoated as a people.

Like many journalists, then as now, Teller was never quite kempt. His bow tie was a little crooked, his suits slightly crumpled, but he had eyes that told stories of the pain he'd seen, the hope he held, and the future he feared.

And that was pretty much the way he looked when Mendy Weiss and Blue Jaw Magoon from Midnight Rose's back room showed up at Teller's newspaper office, looking like they were going out of their way to be on their best behavior. They took their fedoras off, revealing well-combed hair. Magoon's jaw wasn't all that blue, which meant he must've shaved in the last five minutes.

"Who are you?" Teller asked softly, tapping his meerschaum against a huge glass ashtray on his desk.

"I am Emanuel Weiss, and this is my associate Seymour Magoon."

"Pleased to meetcha," Magoon said.

Weiss continued: "We have been assigned to take care of the Nazi bastards who march in Yorkville."

"Assigned? Who sent you?"

"We are with an organization called Murder, Inc. We are looking for the list."

Teller knew what Murder, Inc. was, but he tried not to show his concern as he thumbed fresh tobacco into his pipe.

"Which list? I have no list."

"It is a list of Nazi bastards who need rubbing out. We were told you had a list."

"No."

As Teller later recalled it, the men were wide-eyed, out of their element, and held their hats against their chests as they asked. Teller didn't much like having these guys in his office, but his sixth sense for news was going berserk. Gangsters versus Nazis. What a story.

"I'll tell you what. I'm a reporter, as you know, damned good at finding things out. If there is a list, I will find it. How do I get in touch with you?"

"We'll be in touch. Thank you, Mr. Teller," Weiss said.

"Pleased to meetcha," Magoon added.

So Teller went to the bearded "Jewish communal leaders" to ask about the list. Those leaders didn't like the Murder, Inc. angle at all. They were embarrassed by the fact that some of the best-known—and respected—Jews in New York were criminals, professional killers.

"Children idolize these men. It brings every Jew down," they said. The second a gangster smacked around a German, the police would be notified and the anti-Nazi effort would be shut down.

Teller left the meeting feeling rejected and dejected.

A few days later, Teller's phone rang. It was Meyer Lansky himself.

"We ain't going to ice the bodies, only marinate 'em. Just watch. No one will shut us down." Only a few attacks would be needed, Lansky maintained, and the attendance at Nazi rallies would shrink and shrivel. They were cowards, bold only in numbers. Individual Nazis would be afraid to walk the cracked sidewalks of New York with their uniforms on.

"I'll get the list," Teller said.

Again, the journalist got on the horn, made a few phone calls of his own—the Anti-Defamation League may have been one of them—and the following day, in the afternoon mail, Teller received "the list."

Soon thereafter, Weiss returned to Teller's office, this time without Magoon. "You have it?"

"I have it."

Teller handed Weiss a sheet of flimsy paper on which was a carbon copy of a typed list. It consisted of the names of Bund members in the city of New York, with home addresses.

"Thank you."

"Do me a favor, invite me along. I'd love to observe."

"You would have to ask Mr. Lansky about that," Weiss said. The men shook hands, and Weiss was gone.

In the days that followed, the boys set up almost daily operations, staking out Nazi homes in Manhattan, Brooklyn, and the Bronx.

And when they caught these guys out on the street alone, mugging them.

"Hey, Fritz!" they'd say, approaching hot and with a slight crouch.

It wasn't as much fun as murder, but it was close. What it lacked in finality, it gained in glory. They were beating up krautheads for a *cause*. It wasn't like they didn't know how to beat a guy up. They'd been doing it since they were kids, collecting debts. A dead man never pays his debt.

They braced a Nazi and left him bent over, puking on his shoes. As a parting gesture, they'd kick him in the shin and tell him he was fish food if he called the cops.

CHAPTER EIGHT
Yorkville

The German Americans' original home neighborhood in New York City was Kleindeutschland (Little Germany), or what is now known as the East Village and the Lower East Side, downtown, where the St. Mark's Evangelical Lutheran Church was the epicenter of activity. But tragedy struck when much of the neighborhood went for a ride around Manhattan aboard the huge side-wheel paddleboat *General Slocum* on June 15, 1904. As the *Slocum* was headed up the East River toward Long Island Sound, a fire broke out and spread rapidly. Passengers had a choice of burning to death or drowning, as few of them could swim, and the women were dragged down by the weight of their 1904 clothing. The *Slocum* sank near North Brother Island, taking 1,021 souls with it, the deadliest incident in New York history until 9/11. The old neighborhood was hauntingly empty and laden with despair, so the survivors moved uptown to a neighborhood known as Yorkville, on Manhattan's Upper East Side.

By 1938, New York City had the third largest German-speaking population in the world, behind only Berlin and Vienna, and most of them lived in Yorkville, which by this time was commonly referred to as Germantown. There were German neighborhoods in the outer boroughs as well, such as Williamsburg and Bushwick in Brooklyn and Ridgewood and Glendale in Queens, but they

were tiny in comparison. East Eighty-sixth Street, nicknamed
Sauerkraut Boulevard, was Yorkville's main drag.

On Wednesday evening, April 20, 1938, Meyer Lansky himself
accompanied a squad of fifteen gangsters on one of their first
anti-Nazi missions. A Bund meeting was scheduled, a big, cheerful one, full of celebration. It was Hitler's forty-ninth birthday!

The gangsters congregated a few blocks away, circled around
Lansky, who was on one knee and pulling open a pasteboard box.

"If anyone from the press asks, say you're a patriot, a veteran,"
Lansky instructed as he pulled from the box a stack of crisp
brand-new American Legion hats.

"Put these on. You are legionnaires, and the legion is the crew
with the beef."

To help sell the cover, they brought along Joseph Greenwald,
who was the Bronx County commander of the Jewish War Veterans. Also on hand was Judd Teller, the journalist who'd supplied
"the list," with a well-thumbed notebook and stubby pencil in
hand.

The Bund rally would be held at the Yorkville Casino on East
Eighty-sixth Street, between Second and Third Avenues. The
Bund was on home turf here and very comfortable. Their national
headquarters was just around the corner on Eighty-fifth. Because
it was a special occasion, there was to be a parade!

Yorkville Bund parades mustered at Carl Schurz Park, an ap-
propriate staging area for a German-pride event. The fifteen-acre
park covered the land along the East River at the foot of Eighty-
Sixth Street and was named since 1910 after a German-born secretary of the Interior. When parades were about to begin,
neighbors could hear the tubas warming up with a little "O Mein
Papa." East River Drive (now FDR Drive) was then under construction, built to go under the park through a tunnel. The park
was closed for tunnel blasting, so this day's Bund parade stayed
close to the East End Avenue entrance.

From their gathering point at the park, the Bundists would
march—as militaristicly as possible considering the level of ine-

briation—westward to the casino for the big rally, after which there would be more beer and charming young girls who'd sit on the lap of anyone in a brown shirt.

Many of the Bundists wore nameplates clipped onto their breast pockets, first name only, usually, along with their occupation. These were meant to be conversation starters. Bund meetings were designed to be as social as possible, good places for men of business to network.

The Yorkville Casino was a six-story building built in 1904 by the Musician's Mutual Protective Union (forerunner of Local 802 of the American Federation of Musicians) as a social center for both German and Irish immigrants who lived in the neighborhood. The word *casino* in this case did not mean a house of gambling but rather a place for meetings and dances. The casino was a place for fun, and most of the German American events held there were just that. Bands played, schnitzels and wursts were served, and the beer flowed freely. (The casino continued to function as a dance hall until the mid-1960s.)

The building had two ballrooms. The smaller of the two was used to show German-language movies. The larger one had a fifteen-thousand-square-foot dance floor, and it was there that the Bund meeting was held. The dance floor was covered with neat rows of folding chairs, and the bandstand was empty, with the exception of a single podium.

According to Teller, the squad of invaders divided into three teams. One—consisting of Lansky, Buggsy, Pep, and Mendy—went into the arena and took seats among the enemy, trying to look inconspicuous. The second—Tic Toc, Drucker, Workman, and Magoon—remained outside the hall. The outside crew held baseball bats and sawed-off pool cues. The inside crew brought their fists.

A third group managed to climb a fire escape and entered the building through an upstairs window.

Inside the ballroom, Lansky looked around and was enveloped by rage.

"The stage was decorated with pictures of Hitler, the fucking birthday boy," Lansky recalled.

Large swastikas hung from the back of the stage and formed the backdrop. There were swastikas all over the place, a man on stage delivering a speech as much like Hitler as he could, with arms waving and spittle spewing from his lips.

All eyes were on the speaker. The inside crew didn't just plow into the crowd and start a brawl—although that eventually happened. First, they gathered in the hallway outside the main ballroom and attacked stragglers, late arrivals, and guzzlers hitting the can.

A man, not connected to the gangsters in any way, began to heckle the speaker.

"Are any of these speeches going to be in English?" he cried out three times before he was shushed back into his seat.

Seconds later, the inside gangsters entered the ballroom and aggressively approached the stage. The outside crew overwhelmed the sentries posted at the front entrance and stood ready for the inevitable emergency evacuation.

The fire escape group whooped and hollered as they came down the stairs to join the fray. In seconds, it was on. The Nazis found themselves being attacked from three directions.

Eventually, there were fifteen fistfights and a lot of Nazi panic. If the Nazis had stood their ground and put up their dukes, they might have done okay because they heavily outnumbered the gangsters. But they were weak and keened like banshees.

There was one mouthy Nazi. He had a salesman's frozen smile, and his nameplate read "Fred. Retail." He ran up the stairs to avoid the violence. Buggsy was hot on his trail and planted a nice combo—thank you, Gleason—on the guy's jaw, causing him to sag against a wall. Fred slid down the wall like vanilla ice cream rolling down a cone. Once he was on the floor, Buggsy kicked him in the ear.

"Mr. Retail, you're a lucky man. You are getting a beating *wholesale*," Goldstein exclaimed with a bright grin.

Drucker, who up until that point hadn't done much, ran up the flight of stairs to see if Buggsy needed help. The gangsters worked as a team, and they dangled the semi-conscious Nazi out a second-floor window. There was a brief discussion. Should we or shouldn't we? Then—what the hell—they dropped the guy to the sidewalk below, and he landed right foot first, causing his leg to accordion.

The crowd quickly thinned as Nazis, many of them bleeding, fled out the front door and returned to their homes in the East Eighties.

Lansky remembered that the job ended with his boys chasing three Nazis down the street.

Not all of the Nazis fled. Some were left where they'd fallen, unconscious from a blow to the head or grotesque and screaming with compound fractures. The Nazi who'd been dropped out the window had a busted right femur.

Teller later said it didn't last long, five minutes tops, but it was an action-packed few minutes. When Teller himself turned and moved to a safe distance, the hall was already mostly empty, but scattered about were injured Nazis. So much blood.

Teller hung out at the other end of the block to observe the aftermath. The police arrived just late enough to do no good. The men in blue were scratching their heads and wondering what the hell happened. There were a handful of arrests, mostly of Germans who were very brave now that the attackers were gone.

The gangsters dropped their weapons and legion hats on the sidewalk as they left, and sure enough, the papers the next morning blamed the American Legion for the riot. It would be years before Lansky would admit to his role in the brouhaha.

"I must say I enjoyed beating up Nazis," Lansky later commented. "There were times when we treated some big anti-Semite in a very special way, but the main point was to teach them that Jews cannot be kicked around."

Of those arrested, the most serious charge went to the blond and German-born Otto Geissler, who was held for violation of the Sullivan Act, best known as a gun-control law, but also prohibiting a man from carrying a knife in a scabbard. Or any other "dangerous weapons", for that matter.

Both Geissler's defense attorney and the prosecutor were Jewish, and the judge was a veteran of the World War. Geissler's lawyer was Joseph Ellison of the Voluntary Defenders' Committee of the Legal Aid Society. He stood up for several of the battered Nazis, all in a day's work.

Judge Matthew J. Troy looked out into his courtroom and saw a bunch of sad, bandaged men, and one by one, after making each sweat a bit, sent them home, warning them to play nice from now on. The judge discussed the irony of an anti-Semite being defended by a Jewish lawyer.

"This all demonstrates the worthwhileness of Americanism," Judge Troy commented. If the judge knew that his colleague, Judge Perlman, had instigated the fracas, he kept his mouth shut about it.

CHAPTER NINE
White Plains

The next Bund rally, this one called a German Day Fete, was moved outside the five boroughs of New York and into Westchester County, in the town of White Plains, in an arena on the Bronx River Parkway known then and now as the Westchester County Center.

Of all the venues for Bund events during the Depression, this is one of the few that still stands and still serves its community much as it did in 1938, although it did get spruced up in 1988 thanks to a $16 million renovation.

The architectural firm of Walker & Gillette designed the art deco structure. It cost $785,000 to build and opened for business in 1924. (It is the current home of the Westchester Knicks of the pro basketball G League. It's hosted more than five hundred boxing cards and concerts by Judy Garland, James Brown, and Janis Joplin. And, in 1938, one happy, happy Nazi party.)

According to posters, the Nazi event was held under the sponsorship of both the German American Bund and the United German Societies of Westchester County and Connecticut.

Because of the Yorkville riot, the NYPD was on high alert for the Sunday evening event "upstate." More than one hundred uniformed patrol officers and detectives were in the Grand Central Station area, keeping a close eye on the anticipated one thousand Nazis thought to be getting to the rally via a chartered train.

There were the normal number of homeless (referred to in 1938 as "loiterers") in the station, and they were cleared out to prevent anyone in a bummy disguise from attacking the Nazis. Officers even worked outside Grand Central to make sure pedestrians on Lexington and Vanderbilt Avenues kept moving.

Three sides of the huge railroad station were cordoned off, as was the stretch of Forty-second Street from Second Avenue to Madison Avenue. There was an impressive police presence on both the upper and lower levels of the station, while other officers guarded the IRT subway station under Grand Central and the elevated station at Third Avenue and Forty-second Street.

The Yorkville brawl had squelched the Bund's New York momentum. As Lansky had predicted when speaking to Teller, attendance in Westchester had shrunk and shriveled. A thousand Nazis were expected to ride the chartered train but only about a quarter of that boarded.

The train left at six. The event began at eight. The ride was about thirty minutes. At first, the train traveled northward underground, but then it rose into the daylight at Ninety-sixth Street and Park Avenue, where more police were stationed to discourage rifle-armed rock throwers.

We don't know if there was a planned attack on the Nazis as they went to the White Plains rally, but if there had been, the heavy police presence discouraged it.

"There was no demonstration or disorder," a police representative said the next day about the Grand Central Station op.

It was a different story up in Westchester. There was definitely an attack planned there, featuring a roster of hoods pretty much the same as those who had busted up the Yorkville Casino birthday party.

But, unlike Yorkville, where the police arrived after all was said and done, the police presence at the Westchester arena was so tight that the gangsters' initial plan to bust heads was scratched.

The Nazis who trained to the event marched the half-mile from the White Plains train station while guarded by twenty uniformed

White Plains police officers. The gangsters didn't want to let the Nazis think they'd gotten away with something, though, so Lansky quickly formulated a Plan B.

He spotted a pair of fresh-faced teenagers in baggy and patched dungarees.

"You boys Jewish?"

"Yeah, what about it?" Turned out they were from Bronxville Manor and attended Bronxville High School.

"No, that's good, that's good. Us Jews, we got to stick together. You know who's in that building?"

"Yeah, Jew-haters."

"That's right. You guys want to make a dollar?"

"A dollar each?"

"Sure, sure."

"Let's see it."

Lansky pulled a wad from his jacket and watched their eyes pop. "One for you, one for you. Here's what you got to do."

Lansky pulled something out of his other jacket pocket, looked like two vials from a chemistry lab, with corks in them.

The White Plains fete had been billed in advertisements as a fun observance of a milestone in the history of the "German-American element in this region." Inside the arena, however, things didn't feel all that fun. There was apprehension in the air. Veterans of the Yorkville riot were in the audience, men in slings, men with the visible green remnants of shiners.

As was foreshadowed by the largely empty charter train, there were many no-shows. The arena had a seating capacity of five thousand but was less than half full. If a Nazi spoke loud enough, he could hear an echo.

Some in the arena thought there was going to be trouble when nine members of the American Legion, real ones in their telltale hats, entered. But there was no excitement as it was announced that the men were there at the invitation of H. H. Greve, president of the United German Americans of Westchester. They were greeted at the door by storm troopers who escorted them to a box near the stage.

Lansky's teenagers took seats in the back. No one paid any attention to them. Right on time, the band started to play. The United States and German national anthems were performed while everyone stood.

Teenaged girls cartwheeled down the aisle, and a chorus filed onto the stage and sang a couple of German songs. Then the first speaker took to the podium. That was when Lansky's young soldiers went to work.

The teenagers stood and shouted, "Hitler's got one ball!" And each pulled out their vial and threw it toward the podium. They were "stink bombs." The boys didn't even wait for the vials to break; they turned on a dime and hightailed it toward the exit.

The police snagged them, however, and charged them with disorderly conduct. They didn't rat out Lansky, however, if they even knew who he was.

"Why did you do it?" a cop asked as the boys were placed briefly in a White Plains jail cell.

"It was our sworn duty as true-blooded Americans," one of them replied.

A reporter came to the jail to interview the youthful Nazi-haters. Again, they were asked why they broke up the meeting.

"How would you like it if those guys came over here and took control?" one of them said.

Back at the arena, there was an evacuation, an airing out, and then festivities resumed. There were more empty chairs than ever.

A photo that ran in newspapers around the nation the next day showed American citizens in the audience giving the Nazi salute at the "passing of the colors," a swastika flag carried by a color guard down the aisle during the rally.

Organizers (ignoring the stink bombs) bragged to reporters that the rally, which "called for a return to the ideals of George Washington," went on "without significant disruption."

Those mainstream newspapers largely ignored the obnoxious politics discussed at the meeting and wrote that among the German American groups attending were "singing and gymnastic" clubs.

As the meeting resumed, a picket line formed outside. A group of young men and women representing the Westchester division of the American League for Peace and Democracy marched in single file outside the arena, carrying signs that read:

KEEP HITLER OUT OF AMERICA

NO ROOM FOR NAZI MURDERERS

EXPOSE THE NAZI SPY RING

The protesters did not adversely affect the meeting inside, but they did cause a traffic jam as homeward-bound drivers tarried and rubbernecked to see what all of the fuss was about.

Simultaneous to the White Plains event was a Manhattan gathering of the Kings County and New York County Jewish War Veterans. One of the highlights of the meeting was the election as commanders of two members who had participated in the "Battle of Yorkville" just days earlier.

Among the speakers was Jean Mathias, whose heckling ("Are any of these speeches going to be in English?") seemingly triggered the Yorkville melee. He pledged that he was going to continue to attend both fascist and communist meetings as part of his ongoing investigation into "treasonable activities."

Other speakers included Kings County Commander Abraham Cohen, now the man in charge at the East Flatbush Community Center on Linden Boulevard, who said, "We must awaken the American public to the realization that there is no room in this country for Nazism. The bunds are made of blackjack-wielding fomenters of racial hatred. I call for measures that will wipe out subversive groups in New York City."

City Councilman Abner C. Surpless and Representative Donald L. O'Toole of Bay Ridge, Brooklyn, also spoke. O'Toole told the gathering to continue to "fight for American democracy" and urged the United States to halt relations with Germany "and any other nation that persecutes minority groups. And we must acknowledge the existence of an armed, uniformed, terroristic, anti-democratic, un-American fascist force in our city."

Representatives of the Sons and Daughters of Liberty and the American Gold Star Mothers also addressed the gathering. At one point, there was a complaint about unauthorized use of American Legion hats at the Yorkville riot. Nobody knew who those guys in the hats were, but there was agreement that they should get a pass because they were such good fighters.

Then a man from the Communist Party got up there and said that they didn't want to be lumped in with those Yorkville creeps, and he pledged that the communists would fight "for the protection of our basic American values." The message was met with only polite applause as many attendees were all too aware of the Nazi claim that communism was a Jewish conspiracy to control all the money.

Perlman had promised to stop the negativity about Lansky in the Jewish newspapers and to defend his anti-fascist activities, which, though violent, were for a great cause. And the judge tried, but that didn't mean that Lansky was happy.

One never knew what a gangster was going to be sensitive about. These men, many of them, lived double lives, with wives and children who had no idea what they did for a living.

The Jewish papers quoted Rabbi Wise, who was there when Perlman met with Lansky, who said that the "Yorkville Bund Busters" were a bunch of "Jewish gangsters." Lansky was furious. How dare he use that word? Why didn't Perlman protect him the way he said he would? Lansky felt double-crossed.

Lansky later claimed that this was the first time *anyone* ever called him a gangster. Could it possibly have been true? Surely,

Lansky had been called a gangster many times—but maybe always behind his back. Maybe he just meant the first time in public.

What Lansky said was, "They wanted the Nazis taken care of but were afraid to do the job themselves. I did it for them. And when it was over, they called me a gangster. No one ever called me a gangster until Rabbi Wise called me a gangster."

It may have been Lansky's snit fit that resulted in the Bund getting off one last 1938 New York rally unmolested. The meeting was held just on the other side of the East River from Manhattan—at the Turner Hall in Astoria, Queens—and drew seven hundred Nazis, including Fred the Retailer, who was still on crutches with a plaster cast up to his waist. There were an estimated three hundred protesters outside the hall, peacefully protesting, and about a hundred cops guarding the doors. Inside, feeling safe and cozy, an attorney named Herbert Roth concluded his anti-Semitic speech by saying, "Fellow Bundsmen, it is time to smash the shield of Abraham once and for all." Fritz Kuhn, sitting at a dais, thrust his chin in the air in approval. When the quote was relayed to former magistrate Joseph Goldstein, he threatened to file charges against Roth for inciting a riot. The Nazis considered the meeting a great success. For once, they all got to go straight home without stopping at the emergency room for first aid.

The greatest symbolic win over Hitler in the New York City of 1938 didn't happen at a Bund meeting. It happened at the big ballpark in the Bronx: the heavyweight championship fight between African American Joe Louis and the undefeated German Max Schmeling in Yankee Stadium on June 22, 1938. It was a rematch. Schmeling had KO'd Louis in the first bout. That made Hitler strut with his chest puffed out as tears fell in Harlem.

The buildup to the rematch was huge. Never before or since had there been a fight quite so symbolic. American versus German, black versus white, Democracy versus Nazism.

There were many Jewish boxing fans in New York who did not tend to root for the black prizefighters, but in this case they made an exception. Almost all Americans did. Yankee Stadium was packed, and the rest of the country, seventy million of them, anyway, listened to announcer Clem McCarthy call the fight blow-by-blow on the radio in his "whiskey tenor."

(To be fair in the retelling, Max Schmeling was not a Nazi and was by all accounts a good guy. But he was German and Hitler's pride and joy. As far as the world was concerned, only his alabaster skin mattered.)

The fight itself was quick but brutal. Louis went to work early and hard, throwing devastating left hooks, four to the head and one to the body that landed with a sickening thud that could be heard in the stadium's third deck. Schmeling cried out in pain. The German sagged with one arm over the top rope. The ref paused the fight until Schmeling could stand up straight.

After that, the end came swiftly. An overhand right to Schmeling's kisser sent the German to the canvas for the first time, but he was up at the count of three. Louis threw a three-punch combo, with all of them landing on the button.

McCarthy had America riveted with his impossibly fast tommy-gun delivery: "A right to the head, a left to the jaw, a right to the head, and Schmeling is *down*!"

This time, he was up at the count of two. A third knockdown followed immediately, and at the 2:04 point of Round One, Schmeling's corner tossed the towel. Louis had thrown forty-one punches, landing thirty-one of them. Schmeling threw two punches and landed one, a decent right to the face that Louis walked through without blinking. Schmeling spent the next ten days in the hospital.

Mayor Fiorello LaGuardia was the sort of politician you don't see anymore: a liberal Republican who'd risen to power on the coattails of FDR's New Deal. He was a short, round man, with a deceptively friendly manner.

One day, while sipping orange juice at his breakfast table, La-Guardia opened a letter from a very whiny Nazi who said that Jewish goons were infringing on the rights of the Bund to peacefully assemble. LaGuardia knew the guy had a point. From a legal perspective, the Jewish fighters were fully in the wrong. It was only the intrinsic immorality of Nazism that muddied the issue. LaGuardia couldn't stand the Bund. All of that hate made his skin crawl.

The mayor told the Nazis okay, we'll keep the Jews off your back, but with a few caveats. The Nazis were forbidden to wear uniforms, display swastikas, sing songs, and march to drums. Keep the tubas home, too, he might as well have said. And they had to stick to their own turf, that is, Yorkville.

The Nazis agreed, and that was supposed to be the end of the gangster campaign of pain. LaGuardia assigned Jewish cops to Yorkville events, so if trouble erupted, the Nazis would be made to feel as uncomfortable as possible. The mayor took it a step further and made sure Jewish cops were assigned to security duty whenever a German Nazi dignitary visited New York.

It signaled the end of Lansky's battle but just the beginning of the war. The Bund took its act on the road, and Perlman made other phone calls to other gangsters, so that wherever the Bund tried to hold a noxious meeting, the boys would be there to dish out the hurt.

PART THREE Chicago

Get in there and fight, you punk.
—DAVEY MILLER

CHAPTER TEN
Father Coughlin, Radio Priest

Anti-Semitism was nothing new in Depression-era Chicago. According to Irving Cutler—a professor emeritus at Chicago State University and also author of the book *The Jews of Chicago*—anti-Semitism in the Windy City dated back to the turn of the century, a time when Jews had to daily face vicious hatred. Kids would run up to aged Jews and pull their beards or throw their chewing gum at them. (Gum in a beard couldn't be removed without pain, and often a scissors.) The Jewish community stood out and made easy targets because they looked different and tended to wear Old Country–style clothes.

But by the late 1930s in Chicago, anti-Semitism was not confined to the insults of street bullies or the ignorant proclamations of juiced-up bigots. Hate talk was in the very air, in the airwaves, coming out of every radio in the city. One spewer of the sewage was a Catholic priest named Father Charles Edward Coughlin, who gave his sermons over the radio on Sunday afternoons, right between the *Rhythmic Ramblings* program and *Design For Dancing*. They called Coughlin "the Radio Priest." Coughlin had a velvety soft voice and tenderly wrapped his hate speech in a warm security blanket of tone and comfort. He wore small, round glasses, and when he smiled, he emanated a shallow kindness, one that dissipated if you examined his eyes. The guy was nuts.

Father Coughlin was born in Canada in 1891 and attended seminary school in Toronto. He was a star pupil. After he was ordained, he taught for a few years before being assigned to the Detroit diocese.

His first flirtation with the public eye came in 1926, when he was thirty-five years old. He arranged for the construction of a Catholic shrine in a Detroit suburb where there were only a handful of Catholics but an active KKK. To keep the shrine from being smashed, Coughlin recruited sports stars, including Babe Ruth, to make personal appearances at the shrine. After the Shrine of the Little Flower was built, Coughlin had cleared ten thousand dollars on the deal and frequently had his name in the newspapers.

In September 1926, Coughlin asked a Detroit radio station for free airtime so he could "raise awareness of his church." The station agreed. Coughlin and radio turned out to be a perfect match. His baritone voice with perfect enunciation made him a pleasure to listen to—as long as you paid no attention to what he was saying.

The first sign that Coughlin was special came in the form of pilgrims, people from all over who journeyed to visit the Shrine of the Little Flower. He had built it, and they were coming, and once they got there, they discovered Coughlin's offertory basket was always out.

He created the Radio League of the Little Flower, and anyone could become a member by sending Father Coughlin one dollar. Since Coughlin considered himself a charity, it was all tax free.

In 1928, he met with New York architects to build a new church at the corner of Woodward and Twelve Mile Road in Royal Oak, Michigan, a combination place of worship and headquarters for Coughlin's syndicated radio network.

His popularity grew. He was an influential broadcaster in Detroit, then Chicago, then from New York to Los Angeles. His program was carried on forty-six stations across the United States, without the benefit of a major radio network. His first shift from the religious to the political came after the stock market crashed and the nation plummeted into despair. He advocated, on the air, a fresh printing of money at the US mints, which he claimed would cause inflation and give the economy a boost. FDR thought the idea ridiculous and said so, at which point Coughlin began a never-ending rant about FDR being un-American.

The US Treasury Department responded by investigating the Radio Priest, then publicizing their findings. They'd discovered that the private citizen in Michigan who owned the most silver (a half-million ounces) was Coughlin's secretary. You know, in case anyone was wondering where all of those dollar bills were going. Coughlin responded by calling FDR a "tool of Wall Street."

In 1936, Coughlin exploited his media clout to launch his own political party, designed to run a candidate for president against FDR. It was called the Union Party, but it wasn't all that pro-union. He couldn't find a candidate who wasn't Catholic, and the common wisdom at the time was that Americans wouldn't vote for a Catholic for president. (There have only been two Catholic presidents—John Kennedy, who was assassinated, and Joe Biden.) He finally found a body to fill the tickct in William Lemke, a North Dakota Republican. Coughlin didn't really think Lemke would win, but he had hopes of deadlocking the Electoral College, which might have resulted in FDR's ousting. The reality was that Lemke drew fewer than a million votes and FDR beat Republican Alf Landon in a landslide.

So Coughlin returned to his radio microphone. His themes tended to repeat, and one concerned Jews.

There were indications that the radio was becoming more powerful than newspapers ever were or could be. On October 30, 1938, the night before Halloween, America had listened to Orson Welles's *War of the Worlds* on the radio, a theatrical piece about a Martian invasion of Earth set in New Jersey, and many people had panicked because they thought it was real.

Just a few weeks later, the Radio Priest broadcasted a strong defense of Nazi Germany. In particular, he praised the way Nazis dealt with Jews. The priest said that he was against all forms of religious persecution, of course, but the Germans' treatment of the Jews was a natural reaction to the communist threat that the Jews represented.

It is unclear whether Coughlin was aware of the genocide underway when he said this, but he certainly knew about Kristallnacht, the night of November 9 and into November 10, 1938, in which Jewish neighborhoods were smashed and many of their residents killed. Coughlin told America that he wasn't pro-Nazi; he was anti-communist. He named the names of two dozen Jewish men who were involved in the "Russian revolution." The Jews had money and were backing the communists. The Jewish religion and communism, in fact, had become synonymous, and the power of that combo was making Germany sick, like a cancer. Was it any wonder they wanted to cut it out? Without any sense of irony, he said that many Jews in Germany had become powerful by using their talents to acquire positions in radio, on newspapers, and in international banking. The Jews, he said, were dangerous because of their solidarity. It was one-for-all with those people, so that when they wanted to be aggressive, they could hurt Germany. He pleaded with FDR to pull American ambassadors out of all communist countries.

Coughlin's ratings were through the roof. The show was called *Golden Hour of the Shrine of the Little Flower*, and the Gallup poll said twenty-two million listened in—which could have been a record for that time. Many Americans took it all very seriously. How could Father Coughlin be wrong? He was a priest! He made the sign of the cross before and after his sermons. He threw in a Latin phrase now and again, and when he wasn't calling for the extermination of a race of people, he led the nation in prayer. He was keenly aware that his audience was poor and had been poor for close to a decade. They were immigrants and sons and daughters of immigrants, not just German but also Irish and Italian and Polish. When he discussed the impending war in Europe, he naturally thought the United States was best to stay out of it. The conflict, he opined, was over money, capitalists fighting over a bigger piece of the pie. The subject of the barbarism of Nazi domination never came up. He prayed for the poor masses, he said, prayed that they would remain safe from the greedy interests of FDR and global banking. He was, he said again and again, *vox populi*, the voice of the people. That message, oddly, melded into another: he questioned why elections were necessary and called for a halt to the two-party political system.

WMCA, the radio station that carried Coughlin's program in New York, had asked for and received an advance copy of Coughlin's sermons, so the instant he went off the air, they had a speaker ready, not only with a disclaimer that those opinions did not represent those of the station but also with a rebuttal from a silver-throated member of the Anti-Nazi League, refuting just about everything Coughlin had said.

Eventually, Coughlin went too far, and WMCA announced they were dropping Coughlin's program. The reason: "Unfortunately, Father Coughlin has uttered certain mistakes of fact."

That caused Coughlin's fans, carrying anti-Semitic signs, to picket on the street in front of the radio station's studios.

"We want Coughlin!" one chanted.

"Send the Jews back where they came from—in leaky boats!" called out another.

"Jews are going to be sorry when Hitler comes over here," cried a third.

WJR in Detroit received a deluge of complaints, and the Roman Catholic diocese in Detroit made it clear that Coughlin's worldview was his own. WJJD in Chicago and WIND in Gary, Indiana, stopped broadcasting the show, but wouldn't publicly state why.

"It no longer appears on our program sheets," was the company line.

Coughlin persisted, however: "By their failure to use the press to fight communism as vigorously as they fight Nazism, the Jews invite the charge of being supporters of communism."

Coughlin was an entrenched tile in the 1938 zeitgeist mosaic, mentioned in the lyrics of tunes by Cole Porter (1935's "A Picture of Me Without You" from Broadway's *Jubilee*) and Woody Guthrie (the scathing but unreleased "Mister Charlie Lindbergh"), but he was not a rallying point for other groups that shared his anti-Semitism. To a certain extent, he remained a loner out there on the airwaves because he was Catholic, and to a lot of Jew-haters, Catholics were almost as bad. Coughlin was the subject of an angry Ku Klux Klan rally, after which they burned a cross on his lawn. That said, Coughlin remained more popular than the Protestant ministers who sermonized anti-Semitic messages on the radio at that time, guys like the Reverend Gerald B. Winrod, who also denounced the Jews from coast to coast, but he couldn't match Coughlin's charisma, his media savvy. The only radio voice of hate that could compete with Coughlin was that of Gerald L. K. Smith, a Louisiana political organizer who took over where Huey Long left off after Long's 1935 assassination. But Smith was not a man of the cloth.

As Judge Perlman picked up the phone and said, "Long distance operator, get me Chicago," anti-Semitism was in the air.

CHAPTER ELEVEN
Herb Brin, Fighter of Fascists

During the Great Depression in the Windy City, the most powerful Jewish gangster was Jake "Greasy Thumb" Guzik. It wasn't so much that he was the boss of anything, but he was Al Capone's right-hand man, and Al Capone was boss of everything. Thus, Guzik wielded tremendous power.

If you asked him, Guzik would say he was Capone's business and financial advisor. Guzik was Russian-born (1886), but had no memories of the Old World as he came to America with his parents as an infant.

The Guziks settled in Chicago, where dad ran a cigar store. When Jake was old enough, he took a job tending bar, and sometimes he was a "steerer," aggressively guiding businessmen from out of town in the direction of his brother's brothel.

"You gentlemen looking to have a good time during your stay in Chicago? I'll fix you up," went Guzik's rap.

In 1932, Guzik was busted by the feds and served three years for tax evasion, splitting the stint between Leavenworth and Lewisburg Prison in Pennsylvania. His first chance at parole was rejected as the board found Guzik to be a menace and dangerous.

Dangerous? Ha! Guzik said that was a joke. He'd never lifted a finger in anger.

Upon his release in 1935, he immediately returned to Chicago and resumed his position at Capone's side, doing the math. Now, he was a loving husband, father, and grandfather, known in his profession as "Greasy Thumb" because he was always "counting Capone's money."

It was obvious that Guzik picked up much of his fashion sense from Capone. They both wore dark trench coats in inclement weather and cream-colored fedoras with dark brown bands above the brim. They were both in love with food as well, and Guzik— like his boss—had a pudgy, round face and a double chin.

And so, when it came time to fight the Nazis, Judge Perlman called Guzik. As part of Guzik's job involved "handling judges and politicians," he answered the call with a friendly hello.

Perlman asked, "Jake, do you know anyone who might want to punch out a few Nazis?"

"I do. My boss"—in prison at the time, but still, no name was necessary—"likes to eat at a place next to a boxing gym. Many Jewish fighters. Barney Ross. You heard of him."

The gym was on Kedzie Avenue and Roosevelt Road, on a block where Capone owned a few buildings in a row. There were all kinds of Jewish tough guys hanging around looking for stuff to do. Some ran errands for the boss; some were prizefighters in training, dreaming of fighting someday in the main event at the Chicago Stadium, which despite its name was an indoor arena. There would be no trouble putting together a crew. He'd have to run it past his boss, of course, but he didn't expect a problem.

Perlman said "Great" and hung up the phone. His next call was to the Chicago B'nai B'rith (Sons of the Covenant) and Rabbi L. Elliott Grafman, the founder of that organization's new project, the Anti-Defamation League. Rabbi Grafman, in turn, called a journalist by the name of Herb Brin.

"Go see Richard Gustadt," the rabbi said.

Brin was going to ask why, but the rabbi had already hung up.

Herb Brin was born in 1915, the son of immigrants. His dad, Solomon, was born in 1883 in Konin, Poland. As a young man,

Solomon, against his will, went to battle as a baker with the Russian army during the Russian-Japanese War of 1904 and 1905. He came to America when he was twenty-seven, with dreams of panning for gold in Alaska, entered the country at Galveston, Texas, went to work for the railroad, met Pia, who would become his wife and the mother of his children, and never made it to Alaska.

A little over a year after they were wed, a baby boy was born, little Hymie. During Hymie's infancy, the family lived in a cold-water flat on Lincoln Street in Chicago. When the child was three, they moved to a better apartment in a basement on Claremont Avenue, then when he was thirteen to an even nicer apartment above ground on Claremont.

Solomon operated a plumbing supplies store on Kedzie Avenue. The Brins were moving on up—and then the Great Depression hit.

One day Hymie, when he was about eleven, was walking with his dad down Kedzie Avenue.

Sol said to his son, "We call you Hymie because we love you, but you should pick an American name."

They were passing the Kedzie Avenue Theater, at the corner of Kedzie and Madison. It was built in 1912 for vaudeville and still split programs between live acts and the "flickers," still silent in those days.

There was a poster behind glass on the front advertising the next week's movie, *Burning Gold*. The colorful poster showed an oil well blowing up in the distance while in the forefront a virile young man clenched one fist in fury and used the other to protect the beautiful blonde woman he was with.

The rest of the poster read: "Directed by Jack Noble. Cast: Herbert Rawlinson, Mildred Har—"

Wait. That was it.

"I want to take Herbert as my American name," the boy said, and Herb it was.

Herb attended junior college in Chicago and then the DePaul College of Law, which only lasted until the school realized he couldn't pay the tuition. He tried to get a job working for one of the big downtown department stores and was told sorry, no Jews. In 1935, he bought a beat-up two-hundred-dollar Chevy and headed west.

In California, he took a job as a milkman and, though he was only there briefly, helped the others organize a milk truck drivers' union. He returned to Chicago because his dad was sick and went into the family business, which was manning a series of news-stands on Kedzie Avenue, up and down from Crane's Plumbing Supplies, where Solomon still worked.

It was no doubt during this period that he ran into the Jewish gangsters and boxers who hung out at the nearby pool hall and boxing gym on Kedzie. He remained restless, filled with a young man's wanderlust, traveling first to New York City, then to Phila-delphia, where he worked briefly as a collector for the United Mercantile Exchange. It was there that he met a beautiful blonde violinist named Selma Stone.

In 1938, Herb Brin was twenty-three years old. He had listened to enough stories of the "Old Country" from his parents to know that dangerous anti-Semitism had been around a long time before the rise of Hitler in Germany and the worrisome popularity of his teachings in the United States. One of Brin's great aunts had been murdered and dismembered as a baby on Easter Sunday by "Christians" on a holiday purge.

Brin had been familiar with anti-Semitic culture since he was a kid, when he had to run a gauntlet of Polish goons each morning on his way to school and then again on his way home in the after-noon. One day, he encountered a bully with a knife and came home with a six-inch gash in his leg.

He grew up in a world in which being anti-Semitic was "nor-mal," one in which owners of rooming houses routinely put signs in their window that said, "Vacancy. No Jews or dogs allowed."

Now, Brin was a clean-cut young man who never smoked, was lousy at math, and was holding down a tough job as "gangland reporter" for the City News Bureau, a journalist's dream.

The bureau was known for its hardboiled reporting and later

became the subject of Ben Hecht's play, *The Front Page*. Brin's job took him to both the Italian and Jewish neighborhoods of Chicago, where a reporter quickly learned to walk the thin line between writing about the rackets and being whacked in an alley.

Now Brin—who had the light hair and blue eyes of Hitler's dream child yet hated that kind of thinking with all of his guts—had been summoned to meet with the leaders of B'nai B'rith and their Anti-Defamation League. He had no idea why he was there.

"You know what we do and who our enemy is," said Richard Gustadt, head of the Anti-Defamation League's Chicago branch.

Brin nodded. "Our enemy," he repeated.

"We are the only organization in America who is tracing the movements of the Bund. No one else cares. We alone see the danger here."

"Do you want me to write a story . . . ?"

"No, no story. Nothing written down ever. You have light hair and blue eyes. We are asking a great favor."

"I'm listening," Brin said, already feeling his adrenaline start to pump.

"We would like you to volunteer to go undercover and join Chicago's edition of the German American Bund. We would like you to keep us apprised of the rhetoric they are using, any actions they plan, propaganda they are distributing, and most importantly, the location and time of their meetings. We plan to disrupt their activities at every turn," Gustadt said.

"I'm your man!" Brin exclaimed.

Brin explained that he already knew a little bit about those guys, that he'd once encountered a German American man who offered to take him to the Hausvaterland and other German clubs to demonstrate that "Germans were only against certain types of Jews." The implication was that because he had sandy hair and blue eyes he wouldn't be discriminated against.

"Would you be recognized if you returned?"

"No. I sat in the back and kept my mouth shut."

"Excellent. You will contact the Bund and tell them that you believe in their cause and hopefully they will accept you among their ranks."

"Do I report back to you if I learn anything?"

"No, no no no. You will report to your contact at the Edmille Health Club pool hall. Do you know the place? On Kedzie Avenue."

Ah, Kedzie, his stomping grounds, home of family-operated newsstands, movie theaters with great posters out front, penny-candy stores, traveling crap games, hardcase hoodlums, and the notorious Forty-two Gang, who were juvenile hardcase hoodlums in training. During the Depression, there was also hunger and desperation, blurring the morality of cutting corners to make a buck.

"My dad has a plumbing supplies store down the street. I wasted a portion of my youth there," Brin said with a grin.

CHAPTER TWELVE
Sparky and Barney

The pool hall mentioned by Richard Gustadt was in the West Side of Chicago, in a neighborhood known to the locals as Lawndale, situated along a strip that attracted Jewish members of the underworld and teenaged boys, truants, and vagrants who wanted a starter job like running numbers or handing out and collecting football parlays. Alongside the pool hall and boxing club complex was a restaurant frequented by Chicago's underworld, where perhaps the idea for the St. Valentine's Day Massacre was hatched.

The pool hall in question was Davey Miller's place—Davey Miller the boxing referee, forty-eight years old. Davey's brother Max was a hoodlum, but Davey was mostly legit. He'd been a tomato-can heavyweight in his youth, but he could still handle himself in a pier-sixer with his decidedly non-Kosher hamlike fists.

Miller had a heroic reputation with the West Side's Jewish youth. For as long as anyone could remember, he'd been an enemy of anti-Semitism, often flattening the nose of a Polish thug he saw picking on a Jewish kid.

There are many stories about Miller inside the ring, giving pep talks of a sort to boxers who were having their heads handed to them. One wet-behind-the-ears pugilist named Abraham Marovitz, a Twentieth Ward kid who later became a judge, remembered fighting himself into exhaustion in one fight that Miller reffed.

"I said, 'Mr. Miller, I can't lift my arms to fight another round,'" the future magistrate whined.

"Get in there and fight, you punk," Miller replied.

As our story begins, Miller had just worked his biggest fight, Joe Louis's devastation of Harry Thomas in the Chicago Stadium. At the fight's conclusion, with Thomas taking a snooze and the Brown Bomber standing calmly in a neutral corner, Miller proved he could count to ten with the best of them. Two months later, Louis would fight in New York's Yankee Stadium in what would be called the Fight of the Century.

Miller's pool hall was different from many of the hundreds of Chicago's pool halls in that it had a gambling room upstairs where the poker games ran 24/7.

The widespread belief was that Miller had been in Al Capone's pocket. If Miller was quick to stop a fight, the hoods in the front row grumbled (quietly) that Scarface must have had money on the winner.

Miller had been considered for the ref job for the Gene Tunney–Jack Dempsey rematch at Soldier Field in Chicago back in 1927 but had been passed over by the Illinois Boxing Commission because of his closeness to Capone. The job instead went to Dave Barry. Boxing historians will recall that the referee played an unfortunate role in that fight. With Tunney winning on points in the seventh round, Dempsey trapped him in a corner and unleashed a vicious combo—right, left, right, left, on the button— that felled Tunney, the first time he'd ever been knocked off his feet. Trouble was, there was a new rule in play. After a knock-down, the count didn't begin until the standing fighter had re-treated to a neutral corner, which Dempsey failed to do. Time passed as Barry reminded Dempsey of the rule and the fighter complied. In the meantime, Tunney's head was given a chance to clear, and he returned to his feet before completion of the ten-count. With more than 103,000 in attendance, Tunney then defeated Dempsey by unanimous decision. Thus, the fight became known as the "Long Count Fight." For Davey Miller, not getting the job was a big disappointment, but because of the way things turned out, it might have been a blessing in disguise.

Now, Miller's pool hall was no Bensinger's, the roomy billiard parlor on Randolph opposite the palatial Oriental Theatre. Bensinger's—the inspiration for the 1961 Paul Newman–Jackie Gleason movie *The Hustler*—was dramatically lit, a place where a crowd might gather just to watch Willie Mosconi work out over a rack or two. There were even separate sections for those who preferred snooker and a row of bowling alleys with spectator seating.

Miller's lighting was merely dim. The joint wasn't action free, of course, none of the pool halls in Chicago during the 1930s were, but the stakes were small and the winner of a game of straight pool to one hundred might make enough to fill his flask. It was also a place where you could sit in a folding chair for hours and kibbutz, eventually learning all of the neighborhood's gossip.

Directly next door was the boxing club that Miller also operated, where kids, many of them still in their teens, honed their pugilistic skills while trainers blew whistles and shouted out combinations by number. There, too, a guy could come in off the street and watch all day, but it wasn't free like the pool hall. You had to throw a dime in the bucket at the door. On Friday nights, the price of admission went up to twenty-five cents as Miller put on a series of three-round amateur bouts, usually drawing guys who couldn't get tickets to the pro fights at the Chicago Stadium that night.

Miller was sometimes confused—but not for long—with Davey "Yiddles" Miller, a South Side torpedo known for the mean-spirited and thoroughly professional manner in which he dispatched his enemies. Our Davey Miller had a stronger sense of public relations and had the common sense to name his pool hall the Edmille Health Club. What Jewish mother wouldn't want her son hanging out in a place so healthy?

"Your contact at the Edmille Health Club will be a young man named Jacob Rubenstein. Everyone calls him Sparky. Do you know him?" Richard Gustadt asked Herb Brin.

"The little guy who is sometimes in Barney Ross's corner?"

"Yes."

"I know him. Funny guy. Tough."

"Good. You give your report to Sparky, and he will take care of the rest," Gustadt said.

Brin thought about Barney Ross. The legend. The kid had done all right for himself. He had been born on the Lower East Side of New York in 1909 as Barnet Rasofsky, but the Rasofskys had moved to Chicago when the boy was two, and Chicago remained his home for the rest of his life.

As a kid, Barnet had dreams of becoming a Talmudic scholar or maybe a Hebrew teacher—such a good boy. But that all changed when he was fourteen and watched in horror as his father, a rabbi and grocer, was shot and killed during a robbery of the family store. His mom promptly had a nervous breakdown and was sent to "live with relatives," causing Barnet and his four siblings to scatter, the youngest three placed in an orphanage. Barnet went to live with a cousin, but his days of being such a good boy were over for the time being. He stopped dreaming of being a scholar and teacher, renounced his religion, and turned to a life of crime, running numbers for the racket boys, busting any-one in the chops who looked at him funny, and stealing enough to eat regularly. After a few years of that, his pal Sparky, himself a small-time hood wannabe with a mom who had mental issues, suggested Barnet go see Jack Eile at the Edmille boxing gym. If he kept walloping kids on the street, he was bound to end up in jail, and a gym might help him get rid of excess energy. The name Barnet was turned to Barney on the street, but Rasofsky was switched to Ross only after he became a pro boxer and didn't want his mom (whose health had returned) to know he was fighting for a living.

Not that he was effeminate in any way, but Ross did have a pretty face that he'd inherited from his mom. Having a better offense than defense in the ring, he would start fights looking like a debutante and end them looking like Quasimodo. But, as they say, you should've seen the other guy.

Ross, Herb Brin thought to himself, was the toughest son of a bitch in the city, but maybe he'd had his picture in the paper one too many times to be useful in an undercover operation.

Trainer Jack Eile recalled the first time Ross walked into the Edmille boxing gym. The kid was already partly hood, collecting for the rackets, the awesome size of his hands speaking for themselves when a debtor whined that he didn't have the dough. But he was trying to get out of that scene. He wanted to make it legit.

"He was eighteen, nineteen years old, and he had thick black hair that he combed back, but which tended to flop down over his forehead the instant he began to mix it up in the ring," Eile said. "When he came into our club, he showed little ability, but he was willing to hurt and a sparring partner could hit him with everything he had and Barney wouldn't even flinch. I showed him how to jab and hook with his left—and how to clinch when he forgot to duck."

Barney never became a boxing purist, and his fights were slobberknockers, crowd-pleasers. He had a left hook from hell and almost always won. He traveled to New York City's Madison Square Garden in 1929—with Davey Miller himself as his sponsor—and won the national featherweight division Golden Gloves championship before a packed house. And that was it for him and anonymity. He promptly turned pro and fought prelims in Chicago billed as "Barney Ross, West Side Jew Kid." When he had made enough money, he used it to reunite his three youngest siblings, still in an orphanage, with their recovered mother.

Ross earned his first of three championship belts on March 26, 1933, when he defeated Tony Canzoneri by a majority decision at the Chicago Stadium. The fight was close—so close that the referee ruled it a draw. One ringside scribe called the action "bitter and vicious." There was an unwritten rule that to take a man's belt you had to knock him out, so Ross's victory via decision, not even a unanimous decision, was enough to make the crowd boo. Canzoneri had dominated the first half of the fight but had tired. Ross, known for his endurance throughout his career, came on at the end, including a final round in which he "let go with everything he had," forcing a hurt Canzoneri to repeatedly clinch.

Ross won the rematch against Canzoneri less than three months later at the Polo Grounds, the Giants' horseshoe-shaped ballpark on East 155th Street in Manhattan.

Ross's most famous fights were the three he fought against Jimmy McLarnin, the first two in 1934, the third in 1935, all in New York City, all outdoors, the first two at the "Madison Square Garden Bowl," which was a huge hole in the ground dug in Woodside, Queens (the setting for the 2005 movie about James J. Braddock, *Cinderella Man*), and the third at the Polo Grounds. He won the first and the third, but took a terrific beating in the second, the only fight in his pro career in which he was knocked down.

By 1938, Ross's career as a fighter was just about over. He was only twenty-eight years old, but was battle-worn and past his prime. His final fight was against the champion, Henry Armstrong. The fight went the distance, and Ross stayed on his feet the entire time but endured a fearsome battering. From the middle rounds on, fans pleaded with the referee to stop the fight or for Ross's corner to throw the towel, but Ross told his corner men he wanted to go out like a champion, that is at the final bell and on his feet. When it was over, Ross took weeks to recover and never fought professionally again. Like many ex-boxers who drew a crowd, Ross opened up his own restaurant, and that was where he was when his old pal Sparky Rubenstein said he needed volunteers to kick some Nazi ass.

Rubenstein and Ross had been a team since they were kids.

They had a bleak upbringing in common, a bond made of loneliness and pain, and remained life-long buddies.

Rubenstein's dad had been a medical assistant, a man worthy of respect, but his mom, Fanny Rokowsky, was a pixilated redhead who chattered mindlessly even when she was alone. She was probably bulimic and prone to temper tantrums. Fanny and Joseph Rubenstein, Jacob's dad, had an arranged marriage, so there was nothing like love in the home. There must have been some spark, though, because the Rubensteins had eight kids, Jacob being the fifth in line. Joseph took to beating Fanny in hopes that that would shut her up. She'd apparently fallen on her head as a baby, and Joseph hoped maybe another crack on the noggin would snap her out of it. But it never worked. When Jacob was four years old, Fanny had Joseph arrested multiple times and twice charged with assault. Fanny was eventually institutionalized; her illness characterized as deteriorating paranoia. In the hospital, she told the doctors she never liked any of her kids. (In 1909, one of Fanny's children, Jeanette, had died at age two from a scalding incident in her kitchen.)

The Rubensteins lived in a cold-water apartment on Johnson Street, now known as Peoria Street, in a neighborhood known at the time as the Maxwell Street ghetto. Jacob learned to fight when the Italian kids visited from Taylor Street in Little Sicily to beat up Jews. Jacob made sure he dished out more than he got. He got his nickname from his sister Eva, who called him "Spark Plug" as a boy, after the horse in the popular comic strip of the day, *Take Barney Google, F'rinstance.* There were also hit songs from 1923 by Billy Rose and Con Conrad based on the same strip: "Barney Google" and "Come On, Spark Plug."

Jacob became a truant, a kid of the streets, an angry kid who tried to stifle his urge to babble on endlessly just like his mother. At sixteen, he was scalping tickets for Bears football games outside Soldier Field and at William Harley's Mills Stadium, the small wooden ballpark at Lake Street and Kilpatrick Avenue west of Garfield Park, home of DePaul University football games,

Negro League and barnstorming baseball, and an annual Fourth of July fight card. He got to know some of the fighters and began hanging around the Edmille Health Club, where a kid could make a buck running errands for the mob guys. Sparky and his pal Barney were given a crisp one dollar bill every time they delivered a message or went to the corner store and bought a pack of cigars for someone, including the number one guy, Al "Scarface" Capone, who pretty much owned the whole block the Edmille was on.

Jacob worked legitimate jobs too, but always in a venue where one was apt to see gangsters. He sold racetrack tip sheets near Capone's off-track betting parlors. He sold candy and cheap jewelry to the chumps at the burlesque shows who thought the almost-naked dancers were sweet on them.

At least three times a week, he'd get into a fight. He was determined to prove to the world that Jews were tough, years before Judge Perlman gave Meyer Lansky free reign to fight the German American enemy.

As a young man Jacob Rubenstein left Chicago for a few years in Los Angeles—a city where the cops and the hoods were often one and the same—to live with his sister, but he could never adjust to all of that sunshine, and by 1937 he was back on Kedzie Avenue working as a union organizer for Leon R. Cooke, who wanted junk business laborers to earn more than fifteen cents an hour. Rubenstein's job was to pick up skim money, but he was again unemployed after Cooke got himself whacked. Rubenstein played pool and worked out in the gym. He kept himself in great shape and liked to brag while working the heavy bag that he could hit harder than Joe Louis. He continued to make most of his income by scalping tickets at all of Chicago's major venues—Wrigley Field, Comiskey Park, Soldier Field, and the Chicago Stadium.

Each Monday and Friday night, Rubenstein attended the fights at Marigold Arena on the southwest corner of Halsted and Grace, on the North Side, boxing Monday, wrestling Friday. The place held two thousand and almost always sold out—but he never worried about having a ticket. If Barney Ross was fighting, Sparky got in free by going in the boxers' entrance, carrying his friend's gym bag. Even on Fridays, when Barney usually wasn't around, Sparky knew the guy at the back door and slipped in with no complaint. Sparky could always get in—a skill that would one day contribute to his legend. By the main event, the air would be so thick with cigar smoke that you could see the fight but not the spectators on the other side of the ring. Betting was plentiful and out in the open. Some guys would just bet one corner all night, or the guys in the white trunks. Irv Schoenwald ran the Marigold shows and knew plenty of cops. He'd comp them when he saw them on the street and never once was anyone busted at his shows, no matter how obviously they were making a fight book. Sparky observed the behavior. There was an advantage to being friendly with the police. You got more with sugar than vinegar.

Herb Brin knew that his appearance meant everything in the world he was entering. Just as racists judged African Americans by the shade of their skin—the cream in the coffee, they used to call it—so anti-Semites judged Jewish people by their appearance. Brin worked for a time at Sears and Roebuck alongside unashamed anti-Semites.

"How can you work alongside me?" Brin asked one of them.

"You're special, you're a *white* Jew," his coworker replied cheerfully. It also helped that Brin was a big guy, six feet, one and a half inches, and not one to be easily bullied.

The idea that the intelligence Brin would gather might result in a few anti-Semites getting hurt didn't bother him. He didn't like to brag about it, but he stomped one of those German American meatheads himself once.

Flashback. Herb Brin is on a bus, standing, holding a strap, and there's one of those guys on there, a loudmouth, "Jews this and Jews that." Nothing clever, just the usual drivel. He's got a seat, sitting next to a gray-haired woman holding a paper sack with a naked loaf of bread sticking out of it.

Eventually, Brin has had enough.

"Shut up or I'll knock you to Kingdom Come," Brin says.

The guy quiets for a moment but just as the bus is passing James Garfield Park, less than a block from the movie theater where Brin found his name, the idiot starts in again, muttering.

Brin takes one step, waits for the sitting woman to get her groceries out of the way, and busts the guy in the chops.

The bus driver calmly pulls the bus to the curb and stops, although this is not a normal bus stop. Brin grabs two handfuls of the guy's shirt and drags him off of the bus and onto the park's expansive greensward.

Brin beats the man from "one end of the lawn to the other" and leaves him laying there, his nose somewhere near where his cheekbone should be. Brin then brushes himself off and gets back on the bus, to thunderous applause from all of the other passengers.

Return to present.

Brin began by attending marches and outdoor meetings that were open to the public at Harm's Park in Skokie, a northern suburb. He would later realize that the gatherings there were especially ugly because the park bordered on a Jewish neighborhood.

He didn't have to try very hard to be recruited. He expressed an interest in learning more about the movement, and everyone was his friend. Each time he held his hand out, someone gave him printed propaganda and advised him of the next meeting place. After his face became more familiar, Brin signed up as a Bund member at the Hausvaterland on Western Avenue.

So Brin found out the details of a private meeting, and one icy Tuesday afternoon, he relayed the info to Sparky Rubenstein at the pool hall. For Brin, it was a nostalgic moment. The place was exactly the same. Even the smell was the same, an oddly pleasant combination of cigars, sweat, and blue chalk.

Less than an hour later, Sparky gathered his volunteers around him. They were kids, most of them, fresh-faced and eager: Milton Marks, Dave Forman, Max Kamm, Herman Lieb, Irv Botnek, Seymour Brodofsky, Aaron Ragins, and others time has forgotten. One familiar face was missing: Barney.

"Where is he?"

"Next door working out."

"Get him."

A few minutes later, a shiny Barney Ross entered the pool hall from the icy street, wearing nothing but shorts and shoes, well lathered with sweat, steam rising from his shoulders. That got a laugh because it was snowing outside and the temperature was in the single digits. Ross had an expression like he was less than enthusiastic about being there.

"What?" he said. His gloves were off, but his hands were still taped. Written on the tape in black crayon was "DM," for Davey Miller. Rule was you had to initial the tape for a sanctioned fight, so Miller got in the habit of doing it even for workouts so he wouldn't forget some night and get a kid in trouble.

"We're making plans to bust up them Nazi fuckers," Sparky said.

"I know, but I can't go," Ross said, sounding genuinely sad.

"Why not?"

"You guys get caught, it's assault. I get caught, attempted murder. My hands are lethal weapons."

Sparky stared at him without blinking for a solid ten seconds, then blinked several times in rapid succession and said, "I got it. You don't use your fists. You use a sap."

Sparky produced from his back pocket a professional-looking

blackjack—a leather sack filled with ball bearings with a leather handle looped and held in place by a metal clasp.

"Thanks, Spark," Barney said, and everyone was smiles. "When?"

"Tomorrow night," Sparky said. "We meet outside the Germania Club, across the street. That's on West Germania Place, Near North Side."

The boys were told that if a scribe asked who they were and whom they represented, they should say they were "Veterans of the Abraham Lincoln Brigade." Or if they couldn't spit that out, "Americans who believed in liberty."

CHAPTER THIRTEEN
The Germania Club

The Germania Club, built in 1889, looked old even then, when it housed the oldest German American organization in the city. (It looks even older now. The building is still there, added to the National Register of Historic Places in 1976 and designated a Chicago Landmark in 2011.) The building has five stories, including a two-story lime base. Architect August Fiedler designed it in a combination of neoclassical and German Renaissance styles. Inside were a grand ballroom, a banquet room, and a bar and restaurant.

The boys rendezvoused across the street, waited until the meeting had started, and then walked in the front door like they owned the place. They sat in the back and tried to look like they knew what was going on, despite the fact they didn't speak German. Most of them knew some Yiddish, and the languages are similar. They didn't catch every word, but they got the gist.

Sitting near the front was Herb Brin, who was undercover and thus could not participate in the disruption.

The featured speaker was Bund PR director Wilhelm "William" Kunze. It was during Kunze's speech that trouble began, and it had nothing to do with the gangsters and boxers at the back of the venue.

Kunze made his usual mischaracterizations of Bund activities:

They were not a military organization, not seeking to change the American government, only emulating the good things about the German government, blah, blah, blah.

"Hitler put six million and five hundred thousand unemployed people back to work. If we can learn something from that, we should take advantage of it," Kunze said.

Freeze frame.

It is important to note here that there were many German American organizations in America's big cities, close to forty of them, that were anti-Nazi to the bone and therefore anti-Bund. In Chicago, some of those organizations consolidated into the Action Committee of German Progressive Organizations, which published a newspaper called *Volksfront*, that is, "People's Front." The ACGPO was dedicated to oppose by lawful means subversive propaganda against the Constitution of the United States of America. The leader of the group was fifty-year-old Eric von Schroetter, professor emeritus of romance languages at Northwestern University, who was sitting five seats in from the aisle in the fourth row as Kunze spoke. Von Schroetter was also the secretary of an organization called the German American League for Culture.

And . . . action.

Kunze had just made his comment about putting the unemployed back to work when von Schroetter stood and shouted, "Sure, they're all in the German army!"

Two brown-shirted storm troopers moved in on von Schroetter, grabbed him, and began to drag him out.

Somewhat simultaneous to this, a group of Nazi bouncers had spotted the boys from the pool hall—Davey Miller, Sparky Rubenstein, Barney Ross with a handkerchief tied around his lower face like an outlaw in a Western movie. There was nothing Aryan about their appearance, and several Germans accosted the group. Feeling clever, they asked the boys to prove they weren't interlopers by giving the Nazi "Sieg heil" salute. Sparky Ruben-stein wasn't impressed. He gave the Nazis a salute all right, a one-finger salute, and the fight was on.

Ross obediently used his leather blackjack and, with his combed hair flopping onto his forehead, sapped down three Nazis right away, without a single use of his lethal weapons. Sparky tried to grab a handful of one Nazi's hair, but it was too short, thin, and sparse, so he worked the move into a headlock and waled away with his free hand while the Nazi flailed weakly, dropping harmless blows to Sparky's back with the meat of his palms.

A photographer with the Associated Press tried to take photos of the melee when Emil Horitz, one of the guards who'd escorted Kunze to the hall, grabbed the camera, threw it to the ground, and stomped it into pieces. The photographer made a mental note of this guy, learned who he was, and later had the cops arrest him for "criminal mischief."

When police arrived, there were five arrests. Nazis under arrest included thirty-year-old real-estate broker William Wernicke and Horitz, the camera smasher. Also arrested were von Schroetter, charged with disorderly conduct, and two Jewish teenagers from the boxing club. The remainder of the Kedzie Avenue crew made a clean getaway. The next morning, Municipal Judge Gibson German—that was his name—dismissed all of the charges and told the combatants to keep their hands to themselves.

The riot at the Germania Club coincided with the resignation of a German diplomat named Ernst Wilhelm Meyer, who said that he could no longer represent the "New Germany" as Hitler had "betrayed what I knew to be the lasting interest of the German fatherland. I can no longer conscientiously serve a government which I saw to be a foe of so many things I had been taught Germany stands for." Meyer resigned during a speech he gave at a dinner held in his honor in New York City by the Federal Council of Churches of Christ in America. "It is disgraceful for a ruling party of a state of seventy million inhabitants to drive a helpless minority of less than five hundred thousand to destruction."

Brin supplied anti-Nazi intelligence for much of 1938 and 1939. Every time the Nazis scheduled a secret meeting or a surprise march, Chi-town's Jewish gangsters knew in advance, and the Nazis were attacked and pummeled.

As for Brin, he didn't just spy. He later told historian Robert A. Rockaway that he participated in some of the later fights as well.

"I marched with the Nazis," Brin said. "But I came back later with Jewish gangs, and we beat them up good."

Many of the dates and locations of these beatings are lost to time. Brin had promised not to write about his efforts and was good to his word, not discussing the Nazi fights until many years later, but a few of the scuffles did make the newspapers.

During November of 1938, several meetings in a row were busted up at a variety of meeting halls in the heart of the German district—three of them in one week.

The first meeting occurred on the same date as the Syracuse, New York, riot that we'll be discussing in chapter 24. The second was invaded during a speech by Dr. Homer Maerz, president of the brand new German American Alliance. Maerz was speaking on the topic of what had happened at the previous meeting and how to prevent it in the future. He should have been more concerned with the present. Several Chicago cops and Bund guards were posted at the front door, but they did no good as the invaders broke through and entered the hall screaming, "Down with Hitler!" and "Down with fascism!" By this time, the Associated Press reporter knew who was doing the busting up, but he protected Davey, Sparky, Barney, and the others, identifying them only as "anti-Nazi protesters." There were eight arrests, six men and two women. The women had started brawling outside the hall when one shouted "Hooray for Hitler!" The other proclaimed herself a Czech sympathizer. All eight were briefly jailed at the Sheffield Avenue police station.

The third of that week's riots took place at a Silver Legion meeting held at the Loyal Order of Moose hall on Irving Park Road, with the guest speaker fifty-one-year-old Field Marshall Roy Zachary. (For more about the Silver Shirts and their founder William Dudley Pelley, see chapter 21.) The guest speaker didn't look like much. He was small, bespectacled, and gave off a timid vibe. But when he spoke, he shook the rafters.

A United Press reporter was on hand to describe the action. Soon after the meeting began at 8:00 P.M., a parade of cars pulled up out front, and from each car three to five angry Jewish men emerged. At 8:35, just as Zachary was beginning his anti-Semitic remarks, a "shouting mass of men charged in" and a "general melee" followed.

In just about all of the other riots, the top Nazis managed to sneak out of the building and allowed the minions to take their lumps. But on this night, with approximately one hundred Silver Shirts in attendance, the boys went straight for the podium, and Zachary was later hauled out with "head injuries."

This riot, which occurred on the Monday after Thanksgiving, was also the occasion when Judge Perlman's anti-Nazis came closest to defying the "no killing" rule. In the midst of what the reporter called "fierce hand-to-hand combat," Aaron Ragins of the Kedzie Avenue crew punched a forty-four-year-old man named Clarence Sutherland right on the button, causing Sutherland to fall and crack the back of his Nazi skull on the hardwood floor. Sutherland was taken out on a stretcher, and it was touch-and-go at the hospital, but he eventually recovered.

Zachary's injury was the headline, however, and the field marshal's photo appeared in many newspapers with a sad piece of gauze held to his forehead by a clumsy cross of adhesive tape.

The police arrived and peace was restored. There were many injuries, mostly bruises and lumps. The reporter referred to the Jewish gangsters as a "nameless organization formed to oppose both the German-American Bund and the Silver Shirts in the manner of vigilantes."

The organization might have been nameless, but the *Chicago Daily Tribune* published the names of those who'd been arrested for busting up the meeting, and most were Davey Miller's boxing students, ranging in age from seventeen to twenty-one.

A reporter and a photographer from the Jewish Press were also busted, leading us to believe that they were doing more during the fight than taking notes and pictures. "Greasy Thumb" Guzik hastily sent lawyers to the jail to bail them all out.

The final Chicago riot of 1938 took place at a hall where Bund members were watching a German movie. Eleven Jews were arrested and scolded, this time by Judge Charles S. Dougherty, who said he "appreciated the motive" behind the attacks but suggested the best way to make the Nazis go away was to ignore them.

There was one last incident in Chicago during the spring of 1939. The Kedzie Avenue crew targeted a large meeting featuring Fritz Kuhn himself. The police, however, had their own spies in place and went to work before the meeting began outside the hall, detaining dozens of Jewish men who, when asked to explain their presence, mumbled something about liking liberty. Only one was arrested, however, and that was because he was found to be carrying a gun.

Sparky Rubenstein, Herb Brin, Barney Ross, and the other Chicago vigilantes had done their job. The number of meetings they disrupted was impressive. It's safe to say that by 1939 every Nazi in the Windy City knew how tough Jews could be.

PART FOUR Newark

Back then there was only one place in America tougher than Brooklyn: Newark, New Jersey.
—Al Nit

Jewish boxers were brave and tough, but they did fear one personage above all others—their mothers.
—Mike Silver

CHAPTER FOURTEEN
Longie Zwillman

Back in chapter 9, we learned that New York's Mayor LaGuardia put a damper on Meyer Lansky's war on Nazis by forbidding the goose-stepping Germans from wearing uniforms, displaying swastikas, singing songs, or marching to drums.

In essence, LaGuardia was kicking the can down the road, in this case, across the river. The Nazis executed an end run around LaGuardia's rules and refocused their efforts on the other side of the Hudson in New Jersey, primarily at first in the city of Newark.

The Depression had been particularly harsh on Newark. More than one hundred banks in the city were padlocked and abandoned. Misery filled the air with its sour scent. Not only were there many Germans living there, but they also were unhappy and convinced that some outside force was responsible. The Bund was glad to tell them at whom they should direct their blame: the Jews of Newark's Third Ward.

The Third Ward of Newark in the 1930s was much like the Lower East Side of Manhattan, rows of houses on narrow, crowded streets. When a baby was born, the family doctor came to the mother's house and the newborn would be placed on the kitchen table. When you got sick, you went to the doctor's office. Cost three bucks. A lady in a nurse's uniform—who might or might not have been a nurse—would come around and collect the money before the doctor—who might or might not have been a doctor—would see you.

Everybody was poor. Possessions were few but precious. Everybody's grandma lived with them, but she spoke no English and kept her ways closest to the Old Country. On Prince Street, every corner had a newsie—"Extry! Extry!"—but here they called out the day's headlines in Yiddish.

No matter your ethnicity, Jewish peddlers came to your door (or stayed out on the street and rang a bell), with a wide variety of wares. Sometimes, it would be the same guy as last week, but now he was selling something different—pots and pans, curtains, bedspreads, whatever he had. By the time he got to your door, you knew what he was selling because he sang about it. If you couldn't pay all at once, he'd make a deal and come around weekly to collect. There weren't supermarkets like today, where you could get everything in one place. Oftentimes, when you needed something, you didn't go anywhere at all. You waited for the guy to come around in his horse-drawn cart. There was an ice-man, a fish man, a milkman, a seltzer man, and a guy who sharpened knives.

If you were used to watching the dainty fetlocks of a thoroughbred running at Monmouth, the horses that pulled those carts looked strange. Not only were many of them too old and weary to run at all, they also stood on huge ankles and hooves. Their job had nothing to do with speed. It was to pull the cart for twenty years before dropping dead in the street, which was how they usually went.

The only merchant who didn't go to his clients was the barber. Barbershops have remained largely unchanged since 1938—a place where men congregated, where a man could keep up on the local news as he tightened up for an evening engagement.

Newark's Third Ward had eighty-one blocks, nine blocks by

nine blocks, and has been called the Central Ward since 1954. Some famous people grew up there:

- Dore Schary, who went on to be a bigwig at MGM and earn nine Academy Award nominations.
- Future New York City Mayor Ed Koch. When he was a poor child, his dad worked for tips in the cloakroom of the local dance hall.
- Author and Pulitzer Prize winner Philip Roth, his dad slogging out a living as a door-to-door insurance salesman.
- And another hero of our story: Abner "Longie" Zwillman, the gangster who ran the Newark rackets and who hated Nazis just as much as Meyer Lansky did.

Abner Zwillman was a bootlegger, born and raised on Newark's Charlton Street, the son of Russian immigrants who came over on the boat around 1900. Dad Abraham sold live chickens on Prince Street. Abner was the third of seven children, grew up hungry, in poverty so painful that as an adult he thought about nothing but his determination to never be poor again.

He attended Charlton Street School and earned his nickname without irony, growing to be six-two by the time he was fourteen, the year his dad died. With dad gone, Longie quit school, got a job, and helped support his mom and six siblings.

The job was grueling, peddling fruits and vegetables from a horse-drawn cart. He quickly learned a distaste for work. He looked around him, saw who the rich guys were, and noticed that they didn't work very hard at all. They were grifters of all stripes—politicians, gamblers, and gangsters.

Zwillman was charismatic, with eyes that twinkled when he spoke to women but turned hard and cold when he was conducting business. His wiry black hair was combed straight back and trained into waves worthy of the Jersey Shore. He was the neighborhood tough and quickly learned that he could make a profit off of his physical superiority and penchant for intimidation.

When Zwillman was just a kid, there would be anti-Semites on the block, ugly-faced Caucasians with boils—Germans, Polish, Irish, whatever. All goyim looked alike to him. They would harass the Jewish street peddlers. Motive? Unclear. They seemed offended by the peddlers' Jewishness. Hating Jews was a thing to do.

Being the huge kid he was, Zwillman often was taken for being older, and once when he happened upon such harassment, he grabbed the anti-Semite by the collar, told him what would happen if he came back, and gave the guy a series of kicks in the ass until he was off the block. Women in babushkas applauded.

After that, whenever someone would make the mistake of jerking around the man who sharpened knives or whoever, a Yiddish-speaking neighbor would yell, "Get *der Langer!*" That meant, "Call the Long One!" Someone would hotfoot it to the Zwillman house. Minutes later, Longie would show up, rolling up his sleeves, and serve up a deli-style knuckle sandwich.

By the time he was a legal adult, he was waist deep in the rackets—policy bank, extortion, backroom gambling—and, like every other hood when Prohibition came, bootlegging.

Zwillman broke into the booze biz by hijacking other hoods' liquor shipments, a very dangerous business, so he made sure he had backup. He located every still in Newark's Third Ward and extorted a percentage.

His gang, the "Longie Mob," enforced his efforts. Eventually, he worked his way up in power and came up with a lucrative plan to ship contraband Canadian whiskey from Montreal, into New York Bay, around the north end of Staten Island, to a pier on the west side of Newark Bay. On land, he transported his hooch in armored trucks, security that would have impressed Perry Brink.

By the end of Prohibition and the start of the Great Depression, Longie was a very rich man. He bought his mom a big house in Weequahic, the movin'-on-up section of Newark. She was so proud of her son who was a successful businessman.

Truth was, he could have bought the whole block: by the end of Prohibition he had a piece of about 40 percent of the illegal liquor coming into the entire country.

Then happy days were here again, and he had to find a different way to make a living. If Hollywood could retool for sound, he could retool for different rackets: sports book, numbers, and coin-operated machines. He never loosened his grip on power.

When Longie got up in the morning, he went to his office, just like any other businessman. That office was in the Public Service Tobacco Company building in Hillside, New Jersey. There, he'd receive visitors, usually Jersey business owners asking forgiveness for loans or explaining why they couldn't come up with the tribute money.

Longie's reputation in Newark was heroic. Not only did he supply the population with alcohol—manna from heaven during Prohibition—but he was also legendarily generous, giving food to poor Jews and donating food to Christian charities on Thanksgiving and toys on Christmas. He was the Jewish Santa Claus. He personally financed a soup kitchen for the down-and-out, of which there were many. Everyone wished him well.

Catholic church ladies briefly squawked about the church receiving gangster dough. "Evil!" they said. But the archbishop of the Newark diocese was a practical man. He said he personally blessed that money. The hungry did not care where the money came from; they were just concerned with being fed each noontime in the basement of one of the diocese's largest churches.

Of the other Jewish gangsters in America, Longie was closest to Bugsy Siegel, and he was a pampered guest at Siegel's luxurious home whenever he was in Los Angeles. Longie once told a colleague that he'd do anything for Siegel, anything, and all he had to do was ask.

For years, you couldn't get elected to a political office in Newark without Longie's seal of approval. One time, he did get busted and went to jail—three months for beating the shit out of a pimp who'd been short with the tribute money and harsh with the talent. But jail turned out to be a piece of cake. Longie had a re-markably pleasant experience. He was allowed to have his meals delivered, and there was a phone in his cell, where it was under-stood he was conducting business. On his way out the door, he gave one of his jailers a new car.

Longie had three brothers and sisters, and he made it plain to them that he was the outlaw in the family and they were not to get involved in the rackets. So, as he controlled Local 244 of the Motion Picture Machine Operators Union, he used that position to get his siblings jobs as projectionists in Newark movie houses.

But he never heard from a tax form—which would be his un-doing. He was called the "Al Capone of Newark," and Scarface didn't pay his taxes either. After Prohibition, Zwillman and Willie Moretti shared Newark gambling in all of northern New Jersey.

Longie had a way with women, and in 1930 met a nineteen-year-old platinum blonde named Jean Harlow who wanted ever so desperately to make it in show business. She was Hollywood-hot, under contract with Howard Hughes to make a series of pic-tures distributed by United Artists, and while on a publicity tour, she came to Newark and met Longie. The pair locked eyes and soon thereafter were scorching mattresses across the Third Ward.

According to legend, Longie "pygmalioned" Harlow to "act with class." He took her to nightclubs he owned—the Blue Mir-ror and the Casablanca Club—so she'd get to see him treated like the boss. Their affair was torrid but brief. Hughes sold her con-tract.

At Penn Station in New York, Harlow gave Longie a locket containing a snip of her platinum pubes, waved a sad goodbye, boarded the Twentieth Century Limited heading westward, switched to the Southwest Chief in Chicago, and five days later reported to the MGM lot in Culver City ready for her close-up. In Hollywood she was a super nova, her career brilliant, notorious, scandal ridden; her life short, dead at twenty-six from kidney fail-ure. (Her mother was a Christian Scientist, didn't believe in doc-tors, and allowed Jean to die reeking of urine.)

And so Longie settled down. He married the granddaughter of the founder of the American Stock Exchange and became a boss whose turf went right up to the west bank of the Hudson River, but not an inch further. The other side of the river was the domain of the Five Families. Longie knew exactly where his turf ended, and he ran a casino in Fort Lee on the Jersey side of the new George Washington Bridge, a quick drive or cab ride from Manhattan.

In 1938, Judge Perlman contacted Zwillman and explained what he wanted. Zwillman remembered those thick men jerking around the Jewish peddlers when he was a kid. He knew these Nazis were those same assholes. In the middle of the night, the German bastards would drive around the Third Ward and post threatening flyers on light poles, trees, and walls. The flyers were horrible. They said German destiny wouldn't be truly fulfilled until Jewish blood ran through the streets of Newark. The flyers were pulled down at dawn by the waking Jews, of course, but they were worrisome, to say the least. Newark Jews received letters from relatives in Europe. They knew what was happening there and feared the same might happen in Newark. Everyone knew these German oafs were marching and drilling in city parks, wearing uniforms, and looking troublingly like an army.

Perlman told Zwillman that Newark was home to an estimated sixty-five thousand German immigrants and their families. For that reason, and the fact that it was next door to New York City, Newark was a priority target for the Bund.

"They are organized," Perlman said to Zwillman. "I want you to be organized, too."

"I'll take care of it. I have a crew that is well-suited to the task," Longie replied. He promised not to kill the Nazis, just make them regret.

Zwillman told the judge about his tough guys. They headquartered out of a boxing gym run by his friend, Jewish ex-boxer Nat Arno, whose birth name was Sidney Nathaniel Abramowitz.

CHAPTER FIFTEEN
Nat Arno

Sidney Nathaniel Abramowitz was born on April 1, 1910, and grew up only a block away from the Third Ward's main drag, Prince Street. When he was fourteen and already at his adult height of five-five, he walked into a Young Men's Hebrew Club in Newark and approached an old guy with a towel around his neck.

"Teach me to fight?"

"Sure," the old-timer said and handed Sidney a pair of training gloves. "Put these on."

Sidney had the right look—wide set eyes, sturdy jaw, and hands like the business end of a sledgehammer. Once gloved up, he worked out on the heavy bag. His punches made that solid thump sound that said the kid had it. His footwork was great right off the bat. His fearsome hands were quick as well. He made the speed bag dance.

Sidney would have been perfect in every way if he'd shown the same aptitude for defense. The second he began sparring, it was clear he couldn't feint or duck. He was a bull of a fighter, always moving forward in the ring despite the incoming. That would make him a crowd pleaser if he proved to have beard—that is, the ability to take a punch—but might not bode well for his marbles. He got up before dawn each morning and got in his roadwork running around nearby Weequahic Lake. He quit school because it was cutting into his sparring time.

Two days after his sixteenth birthday, he made his pro debut, winning his first six bouts easily. Sidney changed his name to Nat Arno so his parents wouldn't know how he made his money. Posters proclaimed him "Nat Arno, Newark's Fighting Hebrew." Unfortunately for him, the poster also showed his face, which his father recognized right away.

Harry Abramowitz forbade his son to fight. That delayed the boy's career some, but not much. He packed a bag and hitchhiked to Florida, an adventure in itself, where he continued his career, fighting one or more times a week. According to legend, he once fought twice in the same night, one knockout victory and one ten-round draw.

Arno fought thirty times in 1926, at least. Records from back then are often incomplete and based on newspaper articles written by lazy journalists. But of the thirty we know about, he won twenty-one, lost two, and fought to seven draws.

He waited for more than a year before he wrote home and explained where he was and what he was doing. His folks were greatly relieved. They'd thought their Sidney was dead. When he returned to Newark in February 1927, he worked out at a boxing gym in the basement of a bakery.

Arno ended up fighting professionally well over a hundred times, and that is just counting the sanctioned fights. He fought in "smokers" as well, nonsanctioned bouts outside the law, for which he was paid ten bucks each. As a pugilist, he was reliable but not spectacular, and his boxing career never took off. Even late in his career, he was fighting jobber opponents during the preliminaries, usually at one of a variety of New Jersey city armories. He took a friend's advice and retired before he grew punchy. In 1938, Arno was still shy of thirty but long retired and working for Longie Zwillman.

If he'd hit it big in the fight game, he might never have become a gangster. But he was badly in need of scratch, and when Zwillman offered him a job enforcing for the Newark mob, he leaped at the opportunity.

Arno found the work easy and exciting. He believed in looking sharp and wore a three-piece suit. It had been years since anyone had seen him without a Robusto cigar, five inches long with a fifty-gauge ring size, clamped in his teeth. He rode shotgun—with an actual shotgun—during various black market runs.

Sometimes, there were shootouts and someone's dead ass was left by the side of the road. He got to beat people up, and unlike a Jersey City armory fight, the guy he was beating usually didn't have the gumption to punch back.

Now Arno, along with chronic ringing in his ears, had his own boxing gym in Newark and was the one wearing the towel around his neck, handing training gloves to tough kids off the street, shouting out combos by the number while filling the air with cigar smoke.

He was considered a good-natured man. If you pissed him off, look out, and, of course, if you paid him to punch someone, he would—but he wasn't the sort to look for trouble. He enjoyed popularity and eagerly sought out opportunities to do good deeds. Just like Longie, Arno couldn't abide a bully, and when a Jewish kid was being picked on, Arno might walk him all the way to school in the morning to make sure he arrived in one piece.

Zwillman walked into Arno's boxing gym with a big toothy grin.

"Hey, Boss," Arno said, and then to two kids sparring in the ring, "Knock off the dancing. Throw!" Then to Zwillman, "What can I do you for?"

"Nat, I want you should assemble an anti-Nazi army," Zwillman said.

Arno's eyes sparked. He knew every tough guy, Jewish and otherwise, in the city. A lot of them just plain loved to fight, and busting up those Nazi creeps sounded like fun.

Zwillman explained that he would pay the bills, of course. And that meant he would handle bribing the police, paying fines, putting up bail, and paying for any medical costs that might crop up.

"I want you to do more than lead the boys into battle," Zwillman said. "I want you to be point man, let the shop owners know what we are doing and why. Talk to the press if they come around with questions. *Don't mention my name.* This is the Third Ward's war, not mine."

"I got you, Longie," Arno said, puffing hard at his Robusto. "Those guys drive me nuts. I can't believe that, right here in Newark, there are Nazis who want to kill Jews. We take care of them, right?"

"Right. But you can't kill them. You just fuck them up. We're working for judges and rabbis."

"You don't need to tell me that," Arno said, although he did. Need to tell him that.

A crisply edited montage: Arno building his army, whispering into hoods' ears on the street. Then in the gym, teaching them to fight. Gathering a stockpile of baseball bats and sawed-off pool cues in the back room of Arno's gym. Longie showing up to get a progress report, burdened with an armful of deli sandwiches. Arno is having a fit because some of his boys are trying to make weight. The boys are hungrily digging in to the corned beef and pastrami sandwiches. Arno slapping himself in the forehead—but then can't help but laugh. "It's good food!" Longie says. "To fight good, you got to fuel the engine! Here, I brought mustard and sour pickles."

CHAPTER SIXTEEN
Arno's Army

Arno's right-hand man, and one of the many who thought beating up Nazis sounded like fun, was Max "Puddy" Hinkes. Puddy stood out in that crowd. Most of Newark's Jewish boxers were compact, with necks that were short, shorter, and shortest. Puddy had an elongated look, as if he'd been stretched on the rack. He'd suffered "giraffe" jokes as a youngster, but kids quickly learned that teasing Puddy was risky. His arms had great length as well, and he could cuff you from around the corner.

Puddy had boxed for a year and a half before the Depression, mostly against easily dispatched cauliflower bait, and by the time of the Nazi fights, he was a full-time hood. His last pro fight, if you could call it that, was on January 14, 1930, after a seven-month layoff. He'd traveled outside of New Jersey for one of the few times in his life to take on a guy making his pro debut named Joey Edwards. Puddy hadn't trained much for the fight; he believed in the myth that a pug could "fight himself into shape." It didn't work out that way. He threw a couple of pawing left jabs and was gassed. The crowd at the Duval County Armory in Jacksonville, Florida, started to boo, as neither fighter seemed much in the mood. There was a lot of circling and clinching. The referee wearied of separating them and gestured for the fighters to mix it up a little. They didn't listen.

"Get a room," someone yelled from the back of the cavernous armory.

The referee ended up stopping the fight in the fifth round. The crowd booed louder than ever, and some threw things into the ring. The "fight" was declared a "no contest" because of "stalling," and afterward, Puddy decided to hang up his gloves and take his skills, with bare knuckles, to the street.

Gangsters were always sitting ringside in those days (and these days, too, to tell the truth). Most of the fighters were "owned" by racketeers, fights were routinely fixed, and there were several fight cards a week in Newark, indoors in the winter, outdoors in the summer, with the most popular venues being Dreamland Park, the Laurel Garden, and the Lyric Theatre.

Dreamland Park was an amusement park on Frelinghuysen Avenue within spitting distance of Weequahic Lake, where Arno did his sunrise roadwork. (It is the current site of the Seth Boyden Housing Project and is now neighbors with Newark Liberty International Airport.)

The Laurel Garden was a wood-framed barn of an arena located on Springfield Avenue, near the intersection of Eighteenth Avenue and South Tenth Street. It was a German beer garden and cinema for German-language films until the mid-1920s, when it was purchased by Charlie Zemel, a Newark-born son of Jewish immigrants from Russia. Following the sale, the arena housed Newark fights, wrestling on Thursday and boxing on Monday, until 1952, when it was razed.

The Lyric Theatre was a 1,200-seat vaudeville theater that opened on Market Street in 1908. It eventually became a movie theater and, for a time, a venue for boxing. The building was torn down in the early 1960s and replaced by a printing plant for the *Newark Evening News*.

When a boxer was on the wrong side of the bell curve, he started looking at future employment opportunities, and bodyguard/driver for a criminal was a great option. That was the route Puddy Hinkes took.

Puddy was owned and had to do what he was told. He'd been a bad kid: breaking and entering, extortion, hijacking, the works. The old cliché is that bad boys take up boxing to go straight and keep themselves out of prison, but in many cases, thugs turned to boxing for extra cash and remained thugs. That was Puddy.

Why did they call him Puddy? No one knew. Even Hinkes didn't know. He thought one of his brothers called him that and it stuck, but he didn't know the significance or even what it meant.

Since Hinkes boxed on Friday nights, successful men who went to the fights knew who he was, so Hinkes was put in charge of making payoffs at City Hall. He knew important political leaders in Newark in a couple of ways. They knew him from watching him fight, but Hinkes was also a good friend of David "Quincy" Lieberman, who ran the city's brothels. Puddy knew every whorehouse in the city and could get a bigwig a girl quick if the randy fellow had a few free moments.

He earned a reputation as a cool customer, neither sentimental nor emotional, but a pro who only worshipped the American dollar. As a rule, he'd fight for whichever side paid him better, but he hated Nazis so much that he'd bust them up for free.

Hinkes told stories of back in the old days when he was an enforcer for the Jewish community. Ruddy-cheeked jerkoffs would come onto Prince Street where the Jewish kids hung out. If an elder were around, they'd pull his beard and challenge the yeshiva bochers to do something about it. That was when Puddy stepped in and kicked goyim ass.

Once when he was fighting at the Laurel Garden, there was a guy in the crowd yelling anti-Semitic comments at the Jewish fighters. Puddy strode into the crowd and stuck his lit cigar into the loudmouth's eye.

Hurting anti-Semites? You bet Puddy would do it for free.

"Puddy, you know anybody else who might want to join up?" Arno asked.

"Sure, Abie Bain."

"Excellent."

So, the third ex-boxer to join Arno's army was Abie Bain, a Russian-born middleweight. Bain was a far better fighter than either Puddy or Arno. During much of his boxing career, which stretched from 1924 to 1936, Bain was ranked in the top ten in his division by *Ring* magazine.

Bain looked like no one to tangle with, even when he had his shirt on, but shirt off, he was especially scary, his iron-hewed biceps popping up like a mountain range when he flexed.

His only title fight came in the fall of 1930 when he stepped up in weight class to battle "Slapsie Maxie" Rosenbloom in Madison Square Garden for the New York State Athletic Commission's version of the light-heavyweight title. He lost, thoroughly, but put up a great fight and sent the crowd home happy. (Rosenbloom later ran a popular nightclub, Slapsie Maxie's, on Wilshire Boulevard in Los Angeles, which was frequented by movie stars like Humphrey Bogart and Jackie Gleason.)

The other highlight (or lowlight) of his career was another TKO loss in Dreamland Park in 1931 to Tony "Two-Ton" Galento, a blubbery brawler who once knocked down Joe Louis in a heavyweight championship fight, only to be subsequently pummeled into submission by the Brown Bomber until his clock-stopping mush wore a clown-like mask of blood and lumps.

Galento might have been outmatched by Joe Louis, but he gave Bain a horrible beating. Before the fight, Bain weighed in at 165, Galento at his usual svelte 235. Outweighed by seventy pounds, it's amazing that Bain lasted until the fourth round before beginning a seven-week residency in a nearby hospital. He was never the same after that. Bain's record after the Galento fight was seven wins, fourteen losses, and one draw. He won none of his last eight bouts and finally retired.

It would later come out that Arno's fight against the Nazis was not limited to busting up meetings. He was in regular touch with Dr. S. William Kalb, who was the head of Newark's legitimate anti-Nazi efforts. The physician's efforts included boycotting German products and recruiting Jews to the cause.

On Sundays, Arno would visit Kalb's home, and Kalb's daughter once overheard Arno saying, "Doc, is there anyone I can kill for you?"

The next Newark gangster to join Arno's army was Hymie "the Weasel" Kugel, another of Longie's boys. The Weasel was best known as a boxing (and later pro wrestling) referee, a job he'd had since 1920. But just because he was the third man in the ring didn't mean he couldn't handle himself in a scuffle, anything from Marquis de Queensberry to no-holds-barred. He was squat, five-two tops, but had a hard-to-defend burrowing style and could bowl over larger men with pure aggression.

The Weasel, too, liked to talk about the ignorant anti-Semites he'd hurt. His favorite tale was the time he and another of Longie's soldiers, Itzik Goldstein, were having a meal at the Ideal Restaurant when three Polish clods came in, all mouth. They found the service slothful, called the proprietor a Jew bastard, and it was on.

The Weasel went into the kitchen and grabbed a heavy iron frying pan. He invited the three men outside and tried to explain to them that they were being disrespectful. When they responded poorly to that, he slapped the frying pan hard across the cheek of the loudest of the three. The guy went down in stages, seemingly folding himself down to the sidewalk. Goldstein hit a second man over the head with a wine bottle, and he dropped as if shot beside the first. The third hightailed it out of there while the Weasel and Goldstein laughed.

The biggest member of Arno's crew was the full-fledged heavyweight Harry "the Dropper" Levine, who stood six-four. In 1936, Levine won the Golden Gloves tournament, the finals of which were fought in Madison Square Garden.

Another was Benny "Bouncing Boy" Levine, no relation to Harry, a bantamweight who fought professionally for fifteen years and lost just about as many as he won. He outpointed Arno in a fight at the Laurel Garden in Newark but received a devastating thrashing from Arno in a rematch two weeks later. They'd been friends ever since. He originally got his nickname because of his bobbing style in the ring, but near the end, the joke was that it was because he repeatedly bounced off the canvas during every fight. He was a feared puncher, but his hands slowed over time. Near the end, he could barely make weight for middleweight bouts, and those guys hit a lot harder. He was on a serious losing streak in 1938 and on a two-and-a-half-year hiatus from the ring. Benny helped Arno out at the gym and now only fought Nazis.

Other members of Zwillman's Third Ward gang were Barney Sugerman, bookie "Mohawk" Skuratovsky, also known as Jacob Mohawk, so nicknamed because of his tomahawk-shaped nose; Julius "Skinny" Markowitz, twenty-three years old; Harry Green, the youngest, only nineteen; Max Leipzig; and Primo Weiner.

The great majority of the crew remained anonymous. Some later claimed to fight Nazis but maybe didn't. Harold "Kayo" Konigsberg said he was right in there, busting Nazis with Arno and Puddy and the rest throughout the New Jersey campaign. Maybe. Trouble is, he was only twelve years old at the time. Kayo was a little nuts, and he once shat himself in court to demonstrate that fact to a judge. He did grow up to be a Jewish gangster though, no doubt about that, a Jewish hit man who eventually went to prison for life for murder, served fifty years, and lived to be eighty-nine, dying on November 23, 2014, in a Florida nursing home.

There were Nazi-fighters of the Third Ward who were neither boxers nor gangsters, men who'd worked on the assembly lines of Newark's factories, workplaces that were boarded up after the stock market crash. These were Jews—and a handful of sympathetic gentiles—who'd suffered more than anyone with the Depression and hated the disinformation artists out there blaming Jews for America's woes. They were out of work and bored, looking to take out their frustration on something, so it might as well be Nazi skull.

Unlike in New York and Chicago, where maybe a couple dozen gangsters were taking on Bund meetings, Arno's army eventually numbered close to a thousand. If necessary, they could defend the city in case of an attempted takeover. It never came to that, but if it had, they were ready.

Once assembled and trained, Arno's army called themselves the Anti-Nazi Minutemen of America, the Minutemen for short, in homage to the Revolutionary War patriots who could assemble and go to battle with only sixty seconds' notice.

One of the Minutemen's first actions wasn't in Newark, or even New Jersey at all. They traveled convoy-style two hours south-ward to Philadelphia, where they busted up a Bund meeting in the Turngemeinde Hall, a meeting held in celebration of the An-schluss, Germany's bloodless seizure of Austria. The hall, built in 1911, was at the corner of Broad Street and Columbia Avenue (now Cecil B. Moore Avenue).

While unrelated protesters from the Citizens' Anti-Nazi Com-mittee were outside the Philly hall carrying signs that read "DOWN WITH HITLER AND HIS U.S. FOLLOWERS," the Minutemen crashed the party while William Kunze was at the podium.

The cops came and broke up the melee, which was described by the Associated Press as "raging fist fighting in the small hall." More than a dozen Nazis were injured, but only one Minuteman—Hymie "the Weasel" Kugel, who suffered a cut over his eye.

All one had to do was look funny at the Weasel's brows and he'd start to bleed because of the scar tissue that had accumulated there over his career in the ring. On the ride home, the Weasel was teased about taking a shot from one of the krautheads.

"It was a head butt! No way nobody got a punch in on me," Weasel complained. Everybody laughed and passed a bottle around during the ride home.

Back in Philadelphia, Kunze was complaining to a reporter that "subversive minorities" had invaded the Bund. He denied that the Bund meeting was a celebration of anything, said that it was just the normally scheduled monthly meeting.

CHAPTER SEVENTEEN
Schwabbenhalle

The Schwabbenhalle on Spring Street in East Newark, New Jersey, sat snug against the Passaic River. The hall was named after Swabia, a former duchy of medieval Germany, which in the 1930s included portions of Switzerland and France.

The big room where the Nazis were having their meeting was on the second floor. There were 150 of them up there, all flush in the face and a little sweaty. It was half empty, as they were expecting late arrivals. The Nazis forced to cross the Hudson by New York's Mayor LaGuardia had yet to arrive.

A dark alley ran along the side of the building. The only light came from the second-story windows above. Unlike most alleys, this one wasn't a dead end. It led to an unkempt backyard. Arno and an accomplice tiptoed their way down the alley, each carrying one end of a ladder. Earlier, the men had darkened their faces and hands with burnt cork. Following the obligatory *shvartzer* jokes (Yiddish for a black person), they were ready to go.

After inadvertently smacking a metal garbage can with one end of the ladder, noisily knocking the lid off and sending a rat scurrying, they arrived at the rear of the building and set the ladder gingerly against the wall under a window that was opened just a crack.

The formal meeting had yet to begin, but the fun had started. It was somebody's birthday, and Arno could hear the Germans' drunken singing, robust and reckless. When "Happy Birthday" was through, they were having so much fun they sang "The Star-Spangled Banner."

"Assholes," Arno whispered. He waited until the bombs were bursting in air and climbed quietly up the ladder until he reached the window. "Okay, you go back to the front and wait for them to come running out," Arno said.

He peeked inside at the half-full house, then lifted the window until it was open about eight inches. He was looking at the back of the head of a man at the podium and at the faces of everyone else. The man at the podium was Heinz Spanknöbel, a member of the National Socialist German Workers Party deputized by Hitler's deputy führer Rudolf Hess to preach and recruit in America.

While Arno was behind the building, there was something happening out front that he and his crew had not anticipated: spectators were arriving in droves. None of the Minutemen had bothered to keep the planned attack a secret from their families, and their families had not bothered to keep it a secret from the butchers and shop owners, who in turn told their customers. By showtime, everyone in the Third Ward knew that that night's Nazi meeting was getting busted and busted hard. Many, of course, decided to go and watch the fun—maybe join in.

A throng arrived by streetcar and bus. Some of the men, even those old and bearded, were rolling up their sleeves, eager for an opportunity to do their part for the cause.

Longie Zwillman himself was out there, wearing his finest three-piece suit, hooking his thumbs in his vest and strutting around like a proud father. A mob mentality bubbled up out of that cauldron to match the one inside the hall.

Arno would have preferred to wait until the hall was full, but he became impatient, as men are apt to do when atop a ladder. So, with athletic grace, Arno pulled a stink bomb out of his pocket and, like a second-baseman completing a double play, hurled it sidearm into the auditorium. Then another. And another.

The room soon smelled like a septic tank, and there was gagging, coughing, panic—then the anticipated mad rush for the exits.

"Help! Call the police!" a Nazi yelled, holding a handkerchief over his nose.

Another ran to the open window behind the podium for a breath of fresh air and found himself face-to-face with Arno, who broke his nose with a short right hand. Arno then, feeling vulnerable on his precarious perch, hurried down the ladder, abandoned it, and ran on quick feet to join the fray in front.

The sounds of coughing and gagging racked the air. Some coughed so hard that they vomited on the hall's hardwood floor, causing others to slip and fall.

Those who made it out of the big room and into the stairwell ran into Hymie "the Weasel" Kugel, Puddy Hinkes, and a dozen others, with Louisville Sluggers, knucks, saps, and crowbars wrapped in the *Star-Ledger*'s sports page.

"Aim for their heads, boys," said Hinkes.

Some aimed for the head, some for the swastikas on the enemy's armbands. Bones were broken, scalps peeled back. The cries of pain sounded oddly like their singing only seconds before, although some of the baritones who'd been walloped low became sopranos. Nazis slipped on blood and tumbled down stairs.

The gauntlet of tough Jews stretched outside the front door and into the street. Some Germans tried to fight back, but they were drunk and the Jewish pugilists easily ducked their haymakers.

At 9:00 P.M., minutes before the first sirens of the police and the ambulance, two buses packed to the gills with the New York Nazis pulled up in front of the hall.

The Nazis retreated for a moment, and reorganized themselves into a flying wedge, a football play long outlawed because it was impossible to defend against and frequently resulted in a brutal trampling. They formed a single human chevron and pushed past the gangsters and into the hall, quickly barricading the doors behind them. It happened swiftly and efficiently, leaving the gangsters momentarily confused. Bats that had previously been held up to the sky were now lowered, blood dripping from them onto the sidewalk. (The flying wedge was outlawed in football in 1905 after its use resulted in nineteen deaths that year.)

Puddy later recalled that night with great nostalgia. He remembered the way the Nazis were stampeded expertly by the stink bombs, sent gagging into a bottleneck and then into the lobby, where the gangsters were waiting with bats and iron bars. He recalled that beautiful sound of the Nazis screaming "blue murder." It was one of the happiest moments of his life, he said wistfully.

"It's just too bad we couldn't kill them all," he concluded with a sigh.

Years later, Primo Weiner remembered a Nazi trying to shout out a "Heil" as he came down the stairs, only to be silenced by several Louisville Sluggers. While the melee was going on, a car full of Jews came down Spring Street, periodically stopping so someone could hop out with a freshly sharpened kitchen knife to slash the tires on the Nazis' cars. Another with a hammer smashed headlights.

Also years later, Myron Sugerman recalled his dad telling him about the great brawls: "So the Jews went in and kicked the shit out of the Nazis. They didn't fight back. They gave up. All of my father's friends participated."

When the police and ambulance did arrive, they found the wounded to be reluctant to talk. Many refused to give their names, for fear that the *Star-Ledger* would print them the next day.

One Nazi who did identify himself was Albert Schley, who was approached by a reporter from the *Eagle* and turned out to be downright chatty.

"Why are you and the others wearing Hitler uniforms with swastikas on them?" the reporter inquired.

"These are sports costumes. The swastikas are not mandatory. They are the wearer's choice," Schley replied, using an already bloody handkerchief to dab at a leaky nostril.

"Why were the men saluting in the Nazi fashion?"

"It is only a gesture. Nothing to be worried about."

"And what is the purpose of this organization?"

"We exist only to promote friendly relations between the United States and Germany," Schley said.

The gangsters had promised not to kill anyone, and they were good to their word—although it was touch and go. According to one eyewitness report, one beefy Nazi was being gang beaten to a pulp and might certainly have been killed if a tear gas bomb tossed by the Newark police hadn't burst nearby, dispersing the Minutemen.

Tear gas is well known today as an anti-riot agent, but during the Depression, it was new and terrifying. The only thing most people knew about gas was that the Germans had used it in the World War and that it killed you. The explosion and tear gas panicked the crowd, causing another stampede.

The gangsters were game as hell, but in the heat of combat made a few regrettable mistakes. They were great fighters but not always perfect at distinguishing the good guys from the bad guys. There was no surefire way to separate the Nazis from the innocent bystanders. Sure, you could say folks in brown shirts and storm trooper uniforms only, but there was a lot of chaos in the riot and bad things happened. At one point, five reporters had begun shouting questions and taking photos. They were turned on by the gangsters and beaten to the pavement. Reporter Jack Aronowitz suffered a split skull and was in the hospital, listed in critical condition.

Unlike other cities' journalists, the Newark reporters had no trouble identifying the crew who was smashing up the Nazis. They were "gangsters from the Third Ward of Newark."

The Nazis had been eager for the police to arrive, but once on the scene, the cops turned out to be unhelpful. Longie Zwillman was a friend of the police and made sure they always had a little extra money in their pockets around the holidays.

Six of the Jewish contingent were arrested, among them Harry Schwartz and Louis Halper, and charged with using blackjacks in a fight. Minutemen Reuben Wilensky, Harry Green, Harry Sanders, and Skinny Markowitz were also hauled in.

As promised, Longie made sure a lawyer was on the scene right away, two lawyers, in fact, William Untermann and William Fogel, who quickly bailed the men out of jail at a price of twenty-five dollars per head.

Judge Ralph Villani of Newark's Fourth Precinct Court, also a Zwillman friend, dismissed the charges the next day. The judge was far harsher with the Nazis, calling them an "alien menace" and denying them bail because they were a "flight risk."

In the end, no one served any real time. Villàni said from the bench, "These fights must be cut out. If there are any more disturbances here and they are brought before me, I shall deal severely with them, regardless of which side they represent."

The next day, a reporter chased down Zwillman and asked for a comment regarding the riot.

"Wasn't me. Wasn't us," Longie said.

"But I saw y—."

"Not me. Us. Every fucking person in the Third Ward. Us."

"But there is a photo—

"Look. I wasn't even in East Newark last night. I was having dinner with a friend at Dinty Moore's in Manhattan."

"Okay, Longie. Whatever you say."

"Here's a tip. Talk to Nat Arno. He'll give you a quote or two. And if you want to stay my friend don't print my name."

"Thanks, Longie."

That reporter kept his promise, but there was another, from the *New York Daily Mirror*, who not only placed Longie at the scene but added embellishment, claiming that Zwillman was posted outside the hall in an armored truck and was directing the attack like a field general moving his troops. No one else remembered an armored truck. The story appeared only in the early bird edition of the paper and was retracted in later editions. The paper subsequently apologized for the story, saying an anonymous informant had misinformed their reporter.

The Jewish press didn't exactly print the facts, either. They said that the attack on the meeting was spontaneous and that the Nazis were the only ones who used clubs and blackjacks.

Spanknöbel was not seriously injured in the melee, but there is an argument that he fared the worst. There were shadowy figures creeping around East Newark that night, the first indication of an FBI investigation.

Spanknöbel had bragged at the hall about his relationship with Rudolf Hess. A week later, the FBI issued a warrant for his arrest, accusing him of operating as an agent of a foreign government. He was never arrested, however, as he slipped quietly onto the next boat for Europe and returned to Germany. Spanknöbel spent the war in Germany and was arrested and imprisoned in "Special Camp #1" by the Russians when they marched into Germany. He died in 1947 of starvation.

The Nazis quickly learned to hold their meetings in secret, but the Minutemen continued to snipe at them if they caught them out and on the streets. After a while, the Minutemen busted up the secret meetings as well.

The Nazis couldn't figure out how they knew when and where. The answer was: the cops. The Nazis always called the Newark cops to ask for additional security when they were getting together, and the Newark cops told Longie Zwillman, who told Nat Arno.

Then, boom, somebody got pummeled and the rest ran. If Arno had a piece of info that the Newark cops lacked regarding the anti-Semite animals, he passed that along. In those cases, the Newark cops made sure that any beat cop in the vicinity of the

Bund meeting would be elsewhere and far, far, away when it came clobbering time.

The Bund-busting ops never lacked for money. Longie saw to that. If Arno needed a convoy of luxury cars to go to and from the scene of the riot, as had been the case when the crew traveled to Philadelphia, Longie made it so.

Sometimes, the Bund bustings didn't even make the papers. There were no police reports. They stayed secret.

Maybe there was one emergency room nurse who figured it out: "You boys again. Here, put this icepack on that."

CHAPTER EIGHTEEN
Irvington

When the Minutemen learned that the Nazis had the balls to plan another rally—this one at the German Cultural Center in Irvington and in celebration of recent successful efforts to keep Jewish candidates off New Jersey election ballots—preparations for disruption began immediately.

Irvington was a suburb of Newark that bordered Newark's Third Ward. The German Cultural Center was on a triangularly shaped block near the confluence of Nineteenth Avenue and Springfield Avenue in Irvington.

Nat Arno figured it would be easier to get his boys to the scene without interference if they came empty-handed. After scouting out the German Cultural Center, he saw that dense shrubbery grew along the rear of the building, perfect for hiding stuff.

During the days before the meeting, Arno, Abie Bain, and Puddy Hinkes took turns walking to the location with weapons on their person—billy clubs, baseball bats, frying pans, wire cable bludgeons, even lead pipes strapped to their inner thighs. When they got to the location, they went to the shrubs and created a cache of weapons.

The meeting was to commence at 9:30 P.M. The New York branch of the Bund boarded several chartered buses in Yorkville and arrived in Irvington a half-hour early. The Nazis that came off the bus were all males, flush with zeal and in uniform—the very uniforms that Mayor LaGuardia had forbidden them to wear in public on the other side of the Hudson. They, too, carried weapons. If the Jews wanted to interfere in their business again, this time they were going to have a fight on their hands. Just to demonstrate their military strength, the Nazis had their buses parked a block away from the hall and the uniformed men goose-stepped their way to the meeting in crisp lines of four. They sought intimidation through similitude and bore identical smirks of superiority.

Those expressions, however, crumpled when they realized that some of them weren't even going to make it inside. A pack of now-armed Minutemen came flying out from behind the building. Near simultaneously, cars carrying other Minutemen arrived on the scene with screeching tires. The street and sidewalk in front of the "cultural center" burst into instant violence.

Military historians have noted that the Third Ward Minutemen were reminiscent that night of their namesakes. In the American Revolution, British soldiers marched in formation and followed the strict rules of warfare, only to be decimated by guerilla tactics. The same action occurred here, and the fighting was savage.

The Nazis might have excelled at synchronicity, but the |Minutemen were an assemblage of pro pugilists and mob enforcers. Men who knew how to march were fighting men who knew how to hurt.

A Minuteman with a hammer in his right hand dug the claw into a Nazi's upper arm and, just like pulling a nail, ripped away his swastika armband along with his muscle from the bone. The Nazi was Robert Michelis. He went down screaming.

Almost none of the Nazis escaped unscathed. Two brothers made it back to the bus and thought they were home free, only to be dragged out by a pair of pipe-wielding Jews, who left them unconscious in the gutter.

Police arrived and charged at the bloody scene with their guns out, but who to shoot? Instead of pulling their collective trigger, they formed a barricade in front of the cultural center so the melee couldn't work its way inside.

All of the sirens in the distance caught the attention of Third Ward residents, and word spread. There was another riot, the grapevine said, even more exciting than the one up north. They flocked to the scene. Some men rolled up their sleeves and had grandiose ideas as they approached, but once there, they saw the carnage and settled into their roles as spectators.

Also grandiose were the crowd estimates, which said that the two hundred or so Jews who stopped by to observe were "in the thousands." Of course, by the next day, there was no one in the Third Ward who would admit to missing the action, although the truth was that most had slept through it. The *New York Times* said that the riot had featured an "uncontrollable mass of humanity."

Somehow order was restored outside the hall. The Nazis who were conscious and could still walk were allowed by police to enter the hall. The Minutemen were kept outside. Arno, used to performing in front of a crowd, gave a rabble-rousing speech that worked the Jewish spectators into a lather. Unlike Bain—who had been magnificent during the fight, cleaning house with his bare fists, unconcerned with their lethal nature—Arno could raise his voice above a tortured whisper.

The result was that several of the spectators went in search of suitable objects to throw—rocks and pieces of brick. Using their skills as baseball players, they threw the objects at the hall's windows, and the sound of shattering glass mixed with muddled cries.

Inside the hall, the Nazis were not celebrating as they had planned. They were trying to figure out how they were going to get the hell out of Irvington. The decision to park the buses a block away seemed incredibly stupid at this point. It would seem even stupider when they tried to leave and discovered the buses gone. Arno and his men had threatened the bus drivers into fleeing.

Arno and several others called for the rock throwing to stop, temporarily at least.

"I want to talk to the police," Arno said.

He found the lieutenant in charge. The copper was busy ducking thrown objects and falling glass.

Arno said, "Lieutenant, no one wants to see what will happen if those Nazis try to get away. It will be unthinkably awful."

The officer, used to suburban problems and nothing like this, agreed.

"Here's the deal. If you promise a permanent ban on these Bund idiots in your town, we will disperse."

There were legal problems with the request. The Nazis were not breaking the law. There was no such thing as illegal "hate speech" back then. They had a right to say whatever they wanted short of yelling "Fire," and their right to assemble was protected by the Constitution. Besides, after the Schwabbenhalle riot, the Germans had made the Newark police promise that they would be protected during future meetings. To broker a deal between Nazis and Jews at this point would be breaking that promise, and even if it were possible, a mere lieutenant couldn't make it stick.

"Can't do it," the lieutenant replied.

Now one of the problems of working a crowd into a mob is that you can't automatically flick the off switch. Just as the lieutenant rejected the peace offer from Arno, someone in the crowd threw a brick that hit a cop in the face.

That turned the tide against the Jews. The cop went down hard. His comrades, including the lieutenant who'd been talking to Arno, pulled their nightsticks and began bopping members of the Third Ward gallery.

A fleet of paddy wagons arrived from Newark. Just as had happened in East Newark, tear gas was propelled into the crowd. Lots of it this time. So much that the entire neighborhood was affected. Irvington residents up and down the street spent a sleepless night trying to wash the fumes from their crimson eyes.

The police, themselves having trouble breathing, now concentrated on getting the Nazis to safety. The Nazis were told that those who had come by bus would have to come with them to the police station because they had been abandoned. Once in the precinct house, they would have the opportunity to make other arrangements to get back to New York.

This was done, but the angry mob that had been dispersed by the gas now reformed outside the police station, threatening to attack both the police and their Nazi guests.

The Minutemen were not among that crowd, but had instead followed a handful of Nazis who were locals and had not come to the rally by bus. That tail job led them to a café miles away. They raided the joint, smashing windows and tables and plates. Innocent diners hid under tables, and there was surprisingly little collateral damage. All of the rearranged faces belonged to the Nazis.

In the papers the next day, Irvington's police chief apologized for all of that tear gas, which had hurt many innocent people. He admitted it was an overreaction and begged forgiveness.

"Sorry we made you cry," he reportedly said to the innocent Irvington neighbors.

The scorecard after the riot showed that seven Nazis and three Jews had been arrested and jailed.

Of the Nazis, the oldest was thirty-one, the youngest twenty-two; all but one from Manhattan, the other from Yonkers. They had all been on the bus of Nazis that came from Manhattan. The men were arraigned the following Friday in an Irvington courthouse before a police recorder.

Of the Jews in jail, most seriously charged was anti-Nazi Jerome Rodberg, who had to pay five-hundred-dollar bail to get out after he was caught smashing a photographer's camera during the riot.

The jail was nowhere near as busy as the doctors. There were hundreds injured, sixty required hospitalizations.

In the Third Ward, there were stories of strange figures at the Irvington riot, men who didn't seem to represent either side but were somehow involved. One spooky figure in particular became the subject of much gossip—and rightfully so. While the wounded were still lying on the ground moaning, this man in a trench coat grabbed a reporter by the elbow and pulled him into a driveway. "I want you to print this, see? Tell them the federal Secret Service has begun an investigation into the cause of this disturbance." The spooky guy then disappeared like a shadow.

That same shadowy fellow was later spotted whispering into Director of Public Safety Edward Ballantyne's ear, and the boys from the press would have loved to have known what that was all about. The smell was that the fix was in. It was subsequently reported that the Secret Service was looking at the American Nazis in many of the places they gathered because they were considered a threat to national security, an arm of Hitler's "studied policy."

The New Jersey government, which leaned to the right, started to make noise. The Irvington riot was a big deal. Irvington Mayor Percy Miller gave a speech condemning the "attempts to incite riots in this city by means of mob violence and gangster methods."

Ballantyne said "strict measures" were going to be used to dish out justice on those (the Jews) who were arrested during "the trouble." Of course, Ballantyne was the man who would then be contacted by the Secret Service and change his tune.

The Jewish papers referred to the "Nazi invasion of Newark" and portrayed the gangsters who fought back as heroes. Jersey Jews idolized Longie, Arno, and the crew more than ever.

From the Minutemen's point of view, the "trouble" was a huge success. The victory over the Nazis, according to the Jewish Telegraphic Agency, was achieved "despite the protection offered by police."

Ballantyne took twenty-four hours to rethink his statements about using strict measures to jail the Jews, and he issued a press release saying that in the future, no Nazi or anti-Nazi meetings would be allowed in Irvington. He added that any future altercations between the two groups would be halted "with a fire hose."

Folks who came out to watch any riot would be treated the same as the rioters themselves, he added.

"We cannot pick the wheat from the chaff," Ballantyne concluded.

The Jewish press said this was a considerable blow to the Bund, which had successfully built up Irvington as a hotbed of Nazi activity.

But in reality, it was more of an inconvenience. Many of the Nazis who had come to Irvington had already been displaced. So what if they had to move to the next town over?

One paper wrote, much to Arno's delight, that the resistance to the Nazi invasion was part of an obviously well-organized group.

Ballantyne didn't have the power to tell the local Nazis that they couldn't live in Irvington. They just couldn't have meetings there. Judging by the Nazis who were nabbed by the local police at the riot, many attendees were visiting from New York, anyway.

Before the Germans were banned from meeting in Newark, there was a hearing, and a lawyer named Hayes spoke on behalf of the Nazis. He was smart enough to skip the nature of the groups' beliefs, although he acknowledged that their message "nourished Old World quarrels" and even smarter to ignore usage of the phrase "freedom of speech." What he did was argue that it was better for the Nazis to have their meetings out in the open rather than move them underground, where they would fester like a carbuncle and emerge volcanically.

Not all Jersey Jews were on the side of the gangsters. The upper crust folk among them were embarrassed that "hooligans were defending their honor," an argument that would seem ridiculous only a few years later when the full extent of the Nazi horror became public knowledge. Known Jewish criminals committing acts of violence, some Jews believed, would fuel anti-Semitism rather than squelch it. The German Embassy in Washington, DC, complained about the injuries suffered by Germans in Irvington.

Arno heard about this and boasted to a reporter that his Minutemen had caused an "international incident." He added, "I would prefer peaceful means, of course, but we are fighters. We can be provoked. My boys are good boys, but they become aroused by anything anti-Semitic or un-American."

Unlike in other American cities, there was gunfire during the Newark war, and it was reportedly a Nazi pulling the trigger. Twenty-six-year-old Max Feilshus, the Minutemen's chaplain, was standing one late afternoon with Nat Arno out in front of his house. The men were on the sidewalk at the corner of South Orange Avenue and Richmond Street watching children setting off firecrackers when a black sedan pulled up to the curb. Arno and Feilshus had their backs to the car.

Witnesses saw two men in the front seat. The one on the passenger side had a .38 in his hand as he called out, "Dirty Jew!"

When the chaplain angrily whirled around to see who it was, the gunman stuck his heater out the window and fired twice.

One shot missed, ricocheting off a stoop. The other hit Feilshus in the right leg.

The car screamed away, barely missing a couple of the kids, and was gone before anyone could get the license plate number.

Arno helped Feilshus into his home, and an ambulance took him to Beth Israel Hospital, where his condition was listed as "not serious."

Some, but not all, speculated that the shooting was in retaliation for the Irvington riot, an event at which both Arno and Feilshus had been spotted and identified. Most of the Newark cops investigating the shooting, however, thought it was a mob thing, not a Nazi thing.

Arno and Feilshus, on the other hand, had no doubts regarding who had fired the bullet. It was a Nazi bullet, and reporters who came to the hospital to cover the story were told as much in no uncertain terms.

The cops remained skeptical. Arno was a smart cookie. Maybe he was trying to kill two birds, burying his own mob connections—he'd been arrested for gambling only nine days earlier—while headlining the Nazi menace.

Arno was adamant. Doctors were still digging the bullet out of the chaplain's thigh when Arno pledged to a scribe that the war against Hitler in Newark would continue even though "they use bullets against us."

"What got you started against Nazis?" a reporter asked Arno.

Arno, enjoying his celebrity status, said, "I was doing my road work one morning around Weequahic Lake when I happened upon a dead Jewish boy hanging from a tree, a swastika carved into his chest," Arno said.

The papers printed the story as fact. Trouble was, Arno just made it up.

The Nazis had plans bigger than bullets, too. One night, Newark firefighters reported to a blaze and inside the building found evidence of Nazi occupation. Investigating further, they found a Nazi party membership book with names and addresses.

Treasury Department agents were called in, and the house was thoroughly searched. The feds opened a trunk and found lab equipment, chemical formulas, and photos of the many bridges connecting New York City with Long Island and New Jersey.

Following the discovery, US Congressman Samuel Dickstein called Newark a "hotbed of Hitlerism."

The Nazis defied the ban on meetings in the Newark area and held a rally—albeit small, maybe two hundred in attendance—in the Irvington YMCA gymnasium. What were they thinking?

By the time the meeting was to start, the Minutemen had the entire block surrounded, sitting in their cars waiting for a signal to attack. None of this was secret. The cops were there, too, on foot, guarding the front door of the YMCA.

As promised, the Newark fire department was on hand as well, plugged in to the nearest fireplug and ready to hose. Arno, as he had that night at the Schwabbenhalle, snuck around in back of the

YMCA, this time in the company of a young beat cop who was in Longie Zwillman's hip pocket.

No ladder would be necessary this time to disrupt the proceedings, as the gym was on the ground floor. Arno's intention was to smash the gym's back window with a brick and toss in both a stink bomb and the brick. There was a note attached to the brick that read "NAZIS KEEP OUT."

But when he and the cop got back there, they realized that the gym's windows, as is common with gymnasiums where projectiles fly around, were reinforced with wire to prevent shattering. Repeatedly hitting the same spot on one window with the brick, he managed only to open a small hole. When Arno tried to push the stink bomb through the hole, he dropped it and it landed at his feet. That sent Arno and the cop fleeing back toward the front of the building.

Now out in front of the building and on foot, Arno ran into a policeman who wasn't in Longie's pocket. The cop blew his whistle and shouted "Halt!" Arno thought he heard a slight German accent.

Uh-oh.

Arno, his legs still strong from his morning roadwork, took off, and the cop fired a bullet over his head. A second shot whizzed past his ear. Arno put on the brakes and held his hands up over his head.

He was arrested and jailed. The attack on the YMCA meeting never happened. At Arno's arraignment, a judge offered him a deal. No jail time if he kept his ass out of Irvington from then on. Arno told the judge he was Nat "Fucking" Arno and he would go anywhere he wanted to.

"Mr. Arno," the judge said. "You will go to jail. Thirty days and twenty-five dollars."

Down came the gavel.

That was it for the Minutemen in Irvington. They'd been ordered to stand down by the Law. But that didn't stop their activities entirely, and they still pounced on Nazis anytime they could find one alone or in a small group.

They raided restaurants where the Nazis ate, staked out homes where the Nazis lived, and always managed to vanish before police arrived. They beat Nazis in the street, sometimes with baseball bats.

Though these attacks were frequent, several per week by some accounts, none were large enough to warrant mention in the newspapers. Finding Nazis to whomp was easier than ever for the simple reason that there were more of them. German Americans were moving to Newark and taking over blocks that only months earlier had been exclusively Jewish.

The Minutemen's activities became increasingly clandestine. As would be true in other parts of the country, Jewish men who could pass for gentiles were sent to infiltrate the Nazi ranks and return with details of their plans and samples of their propaganda. One spy came out of a meeting with a small swastika flag on a stick. He gave it to Arno, who summoned a reporter.

"I fear for the future of our Jewish community," Arno said.

Although small attacks against the Nazis continued, Nazi rallies in New Jersey, in the state capital of Trenton and elsewhere, were allowed to go on without disruption. Arno's arrest and the shooting of the chaplain had had an effect.

Weeks passed, and Arno, Hinkes, Bain, and a handful of others learned of a Nazi rally in Newark at Turnverein (Gymnastics) Hall, and they decided to attend the event. Their ban from Irvington didn't apply there.

There were about two hundred Nazis in the gymnasium, including a couple dozen security guards who eyed the Minutemen suspiciously the instant they entered. They sat in the back.

While Arno and the others drew attention inside, another crew of Minutemen were at a nearby parking garage, bribing an attendant and doing some work under the hood of Wilhelm Kunze's car. By the time they were done, Kunze's car wouldn't be able to make it off the block.

Inside the hall, Kunze noticed that they had guests and edited his usual comments. He spoke only of German American pride without the usual Jew-hating rhetoric. Kunze said that there were reporters in the room and that he hoped they had the courage to print what he had said accurately and not write their usual lies designed to make the Bund seem villainous.

Just before the meeting was over, Arno gave a signal and the Minutemen got up to leave. A disappointed reporter asked Arno why there had been no riot. Arno explained that he'd been waiting for the first hint of anti-Semitism to start trouble and that hint never came.

"But there were Nazi flags, Nazi salutes," the reporter said.

"That's all I've got to say," Arno replied, but there was a twinkle in his eye. The reporter sensed that the evening was not yet done and rushed outside to see what would happen next.

Kunze and other Bund officials scuttled out the back door as those in attendance filed out toward the front. The plan, as it turned out, had too many moving parts. For one thing, the garage attendant told Kunze that his car had been tampered with, so the car's hood went up and the problem was fixed.

"I overheard them talking," the garage worker said. "They are waiting for you one block north with iron pipes."

When Kunze left, his car fixed, he headed south. The Minutemen realized that they'd been crossed up and tried a U-turn but— and eyewitnesses swear this is true—a woman leaped onto the front of their car and screamed for them to stay.

The driver slammed on the brakes and an effort was made to peel the woman off the hood, but she screamed in protest and crawled onto the windshield, drawing the attention of police. The woman eventually got off the windshield and went on her way, by which time Kunze had safely escaped the ambush.

Days later, three younger members of the Minutemen—Minuteboys really, Al Fischer, Louie Small, and Louie Lieberman— ambushed two Nazi brothers, fully grown adults, who were on their way to the post office to mail propaganda.

The lads had taken boxing lessons from Arno and Puddy and outmatched the Nazi siblings despite their youth. In a flash of efficient fists, the brothers were down on the sidewalk, groggily calling for help.

Leiberman got away, but police arrested Small and Fischer, who spent the night sulking in a dank jail cell before a lawyer sent by Longie Zwillman came to bail them out.

The Minutemen next went into action at a Springfield Avenue movie theater, raiding and busting up a screening of a recruiting film aimed at getting German American parents to send their kids to Nazi camp.

No more complicated schemes. No more pussyfooting or jawboning. This time, the attack was direct and violent. The projectionist received a bloody nose, and the projector was smashed.

Following the movie theater incident, Arno's friend Dr. S. William Kalb, now functioning as a spokesperson for the Minutemen, summoned a Newark reporter. "We expect to take the action necessary to eliminate the Nazi element. We do not stand for violence and force and hope it will not be necessary—but we are taking no chances," Kalb said.

CHAPTER NINETEEN
Union City

Fritz Kuhn and his traveling Nazi show last came to New Jersey during the fall of 1938 with a rally held in the German American Bund Hall at the corner of Thirty-eighth Street and Palisade Avenue in Union City, New Jersey. That was just on the other side of the Lincoln Tunnel from Manhattan, easy access for both New York and New Jersey's tough Jews.

In preparation, Nat Arno ordered Harry Green, still a teenager, to sneak onto the golf course at a Newark country club.

"Take this sack and fill it with golf balls," Arno said.

"Huh?"

"Rich gentiles are too good to go into the woods and look for their errant shots," Arno said. "Go there and search by the thick trees and come back when the sack is full."

"Sure thing, Boss," Green said, and off he went. He climbed a fence and searched as he was told, without ever asking why the golf balls were needed. When he got back, Arno told him he was a good boy and explained that the balls were easy to throw, traveled more accurately than irregularly shaped rocks, and raised a nice lump when they found their target.

"Some of them are cut up. They have smiles in them," Green said.

"All the better," Arno said.

The police were aware that trouble was brewing and at the last second moved the time of Kuhn's speech up an hour, from 8:00 P.M. to 7:00 P.M., in hopes of getting the event over with before the combatants were fully assembled.

It didn't work.

The Bund event was advertised as a victory fete celebrating the German army's acquisition of the Sudetenland, a portion of Czechoslovakia. When the Minutemen arrived at the scene, they found they had unexpected allies—about three thousand of them.

The other protesting groups consisted of Czechoslovakian sympathizers who didn't seem as interested in physical violence as they were in creating memorable photo ops that would guarantee newspaper coverage.

The Czechs chanted and carried signs. One memorable sign read "HITLER WANTS PEACE—PIECE BY PIECE." They burned Nazi flags and a Hitler dummy in effigy outside the Bund Hall.

One group of protesters didn't have to travel very far to get to the Bund meeting. Their own hall, where Czech societies met, was catty-corner at the same intersection.

On a third corner was the city hall and police headquarters building. The police could have moved the time of Kuhn's speech up by twelve hours and all of the players would still have been on the scene in time. There were a couple of hook-and-ladder trucks from the fire department as well, just in case.

When Kuhn arrived, emboldened by drink, he had to duck thrown golf balls to get inside. Luckily for the Bundesführer, he arrived with hundreds of his best friends, storm troopers who surrounded him and tried to shield him from attack. The arriving Nazis were also protected as much as possible by the sixty local police officers on the scene. Some of the protesters had the front door blocked, however, and chaos threatened to reign until police moved Kuhn along the building toward the side entrance.

When the golf balls were gone, the Minutemen charged the building in an effort to get inside. Police barriers quickly collapsed. The front doors were pulled open, and Arno's troops invaded.

The problem at that point was not resistance but the layout for the building. The invasion rapidly bottlenecked, and the Minutemen made it only as far as the bar in the slender lobby before gridlock took over. At the side of the building, Kuhn called out to the police to do a better job of getting him inside. It was 5:45 in the afternoon, and he was scheduled to speak at 7:00 P.M. Kuhn was more or less shoved through the side entrance, where there was another separate small bar and restaurant. Kuhn arrogantly took a seat at a table and called out for schnapps. Before his drink arrived, a group of protesters burst in, one man swinging a belt.

A press photographer—how the heck did he get in there?—stood on a table and snapped a photo that ran in every paper in America the next day. It showed both the man with the belt and the back of Kuhn's head.

Outside, the crowd that couldn't get at Kuhn turned its attention to Kuhn's car and smashed every window.

Also pushing his way through the side door was Union City's Director of Public Safety Harry Little. Avoiding haymakers, Little came upon a startlingly unfazed Kuhn, who was scolding his guards for allowing the "animals" inside.

Kuhn seemed to be experiencing a strange spell of denial. How dare these hoodlums interrupt his peace? He always enjoyed a couple of shots of schnapps before he gave a speech, it was good for his throat, and these lowlifes were making an awful ruckus.

"You can't stay," Little said. "You are disturbing the peace."

"Me?" Kuhn said, highly indignant. "But these *Jews* . . ."

"Yes, you! You are causing this riot. We don't want any bloodshed here. I am hereby ordering you to leave town immediately."

"All right, I'll go," Kuhn said. He glanced around in hopes that he might be served a shot or two of liqueur first, but none of the service staff chose to make eye contact. Glass broke over Kuhn's head as a projectile, looked to be about half of a brick, flew into the room.

"I've got to go," Kuhn shouted out, rising to his feet as he spoke to no one in particular, sticking his jaw in the air. "It is not because I am afraid but because the police fear trouble. I promise I will be back in Union City soon."

He and his guards reversed course and quickly returned to Kuhn's wrecked 1937 Plymouth coupe with its fat running board and whitewall tires, which—though pocked, battered, and covered with broken glass—still ran.

Kuhn got off one infuriating Nazi salute before climbing in, being careful not to cut himself. A fresh barrage—more bricks and a couple of recycled golf balls the size of hailstones—showered onto the car as it pulled away.

With Kuhn gone, police worked their way into the arena, where they informed the assembly that their leader would not be speaking. They also advised those in uniform to change into civilian clothes before going outside or else they couldn't assure their safety.

The next morning, newspapers across the country ran items invariably stating that Kuhn had been "stoned out of town."

The next New Jersey Bund meeting was held in the private mansion of Miss Caroline Meade on the Boulevard (house number 225)—the actual generic name of the main drag—in the borough of New Milford in Bergen County, about twenty-five miles north of Newark. The house stood between Milford Avenue and Main Street, where a street named Kastler Court is today. The toney house was set back from the Boulevard about forty-five feet and fronted by a finely manicured lawn.

The public knew the time and place because there had been a three-column notice in the *Bergen Evening Record* advertising the event, explaining that the meeting was open to everyone and intended to explain "the purposes of the Bund and the principles of free speech."

It was some house. The meeting was held in the home's "ballroom," a feature that many homes lacked. This room was about forty feet wide and one hundred feet long. There were neat rows of folding chairs and a large portrait of Hitler on the wall.

The gangsters had been instructed to kill no one, but they were smart enough to know the other side had taken no such vow. To enter a private home and fight up close would constitute a criminal trespass that could result in gunfire. This attack would have to take place from a distance.

Because the public had been invited, not everyone in the ballroom was pro-Nazi, and there was heckling during the preliminary speeches.

Kuhn interrupted an early speaker and took the podium himself prematurely. He was dressed in his usual gray and black paramilitary uniform, a well-tailored costume that angered some attendees.

"What army do you belong to?" shouted a man near the back.

"What war did you fight in?" cried out another.

"I was born in the United States, and my father and my grandfather were born in this country," the German-born Kuhn lied. "If I can't fight for my own ideas, there is certainly something rotten somewhere. This heckling and yelling is the last resort of men who can't answer any arguments."

"May we debate them?" a new voice called out from the ballroom.

"Order. I must have order," Kuhn said. "Nobody objects to our activities except the bosses of Jewish communism."

Six men rose to their feet and shouted as one: "You dirty rat! You leave the Jews out of this."

The meeting was proceeding in this disorderly manner when the first signs of trouble were heard from outside, the chanting of protesters.

The hostess, Miss Meade, suggested that the protesters be allowed into the meeting. "We're all Americans," she said.

She was quickly persuaded that that was not a good idea, and the first rock came in through a window only seconds later.

Again the hostess spoke up: "Let them break windows. Let

the people in this room see what is wrong with democracy. The Jews are a menace, and you can't have a democracy with them around."

Kuhn and his storm troopers held a quick sidebar away from the podium, after which Kuhn suggested that the women in the room should be evacuated so they wouldn't be cut by broken glass.

Eighty members of the county and municipal police, bolstered by local firemen, tried to cordon off the area, but the Minutemen arrived in numbers and fought their way through the wall of the Law. The town's ambulance, which started out the evening "shiny and new," was the worse for wear and tear by the time the evening was through.

The cops responded with nightsticks and tear gas. There were an estimated five hundred protesters, and about fifty of them made it through the cordon and broke the house's windows with rocks. Minutemen pelted the house with rotten vegetables and rocks. No golf balls this time.

When a fellow named Adam Kunze emerged from the house to shout at the protesters, he was nabbed, dragged to nearby Hirschfield Brook, and tossed into the water.

When the police were informed, erroneously, as it turned out, that the meeting was breaking up, they cleared the front of the mansion, no easy chore. Curious bystanders had joined the protesters. The Boulevard was a bustling thoroughfare. Rubbernecking gummed up the works.

Once the entranceway was clear, the police, accompanied by a soggy Adam Kunze, politely entered the home and told the Nazis that it was now safe for them to leave.

Miss Meade said that would be impossible, as she had just begun to serve refreshments. And so, while tensions outside slowly diffused, Miss Meade's guests had ice cream.

The next day, Arno was savaged in the north Jersey press, called "un-American" and "quick to resort to violence."

CHAPTER TWENTY
Return to the Schwabbenhalle

When Nat Arno made up the lie about the lynched Jew he'd seen with the swastika carved into his chest, it probably never occurred to him that he was putting ideas into the meaty heads of Newark-area anti-Semites.

On October 11, 1938, nine-year-old Bernard Cohen was minding his own business, walking to school, when he was attacked in a park down the street from his Irvington home, dragged into the bushes by a pair of thick-necked cretins, a fourteen-year-old German and a seventeen-year-old Italian.

They used a jackknife to cut a swastika into the yeshiva bocher's forearm. They were going to do the same to his other arm, but the boy's cries of pain attracted attention, so they ran. Little Bernard ran home, his wounds were treated, and he returned to the park to point out the two boys who'd attacked him. They were arrested.

Bizarrely, Judge Thomas J. Holleran let them off with a mild scolding. Did the boys learn their lesson? Two weeks later, a burning swastika hanging from a tree was discovered in that same park.

At the end of October, the Bund, now convinced that police protection would shield them from the Jewish hoodlums, scheduled

a meeting in Newark, their first in a long time. They were returning to the Schwabbenhalle, the scene of the earlier riot. It was a
ballsy move, but again they underestimated the resistance. The
news of the attack on Bernard Cohen in Irvington had infuriated
and radicalized otherwise peaceful Jewish groups.

It was no longer just the Minutemen the Nazis would have to
contend with but also every Jewish organization in the northeast.
Showing up at the Schwabbenhalle would be labor groups, students, even a group of unemployed gentiles.

There were thousands of them, and they'd packed the area
around the hall. A motorcycle cop on the sidewalk made an
abrupt U-turn and knocked a woman ass over teakettle into some
shrubbery. She didn't get up, and an ambulance was called. The
emergency vehicle took forever to get to the woman, as the crowd
had to be parted like the Red Sea.

The small group of Minutemen, Arno and an estimated fifty
others, had arrived early and had a prime spot, standing in formation on either side of the hall's front doors. A cop asked them to
move farther away from the entrance. Arno said no.

"Just make sure you don't block the entrance," the cop said,
and Arno agreed. Wooden horses were brought in to form a
flimsy barricade between the Minutemen and the Nazis.

When the Nazis arrived at the hall and saw the gridlock of protesters, they must have felt an urge to flee. The promised police
protection was there—two hundred officers, some on horseback,
some in plainclothes—but the men in blue were all but lost in the
seething masses. There was a lot of chanting and sign waving.

The Nazis walked by on shaky knees. To get inside, they had to
survive the gauntlet of Minutemen. Some Nazis still bore the
scars of previous fights.

But no one attacked. Arno and his men stood with hands
clenched and ready, but the Nazis entered the building without violence. A few hours later, when the meeting broke up and it was
time for the Nazis to leave, it was a different story.

Following a silent signal, the Minutemen moved as one,

knocked over the police barricade, and attacked. Seeing this, the cops pressed forward, and there was intense action clustered tightly in front of the hall's entrance, looking like the flesh-eating frenzy of piranhas in otherwise still waters. Fists, billy clubs, and blackjacks could be seen rising above the fray.

The top cop on the scene, one John Brady, called for the mounted police to move to the front of the hall and separate the warring groups. The result was a savage trampling as horses moved in fearlessly.

The action was so intense that it subsided quickly, and the mounted police were able to form two rows, between which the Nazis could exit the hall. But the farther they got from the hall, the fresher were their opponents, and objects were lobbed over the mounted police down onto Nazi heads. As had taken place at other gangsters versus Nazis riots, the Nazis' cars were smashed—headlights and windshields shattered and tires slashed.

According to a police report, one Nazi took his abused car to a garage for repairs, only to be beaten up by the Jewish proprietor. There was no sanctuary for a Nazi in Newark.

The Minutemen who were still standing got into their cars and drove away from the hall, seeking opportunities to attack smaller groups of Nazis. About a half dozen Nazis were beaten up at the corner of Bergen Street and West Market Street, a full mile and a half west of the Schwabbenhalle.

The rally, which had gone off without incident, would be remembered as a complete disaster because of the melee that followed it. One Nazi spokesman gave the papers the old rap about their freedoms of speech and peaceful assembly, rights that "meant nothing to that unruly mob."

Two weeks after this riot came Kristallnacht and the stories of synagogues burning as German firemen stood by doing nothing. Tens of thousands of Jewish men were rounded up and taken away. With that news, the last dribble of sympathy for the Nazis in Newark dried up.

*   *   *

That was the last gasp for the Nazis in Newark. Soon thereafter, the Minutemen's services would seldom be needed. The leaders of the Bund returned to New York City for one last major rally (see chapter 27), but it was over in New Jersey. The feds raided Camp Nordland and found evidence of "espionage and weapons violations." And, as we'll see, the Bund leaders began to have legal woes of their own.

Even in Irvington, long considered a Nazi stronghold, praising Hitler became taboo. Of course, feelings hadn't really changed, but right-wing kooks learned to keep their opinions to themselves.

The Bund no longer functioned in New Jersey, but anti-Semitism, minus the Hitler-esque regalia, still existed in Newark. Just as Judge Perlman had wished, they'd learned that being a Nazi could be dangerous.

The Jewish war funded by Longie Zwillman and run by Nat Arno had one more moment in the sun. It was the autumn of 1940, and there was trouble outside a tiny synagogue on Clinton Place in the Weequahic section. Sacred scrolls were being solemnly transported to a new space, in a slow parade that attracted anti-Semitic hecklers. The rabbi paid no attention, which encouraged the ruffians to goosestep alongside him.

True or not, rumors had spread that the harassing crew was part of Father Coughlin's Christian Front and that its members were running a printing press and distributing hateful leaflets out of a building just around the corner from the synagogue.

And that synagogue was where Longie Zwillman's mom attended services.

"Abner, those nasty anti-Semites are back. They are bothering the rabbi," she said to Longie.

"Mama, don't worry about it. They will be taken care of."

Zwillman called Arno. "Put an end to it," Zwillman said.

"My pleasure, Boss," Arno replied with a big smile. It felt good to be back in action.

And so the Minutemen came out of semiretirement. A bit of pre-attack surveillance revealed that the anti-Semites hung out in the same garage where the printing press was reportedly stored.

There were about a dozen anti-Semites hanging out when the Minutemen burst through the door with Louisville Sluggers ready to smash. Marty Cohen had customized his bat so that there was a rusty nail sticking out of the business end.

"Bust their heads and give 'em lockjaw at the same time," Cohen had said with a laugh.

The anti-Semites took the worst of it—about half of them would require hospitalization, most with head injuries, one with a shattered elbow—and all but one of the Minutemen escaped before the police arrived.

Unfortunately, when they regrouped, the Minutemen realized that Mohawk Skuratovsky had gone into the garage but hadn't made it out. He'd been laid out by friendly fire, judging from the nature of the wound, most likely by Cohen's customized baseball bat, and he was one of the unconscious taken away by ambulance. Mohawk was handcuffed even though unconscious, so he wouldn't be able to start swinging if he woke up in the ambulance. He didn't wake up, however. He was rushed to an operating room, and the initial attempt to fix him was botched—he was patched up with a piece of gauze still inside his skull.

When Longie Zwillman learned of Mohawk's injury and the poor treatment he'd received in the hospital, he visited him and made a couple of strained turban jokes because of the huge bandage on Mohawk's head. Mohawk's wife was there. The doctors had told her he probably wasn't going to make it. Longie saw to it that Mohawk was transferred to another hospital and called in a head-injury specialist from Chicago to take charge of Mohawk's care. The expert opened Mohawk's noggin back up, removed the gauze, inserted a steel plate, and although he was in bed for many months, Mohawk Skuratovsky returned to bookmaking.

PART FIVE Middle America

We will undermine the morale of the people of America. Once there is confusion and after we have succeeded in undermining the faith of the American people in their own government, a new group will take over; this will be the German-American group, and we will help them assume power.
—ADOLF HITLER, 1933

CHAPTER TWENTY-ONE
William Dudley Pelley

From the 1880s until the 1920s, Jews came to Minnesota directly from Europe, predominantly from Poland, the Ukraine, Belarus, the Galician sections of the Austro-Hungarian Empire, and Romania. But they also came, second-generation, from the Eastern cities of the United States, where overcrowding in the ghettos sent them fleeing a second time, leaving the urban soot for the breath of fresh air they hoped to find in "the Land of 10,000 Lakes."

By 1937, there were 43,700 Jews living in Minnesota. The men worked with their hands. They made and repaired shoes, worked as carpenters, tailored clothes. They were bakers and grocers. Because of the strict kosher rules, many became butchers whom their Jewish neighbors could trust. The women, if they worked outside the home, were clerks at corner grocery stores or seamstresses in cruel, dimly lit factories.

Many jobs were not available to them, despite their education and experience. The big downtown department stores wouldn't hire them. They couldn't get a job in a bank—ironic in that anti-Semites thought Jews controlled all the money—or in any large manufacturing plant. They were expected to be a self-sufficient set outside the Christian world. They were to buy and sell from other Jews. Period.

They were routinely bullied on the streets in the usual fashion. In state politics, the most anti-Semitic candidate often received the most votes. As was true elsewhere, Minnesota Jews could not even turn on the radio without hearing that they were part of a communist conspiracy to overthrow the American way.

The Minnesota Jews felt anti-Semitism on every street and with every breath.

In the Twin Cities, Minneapolis and St. Paul, anti-Semitism had deeper roots than in many places in the country. The German American community there was large enough and hateful enough to support its own branch of the Silver Legion. As Minnesota Jews realized, having written down the license plate numbers of cars in the parking lots outside fascist meetings, it was the era of the "Nazi next door."

The Jewish communities of the Twin Cities rose up in protest during the early 1930s and the rise of Hitler. They screamed about Hitler's threat to Jews as a race and about the 1935 Nuremberg Laws that denied Jews many rights enjoyed by gentiles. There were marches in the streets, a boycott of German goods, and calls for the federal government to allow more Jews to emigrate from Europe.

"They will die if they remain in Europe," the Jewish protesters yelled, largely into a vacuum.

The government did allow 250 extra Jews entry into the country, a drop in the sadly doomed bucket. The Jewish protesters received a more vigorous response from Minnesota's German American communities.

The Nazis in that area wore silver shirts rather than brown shirts, but the hate was the same. And their meetings were no secret. There were full-page ads in the newspapers announcing the next get-togethers.

The local Nazi organization was the creation of one William Dudley Pelley, who was already an accomplished man in several fields before he became leader of the Silver Legion.

Pelley had a long face and long fingers that fluttered urgently when he spoke. He was a confidence man through and through, with a face that could break into a huge three-dollar-bill smile, using the weight of his artificial charm to lean on his multitude of marks. (Think John Huston in *Chinatown*.)

Born in New England to a Methodist minister and his wife, Pelley rebelled against his dad, and while still a teenager started his own magazine, *The Philosopher*, filled with iconoclastic and antireligious messages. The magazine didn't last long, but Pelley stayed in the business, editing country newspapers in Vermont.

He switched to fiction and did much better, writing adventure stories with strong romantic angles. He grew into a novelist, most famous for *The Fog* (1921), from which a silent film was made in 1923, and *Golden Rubbish* (1929), about an abandoned girl who grows up to be a great Manhattan businesswoman. He won an O. Henry Prize for a short story called "The Face in the Window," which ran in the May 1920 issue of *Redbook* magazine. In all, Pelley wrote sixteen scenarios for produced movies, from 1917 to 1929.

By the time America's movie theaters were converted to talkies, Pelley had moved on to writing nonfiction about his bizarre conversations with the dead—and politics. He was a new man, a man who now only wrote mystical and spiritual prose, enlightened as if struck on the head with a divine hammer, not just a man of vision but also of *visions*, although we suspect his reported conversations with Jesus were merely part of his con-man pitch. Whatever they were, Pelley's claims were nothing if not specific.

For instance, Pelley claimed that at 3:30 A.M. on May 28, 1928, while he was living in a suburb of L.A., he woke from a sound sleep and heard an urgent voice echoing, "I'm dying!" Overcoming a fear that he might be having cardiac arrest, his chest ready to explode, he said he felt something rolling over his skin, as if he'd fallen into a "mystic depth of cool blue." He was naked and stretched out on a marble slab, like a sacrificial altar, and on either side of him were men who called themselves "Spiritual Mentors." They told him he was a man of destiny, a man who would one day lead a "great spiritual movement." For the rest of his life, Pelley claimed the Mentors were steering his every move.

"The Mentors told me to give up smoking, and the next time I picked up a can of tobacco, a mysterious force knocked it from my hand," he said.

The claims evolved from the spiritual to the political. In 1929, he claimed he'd been "given a sign" that a man named Hitler was going to rise to power in Germany and that he himself would become the leader of Hitler's movement in the United States.

Pelley worked on his appearance, tried to make it as iconic as possible, just in case his face one day replaced George Washington's on the one dollar bill. He was always kempt and sported a perfect goatee with just the right amount of gray.

His eyes bright with zeal, he formed an organization that he called the Silver Legion, a "Christian organization" dedicated to politically and spiritually transforming the United States.

Fritz Kuhn of the German American Bund had met with Hitler and considered himself to be carrying out Hitler's orders, but Hitler wanted nothing to do with Pelley. Perhaps he didn't like the religious angle. Perhaps he suspected a rat. That was okay with Pelley. He told his followers that Christ himself approved of his anti-Jewish agenda, and why wouldn't he? Wink wink wink.

Pelley did not openly praise Hitler or wave the Nazi flag as the Bund did. His message was more subliminal, mixing esoteric Christianity with far-right political activism and "anti-communism," a code phrase for "anti-Jew."

Though the Bund and the Silver Legion were separate organizations with separate leadership, there was evidence that they cooperated. If you went to a rally of one, chances were good that there would be someone at the site distributing propaganda printed by the other.

Pelley divided the United States into nine divisions and created a Silver Legion outpost in each. He organized a paramilitary band, "actionists" who were prepared for battle, and he called them his Silver Rangers. He didn't want to be called Supreme Leader or Grand Imperial Poobah. A simple "Chief" was fine.

His "army" wore uniforms that were called silver, but were in reality gray and blue, with a scarlet *L* embroidered over the left breast. The *L* stood for "Love, Loyalty, and Liberation."

He took to calling the United States the "Jewnited States." He wrote a book called *No More Hunger: The Compact Plan of the Christian Commonwealth*, which discussed the "permanent solution to the Jewish problem." The solution was to round the Jews up and put them in "Beth havens," like Indian reservations, and to pass a law that any Jew caught outside his or her haven would be shot. Pelley's own uniform became increasingly militaristic, and he carried a holstered gun on his left hip.

Pelley's complaint about the Jews was familiar: they controlled too much of the money. He preached of an America where he was in charge and the economy was completely in Christian control. All property, he said, would be state controlled, and it would be portioned out to white citizens in shares based on *loyalty*.

He founded a publishing company called Galahad Press and a small college in North Carolina where his supernatural treks and social theories were taught as fact. In 1933, he incorporated the Silver Legion.

The publishing business came back to bite him, not because of the extremist political message but because he was defrauding Galahad shareholders and got caught. He served a brief stint in prison and was released on parole.

He ran for president against Roosevelt in 1936 but was not very successful. He only managed to get on the ballot in one state: Washington. Come Election Day, he only received a smattering of votes. FDR, of course, won big.

Jews were inhabited by demons, he preached—feeling free to quote from deceased figures from history and the Bible who supported his views, quotes gathered during his now regular journeys along the astral plane.

History's wisest people, he said, agreed that Christians of European ancestry were at the top of the heap, with Jews, Native Americans, and African Americans far below.

* * *

Pelley's claims may have seemed ridiculous to critical thinkers—some said Pelley preached the things he did to mask his own feelings of inadequacy—but a frightening number of believers were all in.

A 1934 booklet distributed by the American Civil Liberties Union warned the Jewish community (and all people of good character) that it would be a mistake to take Pelley and his followers lightly: "Pelley is no fool, no accident. He is a clever manipulator of mobs with a distinct talent for popular appeal, and a purpose so single and violent that it carries a conviction of sincerity."

Pelley, the article said, liked to frame his organization as a grouping of Mayflower families, old Protestant Americans, old money, and old and pure culture, but the truth was his gatherings were mean-spirited, wild-eyed, and to any Jewish citizen of Minnesota, terrifying.

He told crowds that the Nazi movement in Europe had begun when one sign painter had climbed up on a barrel and gave a speech. If it could happen in Germany, it could happen in America.

Estimates of how many Silver Shirters there were in the country varied from 75,000 to 2 million. Today, experts say there were about 15,000, with another 100,000 who sympathized with the cause. Many of them were in Minnesota. There was a group of students at the University of Minnesota in 1934 that called itself Swastika.

No matter the number, Minnesota Jews agreed that something needed to be done. Pelley needed to be opposed. At first, the efforts were legal and legit. The Minnesota mainstream press was anti-Silver Shirt, and their ranks were best represented by a young journalist named Arnold Eric Sevareid, who wrote a six-part exposé in September 1936 for the *Minneapolis Journal* in which he laid bare Minnesota's pro-fascist climate.

This is the same Eric Sevareid who would become a top reporter and commentator for CBS News, the same man who editorialized on November 22, 1963, that President John F. Kennedy had been murdered by the city of Dallas, a metropolis he called the "City of Hate."

For his 1936 six-parter, Sevareid went undercover, and he wrote, "The experience was like Alice going down the rabbit hole into the world of the Mad Hatter. I spent hair-raising evenings in the parlors of middle-class citizens who worshipped a man named William Dudley Pelley."

After his exposé was published, Sevareid had to deal with death threats from those same middle-class worshippers.

In New York City, Judge Perlman understood that Pelley's troops, like the Bund storm troopers, needed a punch in the mouth. Once again, that punch would have to come from the Jewish underworld, in this case a crew of gangsters led by David "Davey the Jew" Berman.

CHAPTER TWENTY-TWO
Davey the Jew

David Berman was born in 1903 in Odessa, Ukraine. Berman moved to the United States with his parents as an infant and had no memories of the Old Country. When Davey was a small child, the Bermans lived in Ashley, North Dakota, and then Sioux City, Iowa.

When he was old enough, Berman became a newsboy, selling papers on a street corner. He experienced intense anti-Semitism and routinely busted bullies in the chops, so successfully, in fact, that he quickly became the safety guard for all of the Jewish newsies.

As a teenager, he helped bootleggers truck booze into Iowa. There were reportedly two hundred bootleggers killed in a booze war in and around Sioux City, and Berman's gun was quick. His survival was evidence of that. Though he was still a kid, his power grew until he ran twenty stills, many hidden in the false ceilings of Jewish living rooms throughout Minneapolis.

Booze might have been how he made his money, but gambling was his fascination. He dreamed of becoming a pro gambler. That crowd hung out in the Chicago House Hotel, so Berman hung out there, too, running errands for successful men and absorbing like a sponge all of the trade talk he overheard.

He sidestepped the truancy officer until he was old enough to officially quit school. Book learning he lacked. Street smarts he had plenty. What he learned was how to rig a game so that it wasn't gambling at all. He could mark cards while his opponent was watching. He carried loaded dice in his pockets. He had skills, too, and could hustle at the pool hall at a tender age. His only arrest during his youth was for playing poker in South Dakota, which earned him eight months in jail.

For a time, he was a bank robber, knocking off banks in Laporte, Indiana, and in Milwaukee and Superior, Wisconsin. The Milwaukee bank resulted in his largest haul, more than a quarter of a million dollars.

He lived in New York for a while, became an ally of Vito Genovese while still was in his early twenties, and made big money kidnapping gangsters and collecting ransom. It was an incredibly dangerous game, but he went about it fearlessly. (It was probably during this time that Berman showed up on Judge Perlman's radar.)

Berman got popped for his last kidnapping, and despite the fact that his captive refused to identify him, Berman drew a dozen solid in Sing Sing. He behaved himself and was sprung after seven and a half.

In 1934, he moved to Minneapolis, where his brother Chickie lived. There, he opened a series of gambling parlors that not only catered to Jews but also were next to Jewish restaurants, so a fellow and his date could make a night of it.

By 1938, Berman was accruing power even faster than he was losing his hair. As his hairline receded to the crown, he gained control of all gambling in the Twin Cities.

Davey's biggest competition, largely a friendly one, came from Isidore "Kid Cann" Blumenfeld, who ran the area's other Jewish rackets. Blumenfeld was born in Romania in 1901 and became known as the "Godfather of Minneapolis."

Blumenfeld didn't like bad press. Well, no hood did, but usually reporters were considered off limits for violence. Keep them in your hip pocket, and there would be no bad ink. But Blumenfeld didn't follow that rule. In December 1935, when a publisher named Walter Ligget ran a series of articles in the *Midwest American* about Minneapolis's Jewish mob, Blumenfeld didn't just have him whacked, he whacked him himself, right in front of Ligget's family, which was returning home after Christmas shopping. Ligget's wife identified Blumenfeld as the killer, but a jury took less than four hours to acquit him.

All in all, Judge Perlman preferred to deal with Davey Berman, so it was he who received the phone call.

"Operator, get me the Hotel Radisson in Minneapolis," the judge said.

Berman ran his bustling bookie operation out of the Radisson. The hotel was state-of-the-art at the time, built in 1909 and named after the seventeenth-century Great Lakes explorer Pierre-Esprit Radisson. The hotel's construction changed the face of Minneapolis. The city's downtown area, originally alongside the Mississippi River, moved because of the new hotel to its current location, centered on the corner of Seventh Street and Nicollet Avenue. The "old downtown," renamed the Gateway District, quickly deteriorated.

The Radisson was also on Berman's turf, which included everything from central Minneapolis to the west bank of the river, from the plush to the desolate.

Berman told Perlman it would be his honor to slap those Silver Shirt assholes around, and his first move was to call his competitor Blumenfeld to see if he wanted to join forces for a good cause. Blumenfeld was in, and together the men assembled an anti-Nazi crew.

A no-brainer for the crew was "Ice Pick Willie" Alderman, who prided himself as the greatest ice pick man in pro-killer history. Ice Pick Willie had worked out of Minnesota for years, but as a kid he'd been a New York boy, and he knew Meyer Lansky from those lucrative Prohibition years. He ran a bar up a flight of stairs in Minneapolis, and when in his cups would brag of his

Carrying swastika flags, the German-American Bund parades down East 86th Street in New York City before a large rally at the Yorkville Casino. *(New York World-Telegram and the Sun Newspaper Collection, Library of Congress, LC-USZ62-11748)*

Judge Nathan Perlman was a popular guy. All he had to do was announce he'd helped repeal Prohibition and everyone wanted to buy him a drink. He could also pick up a phone and call gangsters in New York, Newark, Minneapolis, Chicago, and L.A. "Hey, can you help me bust up these Nazi meetings?" he'd ask. The answer was invariably yes. *(National Photo Company Collection, Library of Congress, Prints and Photographs Division, LC-DIG-npcc-03143)*

Judge Perlman was honored by having a Manhattan street named after him. The small lane that runs along the east edge of Stuyvesant Park is named Nathan D. Perlman Place. *(Author photo)*

Judge Perlman's gravestone in Mount Hebron Cemetery, Flushing, Queens, reads JURIST ~ LEGISLATOR / HUMANITARIAN. HIS LIFE WAS FULL / OF KIND WORDS / AND GENTLE DEEDS. And if the cause was just, not-so-gentle deeds. *(Author photo)*

When Judge Perlman decided to fight the Nazi menace in the U.S. with fisticuffs, his first phone call was to this man, Meyer Lansky, who had been instrumental in the formation of both New York City's Five Family system and Murder Inc. *(New York World-Telegram and the Sun Newspaper Collection, Library of Congress, LC-DIG-ds-00979)*

Louis "Lepke" Buchalter. When Meyer Lansky needed a crew to smack Nazis around he used Lepke's boys, a.k.a. Murder Inc. *(Brooklyn Daily Eagle photograph, PORT-0116, Brooklyn Public Library, Center for Brooklyn History)*

Abe "Kid Twist" Reles (left) and Buggsy Goldstein (center) sharing a laugh, something they'd done ever since they were kids growing up on the same Brownsville, Brooklyn, block. *(Brooklyn Daily Eagle photograph, PORT-0744, Brooklyn Public Library, Center for Brooklyn History)*

Seymour "Blue Jaw" Magoon, so nicknamed because of his cobalt-colored five o'clock shadow. At least twice Magoon went out to kill one guy and killed another by mistake, but when it came to punching out Nazis, he always hit the target. *(Brooklyn Daily Eagle photograph, PORT-0582, Brooklyn Public Library, Center for Brooklyn History)*

The leader of the German-American Bund (i.e., Bundesführer) was Fritz Julius Kuhn. He saw himself as America's Hitler, but it didn't work out that way. *(Alamy stock photo)*

The German-American Bund's New York headquarters were housed in this building on East 85th Street, right around the corner from the Yorkville Casino, where they held their rallies. *(Author photo)*

The Yorkville Casino on East 86th Street, between 2nd and 3rd Avenues, has undergone a series of renovations and repurposing over the years, and is now a movie theater, which closed in 2019. *(Author photo)*

Carl Schurz Park, between the East River and the foot of East 86th Street, was the staging area for the German-American Bund's East 86th Street parades. The site was only a stone's throw from Gracie Mansion, where New York City Mayor Fiorello LaGuardia lived. *(Author photo)*

Louis "Lepke" Buchalter and Emanuel "Mendy" Weiss sizzled at Sing Sing fifteen minutes apart on March 4, 1944, and were buried in Mount Hebron Cemetery in Flushing, Queens, only a few hundred yards apart. Lepke remains, by some margin, the richest man to ever be executed in the United States. *(Author photos)*

Before becoming one of
Nat Arno's Minutemen,
Abie Bain fought as a middleweight
and light-heavyweight during a
boxing career that had him ranked
for years in the top ten.
Afterwards he fought in WWII,
then moved to California where
he played boxers in the movies.
(Author's collection)

Barney Ross was the welterweight champion
of the world and a man about town when
his buddy Sparky Rubenstein asked him
to help out with busting up a Bund meeting.
Barney said he couldn't do it: The Law said
his hands were lethal weapons.
"Don't use your hands, use a sap,"
Rubenstein said, and Barney was in.
(Author's collection)

Barney Ross's childhood friend Sparky Rubenstein cracked a few Nazi heads together, but Sparky became best known as Jack Ruby, the Dallas nightclub operator who shot and killed alleged presidential assassin Lee Harvey Oswald in the basement of the Dallas Police Station, on live TV, on November 24, 1963. Here he is moments after whacking Oswald. *(Warren Commission Exhibit 2422)*

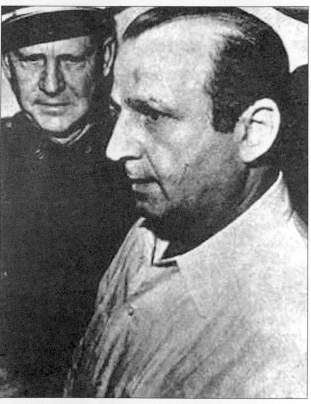

Davey Miller operated the boxing gym, at the corner of Kedzie and Roosevelt, out of which the Chicago anti-Nazi campaign was run. Here Miller is refereeing a fight between Tommy Loughran (left) and Mickey Walker on March 28, 1929, in the brand new seven-million-dollar Chicago Stadium. *(Author's collection)*

Herb Brin and bride Selma on
Christmas Day, December 25
1940, the day they were
married in the YMCA hall
They knew it would be available
(Photo courtesy David Brin)

Herb Brin was a Jewish journalist,
not a gangster, put he did punch out
anti-Semites and even went undercover
in the Chicago Bund so that the boys
would know where and when to attack
the next meeting.
(Photo courtesy David Brin)

Herb's dreams of fighting Nazis with a gun in his hand were shattered when he tried and failed to rappel a cliff with an icy rope during basic training, so he spent the war writing for *Yank* and *Stars & Stripes*.
(Photo courtesy David Brin)

Herb Brin as he appeared around 1960. As an investigative reporter, he broke news concerning Schindler's list, the Kennedy-Krushchev summit, endangered Soviet Jews, and was standing near Robert F. Kennedy when he was assassinated.
(Photo courtesy David Brin)

The formidable Ark Lodge, at First Avenue South and Thirty-first Street East, in Minneapolis, Minnesota was a key location for Nazi rallies during the 1930s. The American flag flew above the structure but grew blurry when Nazi notions were being touted inside. *(Minnesota Historical Society)*

In the United States of the 1930s, one didn't have to go to a Silver Legion or German-American Bund meeting to get their fill of anti-Semitism. All they had to do was turn on their console radio on a Sunday afternoon and listen to Father Charles Coughlin, a Catholic priest who preached a little love and a lot of hate. *(Minnesota Historical Society)*

William Dudley Pelley, seen here addressing his Silver Shirt troops, combined religious zealotry with his Nazi philosophy. He claimed to have talked to Jesus and other wise mentors from the other realm, and liked to say we were all living in the "Jewnited States."
(University Libraries, University of Washington, Special Collections,
Collection: PH 1521.1, Negative no. UW 39259)

William Pelley (in the dark uniform) and Silver Legion members gather in front of the Silver Lodge in Redmond, Washington, in 1936. Note the toothbrush Hitler mustaches in the front and back rows.
(University Libraries, University of Washington, Special Collections, Collection: PH 1521.9, Negative no. UW 39131)

Pelley's troops line up for inspection.
*(University Libraries, University of Washington, Special Collections,
Collection: PH 1521.7, Negative no. UW 39260)*

Mickey Cohen, shown here in his Alcatraz mug shot, didn't need a squad to fight Nazis.
His war with the Nazis ended up close and personal, giving a thorough beating to Nazi leader
Robert Noble and outspoken isolationist Ellis O. Jones when the pair had the misfortune
of being locked inside an L.A. jail holding cell with Cohen.
(Public domain)

ultraneat kills. He would have fit right in playing cards in the back room of Midnight Rose's in Brownsville.

Getting Ice Pick Willie to use his fists in a fight was going to be difficult. He wasn't a big guy, and what there was of him was soft. He looked like a cross between Edward G. Robinson and Larry Fine, with an emphasis on the Stooge. Someone was going to have to keep an eye on him or else, sure as shootin', there'd be a dead Nazi on the floor with his face in the sawdust and the tiniest of all possible holes behind his ear.

Other fighters included Davey's brother, Chickie Berman, and a friend, Nathan Gittlewich, who operated a gambling parlor out of the Eagles club on Fourth Avenue South. Chickie didn't mind a good fistfight now and again, but he liked to have advance notice so he could change into a fighting shirt. At most times, Chickie was a bit of a dandy, smoking expensive imported cigarettes and wearing silk shirts and French cologne. But once he changed into his fighting shirt, he'd roll in the gutter.

The Bermans and Gittlewich worked hand in hand with the legit leaders of Minnesota's Jewish community, the Anti-Defamation Council of Minnesota—later known as the Minnesota Jewish Council and today as the Jewish Community Relations Council (JCRC). It is this organization and their carefully maintained records that are largely responsible for our three-dimensional understanding of the war between the American Nazis and the tough Jews of Minnesota.

Step one was to map and monitor all Silver Shirt activities. In charge of this intense intelligence gathering was Charles I. Cooper, former president of the Jewish fraternal organization B'nai B'rith. Cooper was also one of the founding members of the JCRC of Minnesota. Cooper's man inside the Nazi movement was an undercover agent known to this day only as "SLW."

SLW worked his way deep inside and reported back daily to Cooper. Cooper and his team gathered a list of names, obtained from the license plates of cars at Silver Legion meetings. The list was terrifying in that it included the majority of the congregation of the First Baptist Church in downtown Minneapolis, including William Bell Riley, the church's pastor, who was a local Silver Legion leader. Riley gave sermons in which he advised his seven thousand followers to vote only for Christians.

The Silver Shirt movement in Minnesota leaped forward in 1938. William Pelley was acting less and less like a religious preacher and more like a war general. There were indications that the violent portion of Pelley's campaign was on its way. He now traveled with forty armed bodyguards. Members were advised to keep sawed-off shotguns and two thousand rounds of ammunition handy when it came time to defend their homes, to defend "White Christian America."

The rift between the Jews and the anti-Semites grew, largely because of the news from Europe. In March 1938, Hitler invaded Austria, and there appeared in every newspaper in the world photographs of Jews being forced to scrub the streets of Vienna with toothbrushes. Hitler annexed the Sudetenland section of Czechoslovakia in July. Jews in that area were forced to change their names to Israel so they could be more easily identified. Jewish passports were declared null and void. Hitler's power grew in leaps and bounds, and this in turn caused the popularity of the Silver Shirt movement to skyrocket. Newspaper articles reflected that meteoric rise and the subsequent concern it caused with Jews and Jewish sympathizers. The strong connection between the Silver Legion and the KKK was noted. An editorial in the *Minneapolis Journal* read, "The spirit of the old Ku Klux Klan is being revived in Minneapolis, with a new name and a new kind of shirt."

Minneapolis mayor George E. Leach reacted by banning pro-Nazi parades in Minneapolis. The mayor said, "It is my desire to prevent Silver Shirts, Black Shirts or any other anti-American organization from gaining a foothold in Minneapolis. I have asked the chief of police to enforce this ban. If you are pro-fascist and you want to parade in this city, you will be arrested."

The Silver Shirts weren't showy about it, but they defied the ban. One local Silver Shirt leader was Roy Zachary, and he gave well-attended speeches in Minneapolis on July 29 and August 2, in which he filled the air with unsubstantiated claims and bizarre conspiracy theories.

Zachary told the crowd that "the Jews" had kidnapped and killed the Lindbergh baby. He said that "the Jews" were attempting to take over the US monetary system. It was a problem that needed to be ripped out by the roots, he said. Zachary was fiercely anti–labor union, as he felt that this was part of the Jewish attempt to turn America communist. In particular, he criticized Teamsters Local 574, saying, "The alien forces that are seeking to undermine our constitutional government will take away our right of free speech and deprive us of our liberty."

The mayor tried to put pressure on the Nazis by leaning on the owners of the arenas and halls where they gathered. Two such meeting places were the Ark Lodge Auditorium and the Royal Arcanum Hall, which were on the same block of First Avenue South off of Lake Street. (Both sites are long gone, replaced by the parking lot for an outdoor shopping plaza.)

The managers of those halls allowed the Nazis to use their auditoriums in July and August of 1938 but later claimed they didn't know the nature of those meetings. They were shocked, *shocked* to learn that pro-fascist subjects were being discussed.

The Minneapolis media produced many editorials condemning Pelley's army, but not all of them leaned that way. Some said that the press and the Jews' "witch hunt" to dig out and expose the city's Silver Shirters was even more frightening than the stuff the Silver Shirts themselves were saying.

The press fought back by exposing successful local businessmen who'd worn silver shirts, such as George K. Belden, the president of Associated Industries of Minneapolis.

Albert I. Gordon, who was both a rabbi and a union negotiator, wrote an open letter to Associated Industries, asking them to come clean regarding their attitude toward the Silver Legion and anti-Semitism. The firm said no dice.

*   *   *

Today, the Minnesota Historical Society is in possession of a
typed document from October 1938 on Silver Legion of America
stationery, with Pelley's signature at the top printed as part of the
logo. The document addresses the Minnesota gubernatorial race,
then a month away, and made the most dramatic threat of violence so far against the state's Jewish community.

The document reads:

FLASH! Confidential. SILVER SHIRT operatives, high
in Government service, to-day (October 3) released a short-
wave message for the benefit of Minnesota patriots. Decoded
the message reads: "Governor [Elmer] Benson of Minnesota, yesterday secretly informed Dictator Baruch that Minnesota positively will find employment for, or otherwise
take care of, 5,000 of the 77,000 Jews who will get the
bum's rush for criminal communistic and anti-Christian activities, in new German territories, in the event of his (Benson's) reelection. Baruch, as we all know, is the Jew dictator
who has controlled three national administrations." No, you
won't read about that criminal plot in the Jewish-controlled
daily newspapers of Minnesota. But it's a fact! And what are
you going to do about it? Listen, loyal Silver Shirt, I'll tell
you exactly what can be done. Get out this evening, and
every evening till election day and expose Benson's plot to
trusted relatives, friends and acquaintances. With Jews in
control of all-important business, almost [paper torn] on the
State pay roll, and probably 10,000 being supported by the
taxpayers of this State, we already have a Jewish problem
that probably cannot be settled by peaceful means. If you
don't want Jewish Communism with resulting violence,
blood-shed and civil war (and, of course, nobody does) get
out at once and help defeat Benson and his criminal co-
horts—with Ballots. If it can't be done with ballots, no,
there must be bullets later! Get busy!

The document was signed only with the typed letters "H. G."

Governor Benson was running for reelection as part of the Farmer-Labor party. His opponent was Republican Harold Stassen. The threat from the Silver Legion was clear. If Stassen didn't win, there would be violence and bloodshed. Shooting a Jew would become every decent citizen's patriotic duty. It's impossible to tell how much influence this campaign had on the election, but Stassen was elected governor of Minnesota, and the Silver Legion threats did not need to be carried out.

In the meantime, Charles I. Cooper's list of known pro-fascists grew and now included several Minneapolis police officers. One cop was a Silver Shirt recruiter.

At the Radisson downtown, Berman's crew was ready for action. All they needed was the word of when and where the next Silver Legion meeting would be held, and they were eager to go to work.

CHAPTER TWENTY-THREE
The Elks Lodge Beatdown

One day, the phone rang in Davey Berman's gambling HQ in the Hotel Radisson, and for once it wasn't a degenerate betting the Minneapolis Millers versus St. Paul Saints game out at Nicollet Park. Rather, it was one of Berman's spies with news that the Silver Shirts were meeting that evening at eight o'clock at the Elks Lodge.

Berman contacted his fighting crew and told them to meet at the Radisson at 7:00 P.M. Once they had assembled, Davey distributed the tools of his trade—knucks, bats, sawed-off pool cues.

"Put on the knucks, boys," Berman said. "Hit 'em right in their stupid little toothbrush mustaches."

Berman's crew was twelve strong, a baker's dozen counting Davey himself.

The gang drove in three cars to the Elks Lodge and assembled near the front door. The meeting was underway, and there was a Silver Shirt at the podium delivering a speech about "the Jew bastards in this city."

Taking that as their cue, Berman's gang invaded the meeting. For ten long minutes, they busted Nazi heads. By the time the beatdown was over, all of the Nazis were either on the floor or had managed to find a way out of the building.

Berman went to the podium, his suit spotted with Nazi blood, and delivered a speech of his own to the wounded in the room: "This is a warning. Anybody who says anything against Jews gets the same treatment, and next time it will be worse. Tell your pal Hitler that it is dangerous being an anti-Semite in Minneapolis!"

Berman pulled his gun and fired a single shot into the ceiling.

In 1992, Minnesota Public Radio presented a documentary about the anti-Semitism in Minneapolis during the Depression. On that program, a Minneapolis attorney named Joe Bard talked about the physical campaign to combat the Silver Legion.

Bard had joined a small group of "Jewish businessmen and professionals" to take on the Nazis. He was on a need-to-know basis and didn't know if these brawls were one and the same as Davey Berman's battles, but we can assume they were. All he remembered was that they called themselves the Twenty Club. Bard and the men gathered and plotted strategy as to how to best disrupt a meeting.

Bard recalled being handed a set of brass knuckles and not knowing what they were.

"Put 'em on your hand, like this, punch a guy, break his jaw," some guy, maybe it was Chickie Berman, explained to him.

One tough guy waved off the brass knuckles, explaining that he preferred holding a roll of nickels in his fist. Asked why, he said, "Get caught with knucks, and they know you want to hurt somebody. Get caught with nickels, you say you just need to make a few phone calls."

Bard looked around and saw the men he was with in a new light. These were very special businessmen, indeed, the type who were familiar with the Law and knew how to get around it.

Bard was impressed with the demeanor of the operations. They were executed with patience. Nothing was impulsive. The Twenty Club always worked out a plan with tactics and strategy. They learned techniques, like a military unit getting ready to undergo a suicide mission behind enemy lines. Think *The Dirty Dozen*, with some Yiddish thrown in.

There were Nazi-busting vets in the group, but for Bard his first action came when the crew broke up a Silver Shirt meeting in a hall on Minneapolis's Lake Street. The hall had an auditorium that sat around three hundred in varnished wooden chairs.

"We wore uniforms of a sort," Bard recalled, dark shirts with what they called "Mogen Davids" painted on the front—that is, Stars of David. These were men of steel onions. It was courageous to wear a Mogen David in mixed company.

The SS meeting was underway when they arrived, and they charged in with a whooping battle cry.

"Let's crack some skulls, boys," Bard recalled shouting.

According to Bard, the Twenty Club busted up three Silver Shirt meetings with great success, but the activity never made it into the newspapers nor was it ever mentioned in any subsequent Silver Shirt propaganda. After that, there were no more Nazi rallies in Minneapolis. The cops had been paid off, and none of the brawls resulted in arrests.

From the end of the Twenty Club's campaign until Pearl Harbor, the war against the Minnesota fascists took place above ground. In July of 1939, the Anti-Defamation Council was officially incorporated and renamed the Minnesota Jewish Council. The new executive director was Samuel L. Scheiner. He had operatives throughout Minneapolis, and he was a hard man to keep a secret from.

In office only for weeks, Scheiner wrote to the Anti-Defamation League in Chicago, telling it that he had tentatively identified the Minneapolis distributor of the Silver Shirt pamphlets. His operatives, Scheiner wrote, had determined that a United States postal worker was assisting in distribution, so folks received their Silver Shirt pamphlet with the rest of their mail. Not only was the piggybacking technique cheap, but it also lent credence to the material because it was seemingly coming from an official department of the federal government.

This artificial seal of approval was only the outer layer of the deception. The pamphlets would sometimes come with a Star of David on the cover and claim to be from a real Jewish organization, the Committee for Relief of Jewish Refugees, for example.

The phony pamphlets were found throughout Minneapolis. There was even a Nazi distributing them outside the city's downtown courthouse. Pretending to come direct from the horse's mouth, the pamphlets discussed how a European Jewish refugee resettlement was part of a massive Jewish conspiracy to take over the United States.

The pamphlets urged Jews not to shop in gentile stores and said that prohibition had only been repealed so that Jews could control the booze business. The pamphlet was careful to name as many names as possible, names of prominent members of the Minnesota Jewish community, linking them to the insidious conspiracy.

In his letter to Chicago, Scheiner gave his opinion that the anti-Semites had left themselves vulnerable by distributing the ersatz pamphlet: "This is the first opportunity we have had to invoke the criminal statutes against the leaders of this organization and if possible we do not want to 'muff the ball.'" It was important that matters be handled judiciously and cautiously. If the printer could identify the person who purchased the pamphlets, that suspect could be charged for libel, forgery, and conspiracy to commit and utter a forgery and libelous statements.

In less than a week, Scheiner received key intelligence from an informant named Albert Cyr. The distributor of the vile material was T. G. Wooster, whose name had appeared on a variety of Silver Shirt documents and pamphlets since 1936. Analysis had indicated that Wooster was a passive and insignificant Silver Shirter, but now he would need to be viewed differently.

Cyr was willing to testify under oath that Wooster had bragged about his basement publishing business and the grand cause it served. He showed Cyr that he was in possession of five hundred copies of one pamphlet. Wooster, as he bragged, ended up revealing more about the distribution system than perhaps was smart.

He talked about the ingenious system he had for getting the propaganda to the people of the Twin Cities. He said that he had a team of women who delivered daily newspapers to private homes in Minneapolis and St. Paul. They would insert the Silver Shirt pamphlet inside each newspaper before delivering it. Not only did it get the pamphlets out there, but the system also gave the material a subliminal stamp of journalistic integrity from the legitimate newsprint it came with.

"I'd like to help you distribute your pamphlets," Cyr had said to Wooster enthusiastically.

"That'll be great. I'll print some up for you," Wooster replied.

Cyr said he would return later in the day. When Cyr did return, he brought his landlord with him, a man named George R. Blaisdell, himself a Silver Shirter. Neither Blaisdell nor Wooster knew that Cyr was working undercover for the Minnesota Jewish Council. In fact, Cyr had rented a room from Blaisdell just to get close to him.

Cyr had already reported once on Blaisdell, after seeing his landlord's eleven-year-old son putting Nazi propaganda on the windshields of cars in a church parking lot during services.

Cyr's testimony before a grand jury was key to having Blaisdell, Wooster, and a third man brought up on libel and forgery charges. Scheiner made sure that Blaisdell's indictment read that the material he was distributing was "likely to create violence and a breach of the peace."

Blaisdell, who by now really regretted ever renting a room to Cyr, had his day in court, Minneapolis Municipal Court Judge William C. Larson presiding, where he was convicted of disorderly conduct and sentenced to one month in the workhouse.

Judge Larson said to Blaisdell, "There can be no more potent breeder of public disorder, than a deliberate stirring up of class against class, and race against race. This undermines the patriotic unity of our nation, and is in direct opposition to that tolerance of race and religion which our constitution provides for, and which is a distinguishing feature of the fundamental law of our land, one of its great cornerstones essential to the peace and safety of any community."

The judge's words were of historical importance, as they didn't follow the company line that hate speech was protected by the freedom of speech. The *American Jewish World* periodical, which sounded national but was actually local, praised Larson for being able to see what other judges in Minnesota could not, the "light behind the sound." Larson had merely uttered a simple truth, that hate speech was equivalent to inciting a riot, and the *World* commented, "No matter what legalistic appeals or decisions may follow this ruling, no one can reverse its moral soundness."

The ruling put a major crimp in the Minnesota Nazi movement. Their written materials had been determined to be more than just offensive to civilized sensibilities. Now they were illegal as well.

The Silver Shirts were forced even further underground. A few of them went to jail, based on investigations that began when the subject's name showed up on a list found in Pelley's files.

Not everyone who went to church was a jaw-clenched anti-Semite, of course, and Scheiner pleaded with the clergy to report Nazis in their midst, especially the evangelical fascists seeking to convert others to their way of thinking. There is written evidence that this system worked and that it rooted out some Nazis.

"I heard the guy reciting Silver Shirt propaganda," an informant reported, regarding one of Pelley's men. The subject, it turned out, was a friend of Reverend C. O. Stadsklev, an evangelical minister known for anti-Semitic sermons. The guy was tossed out of the informant's church and told to go peddle his hate elsewhere.

The anti-Semitic clergyman with the most power was still Father Coughlin because of his syndicated radio network. In 1939, the US House Un-American Activities Committee, chaired by Texas Representative Martin Dies Jr., while choosing targets, debated internally and decided to ignore Father Coughlin, whose activities were obviously un-American.

Dies explained the decision, saying it was dangerous giving subpoenas to clergymen because it could be construed as anti-religion. Instead, he set the committee's sights on William Dudley Pelley, who wanted to be thought of as a religious figure but in reality wasn't.

To avoid a public grilling in Washington, DC, Pelley went into hiding, reportedly in Indiana and holed up with some Ku Klux Klan pals. He wiggled out of the jam by telling his followers that the Dies Committee was doing such a great job of rooting out commies that the Silver Legion was no longer necessary and that his members were free to go. That didn't end his legal problems, however. He was found, convicted of sedition regarding the contents of a magazine he'd published, and sentenced to fifteen years in prison.

The Congress might've maintained a hands-off policy regarding Father Coughlin, but not so the FBI. The Christian Front, an organization that Coughlin founded, was busted in New York attempting to, as the feds put it, "overthrow the Government of the United States." The raid, which took place in Brooklyn, revealed that a cell of the Front was gathering weapons and ammunition while making plans to blow up bridges and power plants.

Coughlin responded by saying he had nothing to do with that organization anymore, an absurd notion that the FBI seemed to swallow whole. Coughlin might've gotten away with it if he hadn't gone on the radio the following Sunday afternoon and pledged his allegiance to the Brooklyn conspirators. His ass was saved by the fact that the Christian Fronters were released for lack of evidence, acquitted by juries, or slogged through mistrials, with their charges eventually dropped. Unaware of how things were going to go, one Christian Fronter committed suicide.

In 1940, Scheiner received word that there was an outbreak of anti-Semitic materials under windshield wipers in one Minneapolis neighborhood. The local Catholic priest in that neighborhood was contacted, and he reported to Scheiner that there was a branch of the Christian Front in the neighborhood and they were growing more popular by the day.

Scheiner was a hated man. The Nazis saw him as enemy number one. Their revenge was both pathetic and terrifying. When Scheiner attempted to buy a home in a largely gentile neighborhood, St. Louis Park, he received anonymous phone calls telling him to stick to his own kind, that moving into the Christian neighborhood would be a big mistake.

Crank phone calls. It was the last gasp of a Minnesota Nazi movement that had envisioned world domination.

CHAPTER TWENTY-FOUR
The Great Lakes Cities

In Cleveland, Ohio, on the southern shore of Lake Erie, during the first half of 1938, the primary tool used to combat Nazism was the *boycott*. An organization called the League for Human Rights Against Nazism, led by Rabbi Abba Hillel Silver, organized the tactic, and German-American businesses took a measurable hit.

In that city, rather than fights and riots, it was more a matter of dueling rallies. The Silver Legion had their events, which drew an audience in the hundreds, but the League's rallies drew in the thousands.

Nonetheless, Judge Perlman put together a small Nazi-busting squad that covered the turf along the southern edge of Lakes Erie and Ontario. Perlman's first call went to the number one Jewish gangster in the Cleveland region, Morris Barney "Moe" Dalitz, who shared the power in the region with three others: Morris Kleinman, Sam Tucker, and Louis Rothkopf.

Dalitz was born December 25, 1899, in Boston, but grew up in Detroit. As a youth, he had deep-set and well-shadowed eyes over a beak of a nose and an easy smile that could go cold as ice in the blink of an eye. He was all nose and Adam's apple as a kid but in adulthood grew into his face. He never grew tall, however, stunting at five-three.

As a young man, he worked in his parents' laundry and first turned to crime when he was nineteen, after the Volstead Act went into effect. The family business made a quick transition. Box trucks formerly used to haul laundry now hauled booze.

He worked his way up the syndicate and was a member of the Purple Gang—the notorious Jewish mob of bootleggers and hijackers who terrorized Detroit throughout Prohibition—while still in his twenties. He accrued a huge chunk of a booze empire that encompassed Canada and Mexico and a large portion of the United States. You couldn't drink in Galveston, Texas, without Moe getting a slice.

When Prohibition transitioned with a thump into the Depression, Moe again shifted gears and went into gambling. He knew that in tough times men became desperate and fixated on get-rich-quick schemes—and where better to flex that muscle than over a roulette wheel?

He opened a parlor in Detroit. Moe was afraid of nothing, but there was too much competition in Detroit, so he relocated in Cleveland. As had occurred during his booze days, his business grew and grew. He expanded into Cincinnati, Ohio, and Covington, Kentucky, across the river.

In 1938, when it came time to beat up Nazis, he was operating a chain of parlors in Ohio, Indiana, and Kentucky. Plans were in the works for a new one to open in West Virginia. Moe was still married to his first wife, Edna. Two more wives and a live-in girlfriend would follow.

First to be volunteered for Dalitz's Nazi-busting squad was Alex "Shondor" Birns, the Cleveland racketeer. Birns was once called Cleveland's "Public Enemy Number One." You can't buy publicity like that.

Birns was born in 1907 as Alexander Birnstein in the town of Lemes, which was in Austria, Hungary, or Czechoslovakia, depending on when you looked at the map. Of all the Jewish hoods, Shondor was the one most apt to be mistaken for a gentile. He looked Irish, with light hair and a flat face, small eyes, and shell-

like ears. When he was angry, his face reddened to the point that
it glowed. When that happened, somebody was in big trouble.

His nickname, Shondor, was short for Alexander, but with a
thick accent. He came to America with his parents as a child and
lived in the Jewish section of Cleveland, which flanked Wood-
land Avenue. He was athletic, a swimmer and baseball player.
When he was thirteen, his parents operated a ten-gallon still out
of their home, making rotgut. His mother died horribly when
their still exploded and she caught fire. She ran into the street—a
human fireball—and died the next day.

After a brief stint in an orphanage, he quit school and joined
the US Navy, but he was discharged after half a year when they
discovered he was underage. He returned to civilian life an angry
kid and developed into a vicious street fighter, a skill that would
serve him well in his 1938 patriotic endeavor.

He was caught stealing a car in 1925 and served eighteen
months in the Mansfield Reformatory. Days after he was released, he was back in trouble, charged with assault after breaking some schlub's jaw in a road-rage incident.

In 1933, he joined Maxie Diamond's gang and worked his way
up the mobster ranks. He was charged with manslaughter in a
drive-by shooting incident but was quickly acquitted by twelve
jurors who knew what was good for them.

When Dalitz gave him his new Nazi-busting assignment, he
was working protection for Cleveland's whorehouses and was by
all accounts popular with the ladies. These were high-class joints
with clients who were judges and politicians. Birns was perfect
for Moe Dalitz's purposes.

Dalitz next recruited Hyman "Pittsburgh Hymie" Martin and one
of his primary competitors, Louis Rothkopf. Unlike Pittsburgh
Phil in Brooklyn, Pittsburgh Hymie had actually been to, had
even killed in, the Steel City. His most noteworthy facial feature
was his schnozz, straight as an arrow and pointy as an arrowhead
at the tip.

Rothkopf came to Cleveland via Brooklyn and had been a member of the Bugsy and Meyer Gang as a kid. He was wide and tall, with a widow's peak hairline. Too cumbersome to be a boxer, Rothkopf could have made a living grunting and groaning in pro wrestling had he chosen to. Fighting Nazis, that grappling body would serve him well.

Martin, Rothkopf, and Dalitz had worked together before and were suspected to be the triumvirate behind the assassination of Cleveland City Councilman William E. Potter in 1931, back when everything still had that new-Depression smell. Hymie was the only one of the three arrested, however.

Here's what happened:

Potter was under investigation regarding corruption in a land deal when he disappeared. After five days missing, he was found dead in a recently rented apartment, a single bullet through his head. The landlord at the death scene said someone calling himself "M. J. Markus," a fellow who looked a lot like Hymie, had rented the apartment—so Hymie was the one arrested. As Hymie was being cuffed, he wore a light gray fedora with the brim turned down low, a brown suit, a long blue chinchilla overcoat, a white scarf, and "highly polished" pointed shoes.

He denied everything. In fact, he was offended at the very notion of his guilt.

"How could you think me a killer?" he asked, placing blunt fingertips on his vest. "I'm a rumrunner, a gentleman," he said, chin up.

Rum was the key to his alibi. He claimed he was moving a load of whiskey and was with several people who would alibi him.

Hymie was convicted at his first trial on the jurors' eleventh ballot and sentenced to sizzle at the Ohio State Penitentiary in Youngstown. An appeal earned him a new trial, at which he was acquitted after Martin's defense attorney—William Minshall, later a congressman—successfully argued that Potter killed himself.

Rothkopf, the third member of the alleged team, was also a

bootlegger who'd moved onto other scams—gambling, real estate—since the end of Prohibition. He did not operate a series of
stills like many gangsters. He operated only one, but it was the
largest in the United States, perhaps the largest still ever in the
United States.

As had occurred in other U.S. cities, Rabbi Silver placed spies
inside Cleveland's local Silver Legion lodge. When the Jewish
gangsters disrupted "secret" meetings, the Germans looked around
for the mole who was ratting them out. The internal distrust was
more harmful to the Nazis than the actual attacks. Now everything was shrouded in suspicion.

Dalitz's crew was familiar with protection rackets, so the first
phase of their operation was simple. They made bad things happen to businesses owned and operated by Nazis.

The most violent encounter between the Cleveland gangsters
and the Silver Shirts occurred at a meeting held in a private
home, the Martin Gall home on Riverside Avenue in the Brooklyn Centre section of the city. (The house is still there and now
rests on the south bank of the Medina Freeway.)

To remain surreptitious, the Silver Shirts crammed as many
people as they could into each automobile, so the number of cars
parked outside would not indicate that something was going on.
Cars arrived holding so many Silver Shirts that you would have
thought they were clowns in the circus.

This meeting had about forty-five Silver Shirts in attendance.
All of the curtains were drawn. The two front rooms were emptied of furniture, and rows of chairs were set up. The gangsters,
who knew all about the time and place of the meeting because of
Rabbi Silver's spies, did not enter the home, but rather stayed
outside and "accosted" the Nazis as they came in.

One Nazi, a fellow named Hugh Stanley, arrived at the meeting
disheveled and bruised. He told the others that the men who had
smacked him around outside were the same ones who were attacking German businesses in Cleveland. Stanley explained that

he knew what he was talking about because he'd served in the US Army Intelligence Service inside Germany during the First World War and knew a little something about infiltration.

Again, the Nazis looked at each other. Who was it? Who was the man who was betraying them?

A Western Reserve University professor at the meeting stood and openly accused another attendee of being a spy. The main speaker at the meeting was William Pelley's adjunct, Field Marshall Roy Zachary, who laid out the future plans of the Silver Legion, and sure enough there was a spy in the audience.

We know because details of the meeting appeared, including verbatim quotes from Zachary's speech, in the next day's Cleveland newspapers, including Zachary's conclusion that it was inevitable that one day Nazi Germany would conquer the world.

In the meantime, the Bund took a quick look at Cleveland, saw how Pelley's crew was struggling there, and decided to pass the city by. Fritz Kuhn ordered his traveling Nazi circus eastward, setting his eyes on other medium-sized Great Lakes cities in New York with notable German-American populations: Buffalo, Rochester, and Syracuse.

In Buffalo, a group of 150 agitators infiltrated a Bund meeting. This included Dalitz's crew, who, like Meyer Lansky's crew in New York, donned American Legion and VFW hats as disguises.

Also filling the back rows were Jews from the legitimate world and gentiles who didn't like Hitler just because. In fact, joining the cause were American patriots of all stripes who thought that flying a swastika next to an American flag was a good reason to get your nose busted.

According to contemporary reports, this was no sneak attack. The outsiders pushed their way into the hall and immediately began to heckle the main speaker, Kuhn's second-in-command, William Kunze, who had just reached the podium.

Kunze had managed to say nothing more than *danke schoen* when the trouble began. The heckling intensified each time

Kunze started to speak, and he never really got a sentence out. The speech went undelivered.

Assemblyman Frederick Hammer of Buffalo ran down the aisle, rather athletically leaped onto the stage, and began to deliver a speech of his own. As Hammer was a man with iron lungs, his words rang clear throughout the auditorium without amplification.

"I have relatives who fled Germany because they did not like the military aggression," Hammer said.

There came a German-accented voice from one of the front rows: "Coward!" it said.

"Come outside with me, and we will settle that right now!" Hammer exclaimed, putting up his dukes.

The voice in the crowd fell silent, and fists still clenched, the assemblymen turned to the podium.

"I demand Mr. Kunze that you recite the preamble to the U.S. Constitution," Hammer yelled.

Dalitz, Rothkopf, Pittsburgh Hymie, Shondor, and a handful of the other boys from Cleveland shouted to Kunze that he had better salute the American flag if he knew what was good for him. Kunze refused, and that lit the match.

A scuffle began in the back, and there were the sounds of female screams, then a commotion as several women near the back headed for the exit to get out of harm's way.

In the blink of an eye, all of the agitators had found a dancing partner and were unleashing haymakers. A full-fledged riot broke out. As always occurred, the gangsters had an appetite for violence that overwhelmed their Aryan foes. Germans fled and cried and covered their faces with their hands.

A United Press reporter inside the hall at the time of the fight said he was amazed that no one was killed. Eyes were blackened, noses broken, lips split, and skulls well lumped, but no one stayed unconscious for long, and everyone was more or less ambulatory by the time the police arrived.

There had been a puny police presence at the Bund meeting,

fifteen cops outside the hall, and when they heard trouble inside the hall, they were unsure what to do.

According to Buffalo police Lieutenant Alfred O. Gardner, the policemen concentrated on getting the top-rank Nazis off the stage and out of the hall safely. Kunze objected to leaving, but a pair of cops took him each by an elbow and escorted him off the stage and out a rear exit.

The fight was allowed to exhaust itself before police reinforcements arrived, five squads strong. The Buffalo police were pleased to find that their work was easy. All they had to do was blow their whistles a couple of times and everybody who could walk left the hall without complaint.

The Nazis were slower to leave the scene, many of them looking down at bloodstained shirts. There was a lot of blood and blackened eyes, but according to an Associated Press reporter, "No great damage was done."

The hall emptied, and the show did not go on.

Just outside on the sidewalk was a small pile of Legion and VFW hats. The gangsters had slipped away. An Associated Press reporter grabbed one of the now hatless infiltrators and asked who they were, who did they represent, what was their beef with the Bund?

"We're Jewish war veterans, but we are not from any organization. Our activities are private," the man said. He wiped his knuckles on his pants and was gone before the reporter could get out another question.

The reporter continued trailing combatants until he found an agitator who was more eloquent regarding the politics of the matter. This one said that the Jews were there because they objected to Kunze's denunciation of the Committee for Industrial Organization and objected to the swastika flag on display and to the fact that Bundists gave each other the Nazi salute.

Kunze later was cornered by the same reporter and gave his usual public relations bullshit answer: "Our job is to fight subversive influences in the United States. We want to make sure that no small racial minority gains control of the U.S. government. We are also opposed to the CIO and to marriages between Aryans and Asiatics."

No, he went on, they were not Nazis, but they thought the fake news was giving the Nazis in Germany a bad name. Hollywood movies and radio programs were spreading false information regarding events in Germany. The US, he said, lacked a free press.

"The newspapers determine what policies should be adopted," Kunze concluded.

A few days later, on a Tuesday evening, the Bund tried it one more time and held a rally in Syracuse. They quickly learned that trouble was following them. The leader of the Bund's Syracuse branch was Max Haas. An estimated one hundred legitimate American Legionnaires were in the hall as Haas spoke, while outside was a gang of toughs, no doubt Dalitz's boys. The Legionnaires inside disapproved of the Bund's message. They heckled but remained peaceful.

Some of the thugs outside wore Legionnaire hats too, but theirs didn't fit as well, and their commitment to keeping the peace was dubious.

Haas was heckled off the stage with shouts of "Go back where you came from!" and "You're just a dirty Nazi!"

When Haas was escorted out of the arena to his car, the boys outside took over and smashed his headlights.

(Haas subsequently went into hiding. The next day, when reporters sought him for a follow-up story on the riot, Haas was nowhere to be found.)

When the hall emptied, the "protesters" hungrily lit into the exiting Germans. The cops showed up noisily and, to the gangsters' delight, used their batons to lump up a few Nazi heads of their own.

Standing over a fallen Nazi, one hood was overheard to say, "Next time we ain't gonna be so nice."

That was food for fascist thought, as the Bund was scheduled to hold a meeting down the road in Rochester in just three days.

After the Syracuse riot, the leader of the local Legionnaire branch, Ronald Brown of Fayetteville, New York, said he had no idea who those men outside the hall were, but they weren't Legionnaires. (Judge Perlman, reading that in the New York papers, must've laughed.) The Legion, Brown emphasized, had used no violence in Syracuse. They were using the Law not their fists. They were petitioning the county district attorney to have Bund leaders brought up on sedition charges. His men were going to meet and formulate a plan for rapid assembly, just in case a situation came up in which they "were all needed at once." The district attorney, Donald Mawhinney, said his office was investigating the violence outside the hall following the Bund meeting.

In Rochester, on the south shore of Lake Ontario, there was no local branch of the Bund, but there were German Americans, so Kunze thought it might be a good city in which to recruit. Kunze was scheduled to speak in Rochester in a large conference room in the Powers Hotel on Main Street West. The hotel, considered one of the Flower City's finest, had opened in 1883.

The Bund event in Rochester turned into a major flop when only a couple dozen people showed up. This may have been because people were afraid of the violence that had marred Bund events in Buffalo to the west and Syracuse to the east, or it might have been simple lack of interest.

The Bund announced to the press that the meeting had been canceled because of phone threats. This was a complete falsehood. There had been no phone threats, and the meeting wasn't canceled as much as moved to a cozier space where the handful of attendees would be more comfortable and within arm's reach of a fresh beer. The meeting went on, but in the back room of a bar and restaurant on Clinton Avenue North.

Asked for comment, representatives of the Powers Hotel said

they were relieved to be rid of the Bund. Hours before the meeting was to start, they revealed, fifty "shifty-looking men in American Legion hats" had begun cracking their knuckles and flipping silver dollars in the plush hotel lobby, crystal chandelier above and tessellated floor below, making management extremely nervous.

Kunze, some other Bund members, and the estimated twenty-five attendees were escorted out the hotel's back door onto Fitzhugh Street and, via a convoy of Fords and one Packard Twelve, moved two miles northward to the Nazi-friendly bar.

PART SIX West Coast

Hollywood and the Third Reich must have Zusammenarbeit
[collaboration]."
—ADOLF HITLER

CHAPTER TWENTY-FIVE
The Hollywood War

The relationship between Nazis, Jews, gangsters, and the police was far more complex in Los Angeles than in other American cities, so a little explanation is necessary. First off, nowhere in America did the Nazis try to disrupt and take over like they did in L.A.

Nazi Germany's Propaganda Minister Joseph Goebbels had his eye on L.A. from the earliest days of the Nazis' rise to power. He told Hitler that Hollywood was the world's greatest propaganda machine. Hollywood movies, Goebbels explained, were shown not only across the United States but everywhere in Europe as well. To control the message coming out of Tinseltown was to, dare he say it, *rule the world*.

The Nazi infiltration into La-La Land began in 1933. Pamphlets were published, recruiting meetings held. The trouble was, as Hitler eyed Los Angeles hungrily, he couldn't conceive of just how new and *without tradition* the city was.

New York was a tourist town and drew hundreds of thousands of visitors a year, even during the Depression. Visitors oohed and ahhed, partied a little, and went home. It was different in L.A. They had thousands of visitors a year, too, but the great majority of them had no intention of leaving.

They were dreamers who came to become movie stars but

soon found themselves struggling to afford food and shelter yet still desperate to get a foot in the show-biz door. The migration was magnified by the Depression and the dust bowl that uprooted Americans and pointing them west.

Then, like now, L.A. was a city with a conspicuous homeless problem. In 1935, the state senate proposed a bill that would "prohibit all paupers, vagabonds, and indigent persons" from entering the city. The bill, had it passed, would have allowed authorities to kick out anyone who was likely to one day need public assistance. The bill didn't pass, so the corrupt-through-and-through LAPD took charge of keeping the number of bums in the city to a minimum. If you wanted to sleep under a bridge, a cop would give you "the bum's rush."

As our story takes place, fully half of L.A.'s residents had been in the city for fewer than five years, and 90 percent had been in town for fewer than fifteen years. Second-generation Angelinos were few and far between.

From Hitler's point of view, that made L.A. seem like easy pickings. But when his operatives goose-stepped into town, they found that there was no sizeable German American community. There was no Yorkville in L.A. Whereas New York City was a place where the space between things had been removed, L.A. was the opposite. Space seemed infinite, and the city sprawled in the baking heat, gobbling up the valleys and canyons and hillsides.

And then there were the police. Corruption was assumed. Not that New York and Newark and Minneapolis and Chicago weren't corrupt, but Los Angeles took it to a new level. Organized crime and law enforcement were hopelessly blended. Politicians were bought and sold. Police officers paid for appointments. Madams and bookies paid weekly juice to the vice squads.

In 1938, even as Judge Perlman's campaign against Nazis was underway, a private detective named Harry Raymond tried to investigate Mayor Frank Shaw for election fraud, only to have his car blown up with him in it. Raymond took 150 pieces of shrapnel throughout his body, but after a series of operations, he survived. However, he got the message and wisely discontinued the investigation.

The Silver Legion, separate from Hitler's efforts but equally fascistic and anti-Semitic, was active in the area. William Pelley ordered a camp to be built just outside of Los Angeles, a fortress really, in Rustic Canyon in what is today part of Will Rogers State Historic Park, just west of the Getty Museum. At the time they called it Murphy Park, and it was dedicated as the headquarters for Silver Legion operations in the United States. Today, all that remains of the camp are a cluster of derelict buildings, covered and then covered again with Jackson Pollock–like graffiti.

In Depression-era L.A., there were about seventy thousand Jews, the great majority of whom lived in a neighborhood called Boyle Heights, tucked in between downtown Los Angeles and East L.A. (The neighborhood stopped being heavily Jewish during the mid-twentieth century, when several freeways were built through it, including the East L.A. Interchange, which is at one point twenty-seven lanes wide. The construction helped cars get around but changed the neighborhood for the worse, tearing down houses, obliterating main drags, and vivisecting what was left.) Only a relatively few L.A. Jews, the movie moguls and a smattering of stars, lived in the new, posh neighborhood known as Beverly Hills.

It might seem puzzling that Nazis would hope to gain a foothold in a city in which Jews ran the movie business, until you realize the Jews only represented the *new* money. There was already plenty of money in L.A. before the movie studios moved from Brooklyn and Queens during the late 1910s. *Oil money.* There had been a boom starting in 1892. The La Brea Tar Pits were the first indication that "black gold, Texas tea" was bubbling up from beneath the City of Angels. Edward L. Doheny sank the first well in 1892 at the corner of Patton and Colton, and—*boom*, gusher. Within a year, there was drilling going everywhere, more than a thousand oil wells. Those wells clustered most dramatically in two spots, just south of downtown and around La Brea and Wilshire. People with modest homes drilled for oil in their backyards. If you lived in L.A. during the 1930s, there were constant reminders of this, oil fields with dozens of genuflecting derricks pumped new money to put on top of the old for the lucky landowners. And all of that oil money was purely gentile.

The movie people, with their sunglasses and hangovers, lived in Beaux Arts mansions off Wilshire Boulevard, not a fascist among them. They made left-leaning films, explored themselves, coupled and tripled regardless of gender, drank an insane amount, and took drugs—all to the chagrin of the oil folk, who looked down their noses at the ever-growing Hollywood cesspool of sin. There seemed to be no end to it. Invading show-biz wannabes, profligate and vulgar, were pouring into L.A. at a rate of three thousand per year.

It was the puritanical oil snobs—with their riches, already anti-Semitic to the bone—that Hitler wanted on his side. Only with their help could he overthrow Hollywood and transform it into a Nazi propaganda machine.

The moguls, and most of the stars, had kept their heads above water during the Depression. In fact, in 1938, Hollywood was approaching its greatest year, with *Gone with the Wind* and *The Wizard of Oz* simultaneously in production. Hollywood was aware of the Nazi menace, of course, but hesitant to react. There was money to be made in Germany, and the studio heads didn't want to turn off that cash faucet until it was absolutely necessary.

The oil millionaires weren't the only anti-Semitic forces at play. The Ku Klux Klan was active and had among its ranks top cops from both the Los Angeles Police Department and the L.A. County Sheriff's Department.

To further complicate matters, there had been a seamless blend of L.A. law enforcement and organized crime since the 1920s, when most cops were under the thumb of saloonkeeper and rack-

eteer Charlie "Gray Wolf" Crawford. Goodtime Charlie's reign
ended in the usual fashion on May 20, 1931, when he was shot in
the stomach, liver, and kidney in his Sunset Boulevard office just
as his bodyguard slipped away for a snack. There were L.A. citizens who had busy schedules, being that they were gangsters,
cops, and KKK riders. There was the vein for Hitler to tap into.

Soon after Hitler's scouts moved to Southern California, a Jewish
attorney with the alliterative name Leon Lawrence Lewis put together a squad of spies to combat the Nazi menace. Lewis was in
touch with the foreign press and knew that Hitler was encourag-
ing Germans in America to form "active cells."

Lewis was like Herb Brin in Chicago in one important sense.
He was a six-foot-one Jew and no one to mess with. Born in Wisconsin in 1888 and the son of Jewish German immigrants, he
went on to earn degrees at the University of Wisconsin and the
University of Chicago Law School. His first years as a lawyer
were spent representing Jews who were down on their luck. During the Great War, he enlisted and fought in France and was discharged as a captain. After the war, he moved to Chicago and
became the Anti-Defamation League's executive secretary.

Some of Lewis's spies were gentiles because the physical type
for infiltration was so limiting. And not all of them were men.
Years later, it came out that a Navy widow named Grace Comfort
and her daughter Sylvia, an unwed secretary, infiltrated the Bund
and took photos at marches and demonstrations. Sylvia took a job
inside the Bund, working as a stenographer. Her primary target
was schoolteacher William Williams, who taught at North Hollywood High School in the daytime and distributed vicious anti-
Semitic propaganda at night. (Williams eventually went off the
deep end, shooting his wife and then himself in a murder-suicide
after World War II.) The women reported back to not just Lewis
but also the FBI and the Office of Naval Intelligence. The FBI
worked its way into the loop only after Grace Comfort was ar-

rested and explained with proof that she had been working undercover.

The ladies turned over pamphlets they'd snuck out, propaganda that read, "Buy Gentile. Employ Gentile. Vote Gentile. Boycott the movies. Hollywood is the Sodom and Gomorrah where
Jewry controls vice, dope, and gambling."

Grace and Sylvia worked their way up the ranks, became members of executive committees, and were assigned to check ID at
the door of meetings to keep Jews out. They even listened in on
Nazi phone calls that exposed plans for several hate crimes.

Lewis's spies learned that the Nazis were thinking big. They'd
had secret meetings in which they discussed just how they were
going to overthrow Hollywood. They were going to lynch twenty
top Hollywood stars and moguls—an all-Jewish roster including
Samuel Goldwyn, Louis B. Mayer, Al Jolson, Eddie Cantor, and
Charlie Chaplin—and leave the bodies hanging in public places
to maximize the terror.

There were plans to use gas grenade launchers to put cyanide
into Jewish homes, to throw a beer hall putsch just like Hitler's
that would coincide with the mass robbery of munitions from a
National Guard armory, and to blow up a munitions plant in San
Diego.

The plots were so frightening that they cast a new light on the
rallies and parades. In L.A., anyway, the Brown Shirts and the
Silver Shirts seemed like a show, a glitzy distraction from the insidious matters being discussed in private.

The Nazis held their first public meeting in L.A. at the packed
Turnverein Hall on West Washington Boulevard, at a location
that is now in the middle of the Santa Monica Freeway. On the industrial gray walls were mounted electric fans, noisier than they
were effective, blowing the hot air harmlessly around.

The main speaker was Robert Pape, who was the *Ober-
gauführer* of Nazi Germany's L.A. operation, a World War veteran and charter member of the Nazi party. He had his HQ set up

at the Alt Heidelberg on Alvarado Street. Nearby, he opened the Aryan Bookstore, which was the place to go for all of your pro-Hitler propaganda. Actually, it was a place-to-go in general, as Pape built a little entertainment and business complex around the store. There was a beer garden, a restaurant, and an upstairs space for administration offices. They called it the "Brown House" because that was the name of Hitler's HQ in Munich. Like any good proprietor, Pape worked the guests, making sure every glass was full, talking all the time in his thickly accented English. To anyone who would listen, Pape warned of the Jewish-communist conspiracy and predicted that the Jews would try to take over but would fail because the Nazis would rise up as one and "save America." Pape regularly sent "progress reports" to Hitler and Goebbels.

Also walking around shaking hands was Hans Winterhalder, Pape's propaganda chief. Winterhalder also spoke at the Turnverein Hall meeting, telling his audience that there were fifty German American organizations in Southern California. What good was that? If they could just unify, they would be more than one hundred thousand strong and Hitlerism in America would become a reality. The message played very well with the audience.

The Nazi movement was recruiting in other troubling ways. The large basement of the Aryan Bookstore complex was being used to feed and bed German Americans. Many of them were dust bowl migrants. All of them were on the skids.

Such men, the Nazis knew, were mentally malleable. Consensus among Lewis's spies was that the Nazis were building an army. But what to do about it?

Lewis tried telling the LAPD about the plotted espionage and didn't get the response he'd hoped for. The policemen said that Lewis was only interested because he was Jewish and that Jews had made it hard for Germans to compete economically, that the actions of Germany seemed like they were all for the good. They were sure that the Nazis in America would only do good as well.

Lewis left the LAPD encounter horrified. Desperate to find the

good guys, he tried the US government. Surely, it would be interested in what amounted to a plot to overthrow it. He met with
Joseph Dunn, then the Southern California chief of the Justice
Department's Secret Service. Dunn didn't criticize Jews the way
the L.A. cops had, but he didn't help, either.

"My hands are tied," Dunn said. "I'd like to help you, but I
can't start an investigation until there is an overt act."

Lewis realized that to save L.A. from the Nazi threat, he would
have to do it himself. Still, he'd need backing. He took his case to
Tinseltown, where he knew he'd find a few sympathetic ears and
perhaps a deep pocket or two.

He held a secret meeting of his own, at the toney Hillcrest
Country Club on Pico Boulevard—also the golf course where the
Three Stooges had filmed *Three Little Beers* in 1935. Hillcrest
was a Jewish country club, as the other L.A. clubs had restricted
memberships. Wealthy Jews had opened their own club, and Hollywood bigs like Samuel Goldwyn, Louis B. Mayer, Al Jolson,
and the Marx Brothers were members. Still, to have moguls from
all of the studios there at once brought attention. Club personnel
said they hadn't seen this many limos lined up since the last big
premiere at the Chinese.

These guys weren't tall, but they had trouble moving in mysterious ways. Lewis drew an impressive crowd: Louis B. Mayer,
Joe Schenck, Ernst Lubitsch, Jack Warner, Irving Thalberg. Also
in attendance was entertainment attorney Mendel Silberberg. He
was on board right away.

The others impatiently waited for Lewis's pitch, blustering
through cigar smoke about the inconvenience of the emergency
meeting and the bother of keeping it secret. They gave Lewis
their best this-better-be-good look.

Then Lewis started talking Nazis, and the men paid attention.
Lewis told them he wanted to "create a war chest" for his al-
ready-trained-and-in-place spies within the California Nazi scene.
Thalberg, the MGM wunderkind who didn't have long to live be-

cause of a perforated pump, volunteered to help out with the fundraising. He'd been squeezing money out of people for years and supposed he could do it to fight Nazis.

"I had a fucking heart attack in Bad Nauheim last year," Thalberg told the others. "I have witnessed the Nazi repression." Then he volunteered to be the liaison between Lewis and the studio heads. Some of those moguls were in the room.

The decision to combat Nazism was not easy for the moguls because there were just so damn many movie theaters in Germany, and Germans loved Hollywood movies. If they contributed money to combat the Nazi groups in L.A., it would have to be a secret. No problem, Lewis said. Eventually the studios kicked over with money—MGM, Paramount, Warner Brothers, Universal, RKO, Twentieth-Century Fox, United Artists, and Columbia.

The money helped pay for Lewis's ops but came with strings attached. Not only was the source of the cash to remain secret but Lewis also had to promise that his spies would help keep the fascists out of the studios.

And so Lewis's spies were given a new assignment. They would strike at what Lewis perceived to be the Nazis' weakest point, the fact that the three leaders, Pape, Winterhalder, and Herman Max Schwinn, all seemed to be self-centered egoists who saw each other as competition rather than as allies.

Now, in addition to gathering intelligence, Lewis's spies were to carefully spread disinformation, little snarky comments that would sow trouble into the Nazi hierarchy. Lewis's clandestine crew sparked dissension among the Nazi leaders and then poured gasoline on it. As trust in leadership rusted away, operations broke down in the planning stage and infiltration of Hollywood never happened.

The plan worked like a charm. Pretty soon, the leaders all thought the others were double-crossing them, the fighting turned inward, and plans to conquer California stalled.

Even after Pearl Harbor, Lewis's efforts came in handy. When the US government was looking to round up Nazi sympathizers, Lewis had a list that made the job easy.

So one bullet had already been dodged when Judge Perlman picked up the phone to officially make his gangsters versus Nazis war coast-to-coast.

CHAPTER TWENTY-SIX
Mickey Cohen and Bugsy Siegel

The plot to overthrow Hollywood had been staunched, but in 1938 at the time of Judge Perlman's war, both the Bund and the Silver Legion remained active in L.A.

To start the ball rolling on the West Coast, Perlman called a gangster he'd known back in New York, a well-known hood by the name of Meyer Harris "Mickey" Cohen.

Cohen was not a book-smart guy and was known for his tortured grammar and malapropisms. Street smarts he had. No one knew more about the political landscape in L.A. Need a crooked cop? He was your guy. Need an invite to a Hollywood party? He could get you in. Want to run a scam? You better talk to him first, if you know what's good for you. Need a Nazi stomped? No sweat. He'd been taking orders to beat people up for much of his life, so Perlman had him quickly enlisted in the cause. Mickey later said that whomping Nazis was his "patriotic duty."

Cohen was another Brooklyn boy, born in 1913, son of Russian immigrants. His dad died when he was an infant, and mom gathered up the baby and moved to L.A. Mickey had six older brothers and sisters, who remained in Brooklyn, living with aunts and uncles.

At age six, Cohen was selling copies of the *Los Angeles Rec-*

ord (now long defunct) on the corner of Soto Street and Brooklyn Avenue (now known as East Cesar E. Chavez Avenue), a major intersection on the northern edge of Boyle Heights.

Eventually, he did more on that corner than sell papers. For two bits, he'd hold a package for one man to be picked up by another. The package almost always contained a bottle of whiskey, and Cohen was arrested when he was nine for bootlegging.

According to his legend, Mickey also pulled his first score when he was nine, knocking off the Columbia Theater box office with a baseball bat.

As for competition, he usually settled that with his fists. If another newsboy wanted the hustling and bustling corner of Soto and Brooklyn, there was a fight, which Mickey inevitably won.

Sometime around puberty, someone said, "Hey kid, you should be a fighter." So he wandered into a boxing gym and was immediately enchanted by the speed bag's rhythmic beat.

Punches sold quicker than peanuts back then, and it didn't matter how old the combatants. There was an organized tournament for newsies, and the boys who fought over turf got their first taste of gloving up and getting into the ring, three two-minute rounds while chattering men made bets at ringside.

Mickey didn't win the tournament, but he fared well enough to get his name in the papers and a job as a sparring partner. He was fighting professionally as a bantamweight by the time he was thirteen.

He bragged about his boxing career in later years. Officially, he only fought in seven prizefights and won none of them—three losses, four draws. But in reality, there were many more. He fought in four-round smokers, unsanctioned and illegal fight cards held in bootleg clubs. They were cockfights, only with kids off the street instead of roosters.

When he was sixteen, Mickey returned to New York to train at Lou Stillman's Gym on West Fifty-seventh Street, a dank space that had never been cleaned, and smelled like it. Stillman, who doubled as a private investigator, thought the filthiness of his gym toughened up the fighters who trained there.

It was while training at Stillman's that Mickey picked up the obsessive-compulsive habit of washing his hands sixty times a day. He was a guy who was pleased to meet you but didn't really want to shake your hand.

As was true of many boxing gyms of the day, you dropped a dime in the bucket and you could watch all day, and Mickey got to meet those guys, a cast of characters straight out of a Damon Runyon story.

Moving from opportunity to opportunity, Cohen moved westward again. He eventually became Ben "Bugsy" Siegel's bodyguard, which put him on the fast track for success. In addition to guarding Siegel, Cohen also was raking in the dough with his own bookie joint at the corner of Santa Monica Boulevard and Western Avenue. The place was cop-proof on account of the chief of the Hollywood bunco squad had a piece of the action. The joint was wired for the ponies during the day and operated as a casino at night.

Cohen's pugilistic skills might've been less than top drawer, but there was no questioning his toughness or his courage. The L.A. mob boss Jack Dragna wanted him dead, bad. Mickey escaped every assassination attempt. Bullets were fired into his home. Dynamite once blew a gaping hole in his bedroom wall. Later, he would take a shotgun blast to the shoulder. The attempts just made Cohen's fame grow.

In 1938, when Perlman called, Cohen was already a star gangster in L.A. with plenty of clout and plenty of enemies.

Perlman mentioned Siegel to Cohen. Mickey said that he knew for a fact that Ben would love to sock a Nazi, too, that he'd openly discussed, pardon the expression, icing Nazis.

"Relay a message for me, Mickey?" Perlman said.

"Anything you want, Judge."

"Tell Ben I already have Lansky and Zwillman on board back east."

"You are doing a great thing, Judge."

"And tell Ben no icing."

"Takes a little bit of the fun out of it . . ."

"Yes, but it has to be that way. Rabbis will be watching what you do."

Perlman asked Mickey about the LAPD, whose reputation stunk like the La Brea Tar Pits. Mickey assured him there was no problem. There might've been officers who worshipped Hitler on the force, but most only worshipped the greenback dollar bill.

The judge knew the time and place of the next Bund meeting. Cohen jotted that down and said he'd take care of it. He immediately called Siegel to tell him the good news.

Bugsy Siegel was the best looking of the Jewish gangsters, with heavy-lidded eyes, a movie-star jaw, and a cool-breeze demeanor. He was also Meyer Lansky's childhood co–gang leader and had been sent west from New York to set up rackets in Tinseltown.

Siegel loved L.A. because he loved sunshine and convertibles and starlets. His first westward trek came in 1933, when he visited actor George Raft, himself a Brooklyn neighborhood kid from back in the day.

The weather, the girls, L.A., and Bugsy were meant for each other—but Siegel was overseas trying to sell a patent for a new explosive when he first planned to hurt Nazis.

Siegel had been a bad, bad boy dating back to when he first partnered up with Lansky. By the time he turned twenty-one, he had a rap sheet as long as his inseam: assault, drug dealing, rape, robbery, numbers, rubouts, white slavery.

Siegel also had been a professional killer from the time he was a teenager, sometimes whacking guys for as little as fifty bucks. Ah, but he was a good Jewish boy. He never killed on the Sabbath.

As a killer, Siegel was a *gunman*. He didn't go much for hands-on stuff. He saved that for the dolls. But with a gun in his hand, he was about the most dangerous thing known to man. He had a nose like a football player's—these were the days before face guards—and a rictus grin when he diddled the trigger.

When he was told to break a guy's leg, he shot the guy in the kneecap instead. On those occasions, Siegel would grin at his victim. The wails of pain were music to his ears.

His cold blood scared everyone, no matter whose side they were on.

One former crewmate recalled, "When the rest of us were trying to decide what to do, Siegel was already shooting. I've seen him charge ten men, and all ten ran for cover."

His reputation took a quantum leap in 1931, when he was part of the four-man crew that whacked Giuseppe "Joe the Boss" Masseria at the Nuova Villa Tammaro restaurant in Coney Island. The others included Albert Anastasia, Vito Genovese, and Joe Adonis—an all-star crew.

In 1938, Siegel was thirty-two years old and schtupping Dorothy di Frasso, a married Italian countess, in the Villa Madama in Rome, and big-time Nazis were in the hotel, in town to conduct business with Mussolini. Hermann Göring and Joseph Goebbels were just down the hall.

Because of his international notoriety, Siegel was registered under a pseudonym: Sir Bart, a British baronet. Politics weren't Siegel's forte, but he took an immediate dislike to that "fat bastard" Göring because he caught him chatting with his girl.

"Why do you talk to him, Dottie?" Siegel wanted to know.

"He is an important man. I . . . ."

"Fuck him. And fuck that other asshole, Goebbels, too," Siegel said. "I am going to kill the both of them. It's an easy set-up with the way they're walking around here."

"You can't do it, Ben."

"Why not?"

"They would execute my husband, my whole family, in retaliation," Dottie said.

So Siegel backed off, but he didn't forget.

*   *   *

In the days and weeks after Perlman's call, Cohen, Siegel, and others undertook a campaign of guerilla warfare—slinking around the hot city in small cynegetic packs, finding Nazis alone or in groups and pounding them into the desert sand.

It's unknown how they learned where the Nazis were going to be, but given Perlman's relationship with the Anti-Defamation League and the league's network of spies inside L.A.'s Nazi community, the information was no doubt easily acquired.

"Hitler's got one nut, which is one more than you going to have if we see you wearing that fucking shirt again," Cohen would say to the bloody puddle left squirming on the burning L.A. sidewalk.

Some of the Nazis who were tenderized by gangster fists were also cops, not so brave when caught alone.

"We had to fight cops, too. Back in those days, a lot of L.A. cops were Nazis as well," Cohen later recalled.

In another city, Siegel and Cohen would have been busted for attacking a police officer. In L.A., that couldn't happen. Top cops were in business with Siegel and Cohen, and the pair happened to be excellent earners.

The largest Nazi riot in L.A. came on February 22, 1939, months after most of the action had taken place in New York, Philadelphia, Newark, Minneapolis, Cleveland, Buffalo, and Syracuse. On that date, Cohen, Siegel, and a hundred of their best friends surrounded the Deutsches Haus, the German House, on West Fifteenth Street in Los Angeles as a Bund meeting took place inside.

The Bund meeting was advertised as a celebration of George Washington's birthday—the Bund loved birthdays—and the surprise guest speaker was Herman Max Schwinn, a leftover from Hitler's plan to conquer Hollywood. Schwinn's presence at the meeting had been kept secret because the US government was in the process of canceling his US citizenship.

Schwinn was a bespectacled chap whose military cap hid the

great height and width of his forehead. Sometime during 1938, he'd grown a truncated mustache, an homage no doubt to you-know-who. Also scheduled to speak was a writer and pamphlet publisher named David Hall Jr. from Glendale, California.

But all of that George Washington business was just a smoke screen of patriotism that didn't deter a bloodthirsty mob from assembling outside. Along with the gangsters, there were demonstrators from the Socialist Workers Party and the Young People's Socialist League who were carrying signs that read SMASH HITLER, FIGHT AGAINST ANTI-SEMITISM, and BUILD WORKERS' DEFENSE GUARDS. There were a surprising number of women among the protesters, pipingly singing the "Internationale" in clear, untrained voices.

A box truck rolled slowly around the block with a loudspeaker mounted on it. Inside, a man with a microphone broadcasted a relentless mantra, "Down with Hitler! Down with fascism!"

Along with protest signs, it seemed as if every protester had brought a bushel basket full of rotten vegetables, eggs, and rocks. When a Nazi wearing a brown shirt tried to enter the Deutsches Haus, objects both disgusting and harmful rained down on him. The most serious injuries at the riot were Nazis who'd been hit on the head and face by thrown rocks.

Before long, the front steps to the building were slick with rotten-vegetable slime. The protesters kept attendance down as many potential attendees chose safer activities.

The Nazis inside the hall were still not safe, either. Two rocks smashed through front windows and rained glass down onto their delicate pink scalps. For those who did make it inside, slime dripping from their uniforms, there was a second problem: how to get out.

After an hour's delay, there was an attempt to start the rally, and Hall got off a couple of remarks—"Washington was a leader of a revolution who was like Hitler today"—before more broken glass from hurled rocks interrupted him.

Police were called from a telephone inside the building, but when they arrived, seven radio cars strong, they only made a half-assed attempt to disperse the crowd, which barely budged.

With Hall keeping his head covered, Schwinn took the podium and managed to insult FDR and several members of his cabinet before realizing no one was listening because of the chaos outside.

Eventually, the police decided against direct confrontation with the angry mob. They cleared the area surrounding a side door and led the Nazis to safety one patrol car load at a time.

After the Deutsches Haus riot, there was a feeling among the gangsters that their job was through, that the public had picked up where they had left off. Bund membership in L.A. was shrinking and shrinking fast. Siegel proclaimed it a job well done.

In addition to making Bund and Legion meetings dangerous, Cohen later told a writer that he'd also done favors for the left-leaning Writer's Guild, which was having its own Nazi trouble.

A few weeks later, there was a separate incident in La Crescenta, California, about twenty miles due north of downtown L.A., at a Bund meeting that made the out-of-town papers, largely because of a gender angle that so titillated editors back in the day. There was a *woman* involved.

Her name was Mrs. Elizabeth Barber, and we wonder just how much she appreciated getting her name in the papers after she disrupted a Bund meeting. She was lucky in one sense. At least none of the papers published her address, as newspapers used to do all the time, even for witnesses to mob hits.

There were 1,500 people at the outdoor rally in Hindenburg Park (now part of Crescenta Valley Park), and Fritz Kuhn himself was at the podium, gesticulating, when, according to the Associated Press reporter on the scene, Mrs. Barber stood and demanded, "Tell the truth!"

Her voice was loud and clear, and everyone heard what she said. She may have wished she could have crawled under her seat, but she kept her chin up, even as angry Nazis "surrounded her and began to chant in playground bully style, 'Go back to Moscow! Go back to Moscow!'"

Mrs. Barber began to inch her way toward the aisle, and as she did so, she yelled, "We hold these truths to be self-evident, that all men are created equal!"

She picked up her step as she got to the aisle, confident now that these angry fascists were not going to get physical with her.

"We the people!" she cried. "We the people!"

The wire service reporter followed to make sure he got her name spelled correctly in the morning edition. She told the scribe she couldn't help but speak up because that Kuhn guy was not "advocating true Americanism."

Not being reporters who worked for circulation-hungry editors, many others thought the headline of the day was not the woman heckler but rather the low-flying airplane that buzzed the meeting a few times before dropping thousands of anti-Nazi leaflets on the angry crowd.

"Wanted for kidnapping, Adolf Hitler," the leaflet read. "Indicted by world opinion for murder and kidnapping with intent to kill."

L.A. and its surroundings weren't the only place where Nazis were active on the West Coast. Northern California, Oregon, and Washington State also had their share of Nazi recruiting and anti-Nazi violence.

When the Bund held large meetings in San Francisco, they were held at that city's Deutches Haus, which—now known as the California Hall and used as a concert hall—stands at the corner of Polk Street and Turk Street in the then-German section of the city, now known as the Tenderloin. The venue was built in 1912, designed by architect Frederick H. Meyer.

Cohen and Siegel and their crew didn't make the trip north for these meetings. It wasn't that the meetings were secret or that they lacked controversy. The American Federation of Musicians Local Six union in San Francisco had just published an open letter in the local newspapers condemning the Bund for its "religious intolerance and racial hatred."

Best guess is that the gangsters' hands-off policy had to do with money. Riots bring heat, and perhaps the boys had an ongoing op in the Tenderloin neighborhood, something that was best left without scrutiny by the Law.

One factor supporting that theory is that the instant the Bund tried to have meetings in other parts of the San Francisco Bay area, Jewish gangsters were on hand to dish out some all-American punishment.

The Bund, hopeful now that they had found a section of the country where they could gather unmolested, rented out the Hermann Sons Hall on Western Avenue in the town of Petaluma, California, thirty-seven miles north of San Francisco. The speaker was again Schwinn, who was coming up from L.A. for the gig.

The Hermann Sons Hall building was not named for a couple of siblings who owned the hall. It was the name of a fraternal order of German Americans that had been around since the turn of the century. The Sons' object was to "preserve the culture, traditions, and language" of their homeland. They named themselves after Arminius Hermann, a ninth-century German chieftain who fought off the Romans.

Also heading north for the event were Siegel, Cohen, and a couple dozen hoodlums looking for trouble. The meeting was not a secret, and they were not the only Jews up in arms about the meeting.

A twenty-seven-year-old Petaluma teacher by the name of Jeremy Koch wrote a letter to the editor of the *Petaluma Argus-Courier* denouncing the Bund and demanding that the Nazi meeting be canceled. The paper published the letter, and a wave of protest followed. The newspaper subsequently printed its own editorial criticizing the Jews, shouting that they were trying to stifle the Nazi's freedom of speech.

The folks who ran the Hermann Sons Hall said they were innocent, that they knew nothing about terrorism or movements of hate. They had rented out the hall for the showing of a German-language movie. They saw no need to cancel.

Their innocence was feigned, as they knew exactly who was coming to speak and pretty much what was going to be said. There was even a branch of the Bund in Petaluma, said to be one of the most active branches on the West Coast and to which many of the Hermann Sons belonged.

When the meeting finally happened, there were more protesters outside the hall than Nazis inside. The attendance had been held down by talk of trouble. Two movies were shown. One was a cinematic celebration of the Nazi invasion of Austria and the second was *The Aryan Bookstore*, an infomercial about Pape's L.A. Nazi center that instructed Petalumans on how to get their hands on that much-in-demand Jew-hating propaganda.

Schwinn took the podium and said, "We have as little ill feeling against the Jews as we have against a flea. But it takes only one mosquito to spread malaria, so when such a mosquito settles on our body, we do not intend to spend much time wondering whether it is a good one or a bad one."

Unlike the gangster teams working back east, Cohen's boys did not try to get inside the meeting. If they had, the riot would have started right then and there. As it was, Schwinn finished his speech.

The gangsters waited until it was over and went to work on the Nazis as they came out, some of them fairly sloshing with pilsner. The protesters objected to the gangsters almost as much as to the Nazis, screaming "No violence" as the Brown Shirts were pummeled. About a dozen Nazis were beaten before the L.A. boys cheesed it on account of the cops.

There was action even farther north, a physical confrontation between gangsters and Nazis at the Masonic Temple on Capitol Hill, constructed 1915, seating capacity 750, at the corner of Pine and Harvard in Seattle, Washington. Today, it has landmark status and serves as a single-screen art cinema for Seattle Central College.

One of the speakers that night was Hans Otto Giese, a Seattle German American lawyer, who said, "We frankly admire our reborn and united German fatherland of today and its greatest genius, Adolf Hitler, who has accomplished such wonders over there in restoring national unity and peace."

The event was a celebration for sailors from a German warship visiting Puget Sound and a lovefest for Hitler in general. The main speaker was Schwinn, although again his presence was not publicized because he was sought by the feds.

The event drew a crowd of naysayers. The Bund PR campaign had been combatted by King County Judge Samuel R. Stern, who publicized reports of mass murder coming out of Germany.

"It is a real hell on earth," Stern said.

The audience only learned of the protesters outside after the show started. The instant the orchestra began to play, a group of young women ran up and down the aisles throwing anti-German leaflets into the crowd.

Most of the women were out the back door before anyone realized that they weren't part of the show but were really part of the "communist" protest.

A couple of the leaflet throwers were slow to escape and were nabbed by sailors, who whooped and hollered and "roughed the women up" before tossing them out.

When word of the women's mistreatment got outside, the protesters threw down their signs and stormed the arena. Cops were called, and thirty policemen joined the fray.

In the end, the protesters backed off, and order was restored. The show went on. There were only three arrests, one of them a high school kid and another a black man who was busted for possession of brass knuckles. He should've opted for the roll of nickels.

None of the beaten Nazis was Schwinn, who snuck out a back door when he heard there was trouble in the front. Schwinn may not have gotten a sock on the jaw that night, but he soon there-after got one—figuratively, at least—from the US government. He was stripped of his US citizenship for having made a false oath of allegiance, and right after Pearl Harbor, he was placed under house arrest in Chicago as a "risk to military security on the Pacific Coast."

PART SEVEN The Bund's Last Gasp

The far right could never find its American Führer. The country's political parties ensured that none of the leading candidates, ranging from outlandish options like Fritz Kuhn or William Dudley Pelley to more plausible options like Father Coughlin or Charles Lindbergh, would ever get a chance to make a bid for the position.
—BRADLEY W. HART

CHAPTER TWENTY-SEVEN
Garden Party

By 1939, Murder, Inc., the Minutemen, and Mickey Cohen's crew no longer had to disrupt Nazi rallies. It had become the thing to do, and every time the Nazis planned a get-together on American soil, people arrived by the hundreds to protest and attack the Nazi message and the Nazis themselves.

With a sense of satisfaction that they'd done their patriotic duty, the gangsters went back to their day jobs: extorting, killing, eyeing broads on the Sunset Strip, hanging out on Kedzie Avenue, being kings of Newark's Third Ward, and playing cards in the backroom of Midnight Rose's.

But war in Europe was on the horizon, and the American Nazi movement was still *there*, damaged but as bold and well kempt as ever. The imperious Fritz Kuhn wanted to put his Bund on the front pages of every paper in America. He gave a speech in which he said that there would be no more secret meetings. The time had come for the Bund to act without fear of reprisal from the "Jewish militia."

And so he was careful to do all of the paperwork, get all of his permits, and cross his *T*'s and dot his *I*'s, and then he scheduled the biggest rally of all, his "great Americanization rally," to be held on February 20, 1939, in the biggest city's biggest arena: Madison Square Garden, smack dab in the middle of Manhattan.

The arena, he announced, would be packed with like-minded German Americans, eighteen thousand of them, just shy of the capacity for boxing. The plan was to gather the most Nazis in one place in US history. (It should be noted that this was not the same MSG that stands above Penn Station. This was its predecessor, farther uptown, at Eighth Avenue and Fiftieth Street, which since 1968 has been referred to as the "Old Garden.")

The time and place was announced sufficiently in advance for Nazis to attend from all around the country—except for the West Coast, where a second event at the Deutsches Haus in L.A. would be held two days later (see chapter 26). There was also plenty of time for the "Jewish militia" and other anti-Nazi organizations to make plans of their own. Hours before the event was scheduled to begin, angry Jews surrounded the Garden on all sides.

Were Meyer Lansky and Murder, Inc. there? Probably. Everyone else was.

Before the rally, MSG security guards who knew the nooks and crannies of the arena searched for concealed explosives. None were found. The marquee outside the Garden had the unintentionally hilarious description:

TO NIGHT

-PRO AMERICAN RALLY-

HOCKEY TUES NIGHT

RANGERS vs. DETROIT

On the back of the stage hung the now-familiar combination of American and swastika flags and a banner that read:

JEWISH DOMINATION OF CHRISTIAN AMERICANS

In the lobby, a stand usually used to sell programs for sporting events instead peddled the anti-Semitic rotogravure magazine *So-*

cial Justice, published by the Radio Priest, Father Coughlin, that night hawked by teenaged boys.

"Hey *Social Justice*! Getcher *Social Justice* here! Hey *Social Justice*!"

It was a late-arriving audience. Nazis had to fight their way through the crowd to get in. Many of the seats would remain empty as yellow Nazis saw that mob and decided to rally another day.

Those who did get in sat both in folding chairs on the floor of the Garden and along the sides in two decks of grandstand. Journalists were surprised not by the bold staging of a Nazi event in this tremendous indoor space, that was expected, but by the boring nature of the speeches.

The first few speakers—Rudolph Markmann, the Eastern district leader of the Bund, George Froebese of Milwaukee, James Wheeler-Hill, the Bund's national secretary, and the Reverend S. G. Von Bosse, a Lutheran pastor from Philadelphia—were an invitation to snooze.

It wasn't until William Kunze and Fritz Kuhn took the podium that the air began to crackle with evil. Waves of breeze wafted onto the stage from thousands of simultaneous Nazi salutes. *Sieg heil!*

Kunze was introduced as having just gotten back from a successful organizing tour during which he'd added twelve units to the Bund in Texas. He took the podium and said they were there to "celebrate George Washington's birthday." Cheers. "And to grieve for the death of America at the hands of President Roosevelt—or should I say President Frank D. Rosenfeld." That got a laugh. "This country is in a deplorable state when Henry Morgenthau takes the place of an Alexander Hamilton and Franklin D. Roosevelt the place of a George Washington." Boos. Kunze also brought cheers at the mention of Herbert Hoover and Father Coughlin. "Replacing George Washington with Franklin Roosevelt is like, in the cultural life, replacing Beethoven with Irving Berlin and the like," Kunze said. He attacked radio, saying that freedom of speech only applied if communists were on the air. All you had to do was look at the wild criticism of Father Coughlin's broadcasts to see that. "I call for the radio to cease giving people the trash of the Winchells, the Cantors, and the like, and give us the voice of those who do not speak the American language with a Jewish accent." Thunderous applause.

On the street, among the people trying to get inside was former magistrate Joseph Goldstein. After arriving by taxi, he was talking to the police, looking for a police escort into the building, where he planned to serve a summons. The summons, returnable in Bay Ridge (Brooklyn) Court, charged Kuhn with criminal libel. Goldstein claimed that he had been libeled in the official Bund newspaper, the *Deutscher Weckruf und Beobachter*, the contents of which, he alleged, were Kuhn's responsibility.

The crowd outside the Garden grew and seethed. How many were there? That depended on who was doing the estimating. New York Police Commissioner Lewis J. Valentine said the anti-Nazis were about ten thousand strong. Chief Inspector Louis F. Costuma's estimate was exponentially larger: he thought one hundred thousand had gathered. New York and inflated crowd estimates were a tradition. Every year on New Year's Eve about seventy-five thousand people packed into Times Square, and newspapers routinely described the crowd as being more than a million.

The hostility in and around the Garden that night was matched by the global situation. President Roosevelt had been getting his anti-fascist jabs in, saying that if the Germans didn't learn to mind their own business over there in Europe, he might have to curtail his Caribbean cruise, return to Washington, and get busy. That comment brought retorts from all three of what would become the Axis powers. A German diplomat told the press that FDR just wanted to start trouble and that people had long since stopped believing anything that the lying American president said. An Italian representative said that FDR was spouting "clamorous American nonsense," and editorials in Japan were calling FDR's statements "little short of crazy."

Back at the Garden, the show of police force was strong both inside and out. Many protesters were not content with just chanting outside and wanted in, where they could be disruptive. Holding the throng back was "the largest police contingent in the city's history," 1,700 strong.

According to the Bill of Rights, the Nazis could gather and listen to horrible speeches and be evil, and as long as no one shouted "Fire!" they were breaking no law.

The anti-Nazis outside, however, were breaking all sorts of laws. They hit Nazis as they headed in, they threw things, they blocked traffic. Many cops couldn't have hated the Nazis more, but their job was to protect them.

Police Commissioner Valentine said, "I've got enough men here to stop a revolution."

The cops had to worry not only about keeping the anti-Nazis out of the Nazi rally but also about the twenty Nazis—nineteen men and a woman—who had laid low in the doorways on Fiftieth Street between Eighth and Ninth Avenues and, upon a prearranged signal, attacked the protesters in front of the Garden's main entrance on Eighth Avenue. The Nazis had smartened up and were using Murder, Inc. tactics against the Jewish masses.

Even when there were no Nazis in the picture, the anti-Nazis were in a combative mood, so they fought the police instead. That brought out the nightsticks, and several protesters went down, bleeding from the head.

Just then—only in New York, kids—a parade of World War I veterans, a robust if tipsy band blasting George M. Cohan's "Over There" came marching down Eighth Avenue, seemingly oblivious to the riot just up ahead. The cops blocked their path and tried to explain the situation, and the veterans took a right and occupied Fifty-second Street between Eighth and Ninth.

Seeking the high ground, policemen were sent to the parapets above, ready to throw tear gas down onto the crowd if it came to that.

There were so many people in the region, screaming about one cause or another, that the saloons along that stretch filled with men who'd drop in, pound a cold one, and rejoin the fray.

The sounds from the street were similar to those of a fight-night crowd, the kind they usually had at the Garden, the grunts of the combatants blended like whiskey with the aroused cries of spectators jazzed by the violence.

During the melee, the Broadway musical *I Must Love Someone* let out at the Longacre Theater on Forty-eighth Street. The orchestra left the pit and carried their instruments to the Garden area and played "The Star-Spangled Banner" in an effort to soothe the frenzied masses.

As casualties grew, hotel lobbies turned into mini–triage centers, where those who needed a Band-Aid were separated from those who needed an emergency room.

Inside, while Kunze was talking about the blessing of Aryanism, newspaper columnist Dorothy Thompson, the well-dressed wife of Sinclair Lewis, author of the anti-fascist novel *It Can't Happen Here*, threw back her head and cackled a loud laugh of derision.

A nearby man stood and said, "If you don't like it, why don't you get out?"

"I've got as much right to be here as you do," Thompson replied.

Six storm troopers moved as one toward the conflict. Six policemen approached from the other direction. The cops got there first and suggested that Thompson head quickly toward the door for her own protection. She took their advice and allowed them to escort her out.

Once she was outside, newspaper columnist Heywood Broun

joined her and informed the police that she was there as "an accredited press representative" who intended to write about the rally. She was quietly allowed to reenter the building.

Asked why she had laughed so loudly, she said, "I laughed because these Nazis were exercising the free speech which one day they would deny everyone."

A twenty-six-year-old unemployed Jewish plumber from Williamsburg, Brooklyn, named Isadore Greenbaum snuck into the Garden. He bided his time during the drone of the preliminary speakers and felt his anger mount as Kunze made his ugly remarks. Then, as Kuhn stepped up to the microphone, Greenbaum moved surreptitiously and secreted himself at the left rear of the stage.

Kuhn began to speak: "We have made great strides forward in every section of the land. I know that the Bund will march forward with thousands of new comrades in the years to come. Our great cause of national socialism will be and must be better understood. We have many to win to our side, but I am confident the coming year will see a brilliant future for the Bund in America. In nearly every land of the world our Germans are once more marching forward together and hand in hand with their *Vaterland*. It is so in France, in Spain, England, Russia, and the Scandinavian countries. All our Germans in Poland are united and heart-and-soul with the führer. We have advanced so far that now we even have our own schools and our own churches. We speak our mother tongue and we adhere to our ancient German customs. We are still *thoroughly* German. I mention these things to you to inspire you, to show you what really can be done when Germans in a foreign land stand united and fight for their rights. I am certain after having seen the work and wide scope of the Bund in America that the day will come when our American-Germans will also have their own churches, their own language will be freely spoken, and their customs will be observed with dignity."

Kuhn then began his vitriolic attack: "It was the Jewish financiers who sent America into the Great War in 1917, the Jews who exerted pressure on President Wilson."

Kuhn blamed all American casualties during the great World War on the Jews. "The Brandeises, the Baruchs, and the Untermyers are responsible! They sent thousands to France to die under the slogan of 'Make the World Safe for Democracy.' You all have heard of me through the Jewish-controlled press. American radio is censored; it is controlled by the Jews! Wake up! You, Aryan, Nordic, and Christians, must demand that our government be returned to the people who founded it. The time will come when no one will stand in our way."

It was at that moment that Greenbaum could no longer restrain himself. He boldly made his move, charging at Kuhn like a star of the gridiron rushing toward pay dirt.

Greenbaum got to a point where there was only one man between him and Kuhn. Trouble was, that one man was a wall-like security guard with large hands, a barrel chest, and feet wide apart.

Greenbaum dove to the stage floor and went between the guard's legs. Now he had a clear path to the speaker. But he didn't go after the man. He went after his electronics, yanking on the cables so that Kuhn's microphone fell over. Greenbaum then turned to the crowd and yelled, "*Down with Hitler*!"

The crowd exploded in an uproar. Women screamed. Men, expecting gunplay, hit the deck. There was a mad push to the front, causing folding chairs and the infirm to fall.

Greenbaum now moved toward Kuhn, but Kuhn's security guards jumped in as one. When Greenbaum was only three feet away from the Bundesführer, the first storm trooper got to him, grabbed him by the hair from behind, and pulled him to the stage floor.

The others quickly joined in, dragging Greenbaum to the back of the stage and savagely beating him. Six cops then joined the fray, trying to pull the storm troopers off of Greenbaum so he could be both rescued and arrested for disorderly conduct.

In case there was any question as to where the policemen's allegiance rested, a cop belted storm trooper Arthur Grove in the eye.

There was a ripping noise as the Germans pulled down Greenbaum's pants and the crowd laughed uproariously, observing Greenbaum's degradation with dissolving anger and an emerging smirk of arrogance.

The laughter served to calm things down. Those shredded trousers stayed down around Greenbaum's ankles as cops lifted him by the shoulders and ankles and hoisted him out of there as fast as they could move, to a chorus of boos and hisses.

Bruised and swollen, Greenbaum was taken directly to night court and held on one hundred dollars bail. The next morning— now famous, his photo in all the papers—he appeared in West Side Court in Manhattan before Magistrate Harry S. Andrews.

With him were his pretty wife, Gertrude, and their baby son. Gertrude told reporters that her husband was "kind and gentle" and "no troublemaker." Judge Andrews asked Greenbaum why he'd done what he did.

"When I heard persecution against my religion, I lost my head," Greenbaum said.

The judge scolded Greenbaum, saying that women and children might have been hurt in the melee that would have resulted had he been able to carry out his attack on Kuhn.

Greenbaum responded, "You say many women and children might have been killed or injured. Your honor, do you know how many children and innocent persons will be killed if the persecution they were speaking last night were kept up?"

Judge Andrews gave Greenbaum a choice, a twenty-five dollar fine or ten days in jail for his actions. The fine was paid by Sam Maness on behalf of a Manhattan Jewish newspaper called *Jewish Day*, and Greenbaum was set free. Other Jewish leaders in the

courtroom announced that they, too, had been willing to pay Greenbaum's fine, up to one hundred dollars, and a couple of them offered the unemployed plumber a job.

Gertrude Greenbaum told a reporter from the *Brooklyn Eagle*
that she first knew that her husband had gone to the rally when
she was told he'd been arrested. "He is kind and gentle, always
has been to me and the baby. Although I don't know what he did,
I am sure he had good reasons and it was not wrong. He is a good
man and I love him. We've been on a honeymoon since our marriage three years ago and although he was away from me last
night for the first time, the separation is only temporary. Something Kuhn said must have provoked him, for he is not a troublemaker, just a hard-working family man."

She said she met Isadore when he was doing plumbing work at
her home and it was love at first sight. She said he had recently
been laid off from his job because business was slow.

Of the 1,700 cops at the Garden that night, only four were
injured. The worst injury went to mounted patrolman Charles
Kamerman, who was rushed to Polyclinic Hospital for treatment
of deep gashes on his legs inflicted as he tried to sandbag the tidal
crowds. Another cop, Deputy Inspector Martin J. Brown, twisted
an ankle, and Patrolman William Mitchell suffered a fracture of
his left thumb and wrist, broken as he pummeled a Nazi's thick
skull.

There is a tale, perhaps tall, of one Joseph L. Greenstein who
pulled down a Bund banner outside the Garden and was immediately fallen on by thirteen Nazis, but Greenstein fought his way
out and ran for reinforcements, earning him the nickname "the
Mighty Atom."

A Bund press release after the chaotic night not only buried the
lead, it failed to mention it. The release bragged that the rally net-
ted twenty-eight thousand paid admissions—at least ten thousand

more than were actually there—or that the Garden could hold. Everything went great, the press release claimed. What a night for German Americans everywhere!

The press release influenced only right-wing kooks living under rocks. The rest of the country read the rest of the story on the front pages of newspapers from New York to California. There had been a huge "riot." Multiple vocal and disparate groups converged on the arena in a diffuse but intense protest of the Bund. A lone plumber was a hero.

The "Garden Party" made news globally. In Germany, predictably, the pro-Nazi press made the attempted attack on Kuhn the lead story, equating Greenbaum's efforts with the recent assassination of Nazi officials in Switzerland and France. The headline translated into English read: "Jewish Onslaught on Leader of German Americans in New York."

In Williamsburg, the Greenbaums were overwhelmed by their new celebrity status. The buzzer rang, and it was Western Union—a congratulatory telegram from Judge Perlman.

"A judge! Fancy," Gertrude said.

Minutes later, there was another visitor, this time a deliveryman.

"Izzy, do you know anyone named Meyer Lansky?" Gertrude asked, looking down at a small card in her hand.

"Can't say that I do."

"Well, he knows you!" Gertrude said, with the prettiest smile in Brooklyn. "Look at the size of this gift basket!"

In response to the Garden Party, the Council Against Intolerance in America threw a party of its own, this one in Carnegie Hall. There, a crowd of 3,500 listened as religious leaders (Protestant, Catholic, and Jewish) railed against the Nazis. Father Jeremiah Mahoney said the MSG get-together was "an illegal and unholy mass meeting of enemies of God."

The crowd, befitting the venue, merely clapped politely until

Mayor LaGuardia took the stage and called the Garden Party an "exhibition of international cooties." The crowd roared with approval. After that, the audience was more enthusiastic and booed vigorously at each mention of Hitler's name.

By February 1940, the constant attacks on Brown Shirts had the German American Bund in disarray and on the run. The brilliant future that Kuhn had predicted had dimmed, largely because of the gangsters' fists and Izzy Greenbaum's bravery.

A clandestine government investigation discovered that the Bund headquarters had up and moved in the middle of the night from New York City to Mexico City. Kuhn was a wanted man, accused of stealing from his own organization (see chapter 29). His successor, the story went, was Herman Kilper, a German immigrant living in Mexico City. He was described in the investigation's report as a "man of mystery," which meant they'd yet to learn much about him. A report came in that Kilper had been the choice of Hitler himself to run things in North America, but a second report said the first was incorrect, perhaps purposeful disinformation designed to send the FBI on a wild goose chase while the Bund's members scattered to the winds.

During the summer of 1940, nine Nazis who spoke at a rally at Camp Nordland in New Jersey were found guilty of breaking a new "hate law" and sentenced to serve twelve to fourteen months in prison. Two of those sent away were bigwigs, Wilhelm Kunze and August Klapprott, the Eastern leader and Camp Nordland manager, respectively. By late November 1941, that hate law was stricken from the books as unconstitutional, a breech of a man's free speech rights. Kunze was released and fled to Mexico. When war came, he was arrested, extradited to the United States, and imprisoned for espionage and violating the Selective Service Act.

Jewish gangsters had battled Nazis at every turn, long before American and German armies first made contact in Africa. The Bund and other pro-Germany organizations got to the point where they couldn't assemble without worrying about stink bombs and crowbars.

By Pearl Harbor, the Bund was through.

William Dudley Pelley's Silver Shirts were also on the run. Not only had angry Jews disrupted their meetings, but the House Un-American Activities Committee also was hounding their collective ass.

Pelley tried to do some disrupting of his own and attempted to put a Silver Shirt spy inside the Dies Committee's investigative staff—but the attempt was clumsy and quickly foiled.

Pelley's spy was to be thirty-seven-year-old Fraser Gardner, a "Washington political researcher," but the Dies Committee's background check revealed that he was also an employee of Pelley's publishing company, a fact that he'd left off his resumé.

In August 1939, Gardner was called before the committee and nervously chain-smoked as a series of questioners grilled him. He admitted that he knew Pelley, had received telegrams from Pelley, and had talked to Pelley on the phone, but he denied being a Silver Shirt or being employed by Pelley. He was paid by a man who worked for Pelley but . . .

"Do you know where Pelley is now?" US Representative Martin Dies Jr. asked.

"No," Gardner said.

"Neither does this committee," Dies said. "But we're looking for him."

After months of ducking subpoenas, Pelley was found, and in February 1940, he appeared before the committee. As he testified, his cigar ashes fell onto the table before him. He admitted to being anti-Semitic and pro-Nazi. He said that "when the revolution came" he hoped to be a leader of the anti-communist forces. He sat and took it as the congressman lambasted him for "cruelly maligning a great race" and telling his soldiers they might have to "take up arms" against the "Jewish menace." He named the top financial contributors to his Silver Shirt organizations. When Pelley's testimony was through, before he could leave the congressional chamber, he was arrested for an alleged violation of a suspended sentence involving a 1935 fraud conviction. Pelley called his arrest a "Jewish plot." It was a diddly matter, but the committee got what it wanted. Pelley was humiliated, his picture appearing in the next day's papers being fingerprinted by a cop.

And that was how things stood when the bombs began to fall over Hawaii and everything changed.

CHAPTER TWENTY-EIGHT
Pearl Harbor

At 6:00 a.m. on Sunday morning, December 7, 1941, the first wave of 183 planes—forty-three fighters, fifty-one dive bombers, forty-nine horizontal bombers, and forty torpedo bombers—took off from the Japanese First Air Fleet's launch position, 240 miles north of Oahu, Hawaii.

Forty minutes later, the US destroyer *Ward* spotted the conning tower of a midget submarine headed for the entrance to Pearl Harbor. The destroyer sunk the sub with depth charges.

At 7:00 A.M., the second wave took off from the First Air Fleet. Two minutes later, the radar unit at Opana Point in Hawaii picked up a signal indicating a large formation of planes approaching from the north. They were mistaken for B-17s returning from the mainland.

By 7:48, the lead Japanese plane crossed the northern shoreline of Oahu, and the first bombs fell at the Kaneohe U.S. Naval Station.

It had been a sleepy Sunday morning, but the sailors quickly woke up. At 7:55, the full brunt of the Japanese air attack struck. Dive-bombers destroyed all thirty-three planes on the ground. The only survivor was the plane in the air on patrol at the time.

There would be no dogfights. By 8:05, the battleship *Okla-*

homa had capsized. A direct hit on the *Arizona* caused what was at the time a record-sized explosion, instantly killing more than a thousand sailors.

Also put out of commission by the dive-bombers were the *Nevada*, *California*, *West Virginia*, *Cassin*, and *Downes*. All but the *Oklahoma* and the *Arizona* were repaired and eventually saw action in the war.

In all, 2,700 US sailors died. Americans heard the news on the radio, with regular programming interrupted by CBS announcer John Daly, later the host of the TV game show *What's My Line*? Somewhere, Father Coughlin's radio show was interrupted by the shocking news from Hawaii.

In New York, the boys were listening to football, the New York Giants of the NFL playing the Brooklyn Dodgers at the Polo Grounds when the bulletin interrupted the second-half broadcast. Same thing in Chicago, where the Bears were playing the Chicago Cardinals, and in Washington, DC, where the Redskins were playing the Eagles.

And FDR had no choice but to immediately ask Congress to declare war on Japan. In solidarity, Germany and Italy declared war on the United States.

Across America, boys lined up to enlist.

Once the US entered World War II, everything changed on the domestic front. In Minnesota, William Dudley Pelley disbanded his Silver Legion but continued to publish anti–U.S. government propaganda in his magazine called *Roll Call*.

Celebrities like Charles Lindbergh, a Nazi sympathizer who considered a run against FDR in the 1940 presidential election, now kept their opinions private. The great majority of American Nazis went so far underground that they disappeared entirely. Some of them, of course, were drafted, but an effort was made for obvious reasons to send young German American men to fight in the Pacific, where their allegiance would not be questioned. Luckily for those who remained stateside, their whiteness allowed them to blend back into the crowd, unlike the tens of thousand of Japanese Americans who were plucked from their peaceful lives and interned during the war, many of them at the former Camp Siegfried.

Many German Americans changed their names and—when asked—claimed to be of Swedish descent. The Germania Club, the scene of gangsters versus Nazis fighting in Chicago, changed its name to the Lincoln Club.

But going subterranean did not signal the end of the war against US anti-Semites by Jewish gangsters. Jews still took a poke at smug Aryans whenever they had a chance. Take Mickey Cohen. During the spring of 1942, four months after Pearl Harbor, now twenty-eight years old, he was busted for making book and spent some time in a downtown L.A. holding cell awaiting a court appearance. At the same time, the Nazi leader Robert Noble and an "outspoken isolationist" named Ellis O. Jones were brought in by police for questioning. The pair together ran an organization called the Friends of Progress and had made the papers by holding "mock trials" of FDR for war crimes.

Cohen's court hearing that day was to discuss the ownership of a filed-off gun that had been found in his Santa Monica Boulevard bookie joint at the time of his arrest. Cohen claimed that he wasn't initially in the same cell with "those assholes," but after Cohen had a talk with the guards, Noble and Jones were moved into Cohen's cell.

Cohen knew who Noble was; a "real rabble-rousing anti-Jew Nazi bastard," Cohen called him. He'd heard about some of the crap Noble had said in the newspapers. The usual hate speech. He had no clue who Jones was, but he didn't like him much, either. He was just another "weasel bastard."

Now he could hear the two men talking.

"That fucking Douglas MacArthur should be in here instead of me," Noble exclaimed.

Cohen took exception. "That's a hell of a way to talk about the hero of our country," he said.

Noble looked at Cohen and smirked. "Oh, you must be one of those Jews, huh?" Noble said.

"What about it?" Cohen asked.

"You should know MacArthur ran out on his troops at Bataan," Noble said with a sneer.

That did it.

Cohen took a quick look around to make sure no one was watching and charged the Nazis. In a flash, Cohen grabbed both by the head and knocked their skulls together, a move later popularized by George Reeves on *The Adventures of Superman* TV show. Superman only had to knock the bad guys' heads once and they fell unconscious. But Cohen, who was tough but not Superman, had to knock their heads together a couple of times and only managed to make them groggy.

Noble turned his back to Cohen, his hands on his head. Cohen kicked him in the seat of his pants so hard that his face hit the wall, breaking his glasses.

Then Cohen went to work with his fists. He expected some fight-back, but his foes were too stunned to do anything, so he pummeled their faces and ribs. When working their bodies, Cohen imagined he was Jack Dempsey busting up the ribs of Jess Willard on the Fourth of July.

After a time, Noble and his pal tried to escape, which was impossible as they were in a locked room with bars on the door. So instead they bellowed bloody murder. Guards came running.

"Why'd you put us in here with him," they screamed. "The guy's an animal."

By the time the guards arrived, Cohen had returned to his seat and was calmly scanning a newspaper. He told the guards that the two men had gotten into a fight with each other.

"I stayed out of it. I don't know what happened. I didn't want to mix with them," Cohen said, the picture of innocence.

"You're a lying bastard," they screamed, but no one paid attention.

General Douglas MacArthur was also the subject of Noble and

Ellis's legal troubles. They had been charged with libel over a pamphlet that claimed MacArthur fled Bataan in a cowardly manner. An L.A. county grand jury voted to indict the pair. This would be just the start of their problems, which would escalate into an FBI investigation and an eventual indictment for wartime sedition.

With America now embroiled in WWII, the Office of Naval Intelligence was worried about enemy agents infiltrating the U.S. through its ports. Efforts by the government to gather information from dockworkers and fishermen went nowhere, so—just as Judge Perlman had done—the intelligence officers contacted Meyer Lansky, who in turn had a talk with his best friend Lucky Luciano. Word went out, and the dockworkers and fishermen were on board, helping keep sinister figures from entering the U.S. on their watch.

The gangsters versus Nazis war moved overseas as well. After chasing Rommel across North Africa, the Allies planned to invade Sicily and then Italy in what was called Operation Husky. Luciano supplied information regarding the coastlines that was invaluable as the U.S. embarked on history's largest sea-to-land invasion before D-Day.

CHAPTER TWENTY-NINE
Nazi Perverts and Thieves

The year 1938 turned out to be the high point for Fritz Kuhn. Before the year was out, the news coverage of the Bund had shifted. Previously, the critical tone had to do with the political philosophy of the Bund and the distaste many had for its message. But during 1938, the *morality* of the Bund leaders themselves was now questioned. These were not just men of evil politics, they also were men of evil personal habits as well, perverts and thieves who did things that gave a good, God-fearing American the willies.

The reveal began when Kuhn's chief of propaganda, thirty-four-year-old Severin Winterscheidt, was arrested—for the second time—for a sex crime involving a child.

Winterscheidt was a slender fellow with very little hair and the mild features of a hairdresser's apprentice. He tended to walk with one hand, usually the left, thrust deeply into his pants pocket. He'd lived most of his life in Bonn, in the Rhineland, and only came to America in 1930. During the summer of 1938, he lived on Himrod Street in Bushwick, Brooklyn, a German neighborhood featuring the large Rheingold and Schaefer breweries.

His second arrest came when a ticket seller at the Empire Theater, at the corner of Ralph Avenue and Broadway not far from Winterscheidt's home, reported to her manager that a girl and a man had just entered the movies and something was up.

The little girl, the ticket seller explained, moved with a precocious gait, had too much nervous energy, and she didn't call the man Dad, or Papa, or anything like that.

"What did she call him?" asked the manager.

"*Herr Tomate.*"

"I'll call the police."

When patrolman Walter G. McCarthy entered the theater with his flashlight out, Winterscheidt had his Nazi pecker out. He bolted and had to be chased down Ralph Avenue by the policeman. "Mr. Tomato" was arrested and charged with molesting a ten-year-old girl.

During his capture, he ranted, "We need a Hitler in this country. The people here have too much freedom! Heil Hitler!"

Winterscheidt was convicted in special sessions court of indecent exposure and sentenced to six months to three years in the New York County Penitentiary. The *New York Times*, struggling for euphemisms, said that Winterscheidt had been caught "annoying a girl." The paper also reported that witnesses against Winterscheidt, including the victim, received threatening phone calls from men with German accents before they were scheduled to testify.

Winterscheidt had made the news before, and never in a way that put Germans in a pleasant light. In November 1933, he was called before a New York grand jury to testify about the misuse of the US mail by disseminating anti-Semitic messages. Propaganda against a class or race of people, it was determined, constituted defamatory material.

In May 1935, Winterscheidt was the main speaker at a Friends of the New Germany meeting at the Yorkville Casino, and was quoted in the next day's papers as ranting about the "immorality in the Jewish talmud."

In March 1937, Winterscheidt was the editor of the Bund's weekly newspaper, the *Deutscher Weckruf und Beobachter*, and his name came up in an investigation into the Nazi movement in America as an "alien military body" that intimidated US citizens and raised money for Hitler.

In July of that year, when US Congressman Samuel Dickstein announced seventeen names of top "Nazi agitators," Winterscheidt was on the list. His first morals charge came in January 1938, when he was arrested in New York's Penn Station. A twelve-year-old girl told police that Winterscheidt had flashed her. He was held on a thousand dollars bail, convicted, and served thirty days.

Only three months after his release, he was arrested the second time outside the Brooklyn movie theater.

In January 1940, Winterscheidt was secretly paroled when he turned state's witness against other members of the Bund, eventually testifying in 1943 that Bund members had falsified applications for US citizenship. He became a regular at sedition trials throughout the war.

Winterscheidt was not the only Nazi perv. During the summer of 1939, evidence would emerge indicating that pedophilia and child molestation were pervasive among the ranks.

That summer, the House Un-American Activities Committee held a meeting in Washington, DC, about Camp Siegfried, the Nazi youth camp in Yaphank, Long Island.

As if teaching American youth to be Nazis wasn't creepy enough, the committee unearthed another unexpectedly disturbing aspect of the camps. On that day, the committee's witness was nineteen-year-old youth leader Helen Vooros. Described as dark-haired and pleasingly plump, she told the committee in detail about the teachings and beliefs at the camp, and that was all very troubling, but her primary beef with the camp wasn't political but moral.

"The leaders wouldn't leave me alone," she said. "They were making plans to attack me." Her voice faltered and became quiet until she was barely audible.

"They planned to what?"

She took a deep breath. "To *attack* me!" she said.

She didn't need to say "gang rape." Everyone understood what she meant.

For a moment, no one said anything, then Representative Joseph Starnes spoke up. Starnes was a Democrat from Alabama, a former schoolteacher and a World War I veteran. Haltingly, he began a question: "The immorality of the entire movement appalled you so—"

"It disgusted me," Miss Vooros replied. She went on to explain that the boys and girls sections of the camp were only thirty feet apart and that this caused a lot of trouble. Parents had complained, and boys and girls were frequently seen together.

She testified that the camp leader, Theodore Dinkelacker, had told the boys that trying to have sex with the girls (all underage) was a "noble endeavor."

Although he didn't say "have sex," he said *ficken*. That made the girls fair game. It was terrifying.

Dinkelacker himself partook in the noble endeavor and was once caught in bed with an underage girl from the Bronx. When a youth leader named Mrs. Klapprott—who was married to August, the camp director—was told about Dinkelacker's dalliance, she advised that no one should say anything about it.

In what was considered the boring part of her testimony, Miss Vooros described the brainwashing that went on. The kids were told that Hitler's National Socialist party was the only thing that could save America, that German Americans got the short end of the stick in the US, and that it was high time for that to change.

Studying Hitler's biography in detail was part of the teaching curriculum. She said that Camp Siegfried girls were bussed into the city, dressed to look as cute as a button and display as much cleavage as they could muster as they distributed anti-Semitic pamphlets. She had done this herself, assigned a street corner in South Brooklyn.

Miss Vooros said a friend, who didn't discuss the politics of the place in her sales pitch, had recruited her to the camp. The witness didn't learn the camp was pro-Nazi until she got there.

When the Bund abandoned Camp Siegfried, gone in the night, only hours after Pearl Harbor, it again became known as Camp

Upton. The US Army reclaimed the site and used it for an intern-ment camp for Japanese Americans. After World War II, the camp became the home of the Brookhaven National Laboratory, under the auspices of the United States Atomic Energy Commission.

In 1939, New York District Attorney Thomas Dewey was chomp-ing at the bit to prosecute Nazis. During that year, Bund leaders were charged with filing fraudulent tax returns, failing to file sales tax returns, failing to register as vendors, failing to keep records to compute sales tax, and failure to file both personal and business tax returns.

By March of 1939, not long after the Garden Party at Madison Square Garden, there were indications that Fritz Kuhn himself was coming apart at the seams. Feds were calling his bank and talking to his friends. He was a nervous wreck, drinking schnapps for breakfast and behaving peculiarly. One night, he followed in-fluential radio broadcaster Walter Winchell, a staunch anti-fascist and close friend of FBI Director J. Edgar Hoover, into New York's Stork Club, took a seat facing Winchell, and stared at him menacingly for about an hour before leaving, staying long enough for Winchell to mention him in his next day's column.

In 1939, Kuhn was arrested and charged with embezzlement. During mid-May, NYPD Commissioner of Investigations Wil-liam B. Herlands concluded an enquiry into the Bund and the way they handled money. He gave his forty-two-page report to Mayor LaGuardia, who in short order called for the arrest "within twenty-four hours" of Kuhn and several associates on charges of city tax frauds and "other violations."

In addition to Kuhn, the others on the arrest warrant were the Bund's national secretary, the treasurer and secretary of the Ger-man American Business League, the manufacturer of Bund uni-forms, a vice president of a company that imported swastika emblems, and the company that printed the Bund's propaganda.

Kuhn fled the city when he heard the cops were after him, but the Law caught up with him in Krunsville, Pennsylvania, speeding westward in a Mercedes-Benz. Kuhn was taken in handcuffs to the nearest justice of the peace, who happened to be in West Reading.

"I'm ready to face the charges, and I'm confident I'll be exonerated," Kuhn said—and his sorry ass was dragged back to New York, where in addition to the tax charges, he was charged with embezzling almost fifteen thousand dollars from the Bund he ran. The additional charge was brought by a New York County grand jury.

"The latest charge shows that Kuhn is no more than a common thief," Dewey said, adding that if Kuhn were convicted of all charges, he could face spending the rest of his life in prison.

The embezzlement charge stemmed from money raised at the Garden Party, money that was supposed to go to the defense fund for Bund members who'd been arrested and instead went into Kuhn's wallet.

Kuhn made bail easily enough, but trouble followed him like a shadow. He was in Webster, Massachusetts, over the weekend of July 15–16, 1939, accompanied by Count Anastase A. Vonsaitsky, leader of the fascistic White Russians in America. The count, it should be noted, was married to the heiress to a fifty-million-dollar fortune. The men had been drinking in a Webster bar and were entering the count's large luxury car when policeman Henry Plasse noticed their inebriated gait and decided neither was in any condition to drive.

The officer had a short conversation with the men and decided that Kuhn was the more sober of the two and that he should drive. The men got into the car, and as Kuhn pulled away, he stuck his head out the window and said, "Fuck you, *mutterficker*."

Officer Plasse leaped into action, literally, landing on the running board of the car. He reached in the driver's side window, grabbed a handful of Kuhn, and forced him to stop the car. The men were held at the police station until a court clerk could arrive and fix bail at fifty-nine dollars for the pair, which they scraped together from what they had in their pockets.

Kuhn and Vonsaitsky were given a date to come back for their trial. Sober by now, they didn't look like they intended to come back. As soon as they were gone, Webster Police Chief John G. Templeman couldn't hide his distaste for Kuhn.

"He was just another wise guy who thought this was a hick town and he could stage one of them beer hall putsch things and be the dictator in it. We don't let people go swearing at police in this town, drunk or sober."

Things got so bad for Kuhn that he couldn't even testify before a congressional subcommittee without worrying about someone taking a poke at him.

On August 12, 1938, the Dies Committee called to their witness stand Peter Gissible, who testified that he had been a former official in the German American Bund but had left the organization because of fundamental disagreements he'd had with Kuhn.

"I had been in charge of the Chicago branch of the Bund, but became increasingly disenchanted because of Kuhn's relentless anti-Semitism and his commitment to an evil youth movement in which he enjoyed dressing up children in uniforms similar to those of the Nazi army," Gissible testified.

Gissible said that there was a strong link between the Bund and Hitler himself and that several former Bund officials had returned to Germany, where they formed the Foreign Institute of Nazi Germany, which tried to boost the Nazi movement in other places, but mostly the United States.

Next up at the Capitol Hill hearings was Kuhn himself. His questioning did not go smoothly. Trouble started when Representative Starnes asked Kuhn if the purpose of the Bund was not to establish in the United States a government such as that now in power in Germany.

"That's an absolute lie—a flat lie," Kuhn said, his voice sounding as if he'd recently gargled with rocks.

With that, Starnes turned a scary shade of red, sprung to his feet, and shoved photographers and reporters aside as he headed for the witness. A vein at his temple visibly pounded.

"Don't call me a liar," the congressman spat.

Kuhn poured sweat but didn't flinch. He sat in his chair wet but impassive. Perhaps he could tell Starnes wasn't going to make it all the way. A policeman strode into Starnes's path and stopped him eight feet shy of the witness table.

Chairman Dies worked his gavel hard, and order was restored. Representative Noah Morgan Mason, a Republican from Illinois, took over the questioning. He asked Kuhn if it wasn't true that his Bund was composed of con men, that it was "a money-making racket based on the credulity of the American people."

"That is not true," Kuhn replied. "The goal of the Bund is three-fold. We seek to unite the German-American element, to fight communism wherever we find it, and to teach, to give the German element knowledge, a political background."

Mason said, "Hatred of the Jews, it seems to me, is one of the cardinal principles of your organization."

"All we want from the Jews is to be left alone," Kuhn said.

"Isn't it true that your members have pledged to defend by all means the good name of their mother country—Germany?"

"It is," Kuhn agreed.

"You recently destroyed a lot of Bund official paperwork, is that correct?"

"It is. The documents were shredded because of prospective investigations."

"What is the connection between the German-American Bund and the German government?"

"Nothing official. Familial, yes. I have a brother who is a Supreme Court Justice in Berlin under the Nazi regime."

"Getting back to the destroyed documents. What was it about them that you didn't want investigators to know?"

"I have to protect my members. I destroyed the membership lists."

"But why? Aren't all of your members American citizens?"

"That doesn't make any difference." Kuhn paused to light a cigarette, which he then held between his thumb and forefinger.

"So long as you belong to the Bund, you would lose your job, and you know it."

"Can this investigation have a list of the cities in which local Bunds exist?"

"Sure. We have locations in San Francisco, Los Angeles, San Diego, Santa Barbara, Santa Monica, San Bernardino, Portland, Spokane, and Carson City, Nevada."

As this questioning took place, on the other side of the Atlantic, Hitler was celebrating the twenty-fifth anniversary of his entry into the German Army as a World War volunteer.

Kuhn's embezzlement trial began on November 10, 1939, the day after the sixteenth anniversary of a sacred Nazi occasion, the Beer Hall Putsch of 1923. The defendant entered court with a ridiculously large smile—see how happy and not worried I am?

There was reason for optimism. General Sessions Judge James Garrett Wallace had already informed the prosecution that the nature of Kuhn's politics was not to be mentioned in front of the blue-ribbon jury, as it was bound to be prejudicial.

The judge got a big laugh from the gallery when he said, "Mr. Kuhn is not on trial for snatching Czechoslovakia, blitzkrieging Poland, or sinking the *Athenia*, but merely for pilfering money from the organization of which he is supreme dictator."

During voir dire, one fidgeting prospective juror said he could not abide that Hitler guy, to which Judge Wallace said, "Hitler's got nothing to do with it." The man from the jury pool said he wasn't sure of that and was excused. Eventually, twelve men were found, and security was doubled in court.

Handling the prosecution was Assistant District Attorney Herman McCarthy, while Kuhn was defended by Peter L. Sabbatino. In his opening statement, McCarthy said he would show that Kuhn stole the money from the Bund because of a "keenly sentimental" interest he had in a Mrs. Florence Camp. A second girlfriend, the seven-times-married Mrs. Virginia Cogswell, also surfaced during the trial. Kuhn, with a wife and two kids at home, was revealed to be a busy man.

Sabbatino countered that his client was the victim of persecution and was being tried for political reasons: "Since Mr. Kuhn was the absolute boss of the money under discussion here, no crime was committed. He could use that money as he saw fit."

On Tuesday, November 21, Kuhn took the witness stand in his own defense and, literally pounding his chest as he spoke in his thickly accented English, said that it was not he who stole the Bund money from the till, but rather officers from the D.A.'s office, who snatched the dough during a raid on Bund headquarters on East Eighty-fifth Street on May 2, 1939.

He had to sit on the witness stand and listen quietly as his love letters to Mrs. Camp were read aloud.

"I was very, very friendly with Mrs. Camp, but nothing more," Kuhn protested vehemently.

McCarthy glanced at the jury box and saw all twelve panelists waxing skeptical. An Associated Press reporter noted that Kuhn's "shy little wife" was not in the courtroom for her husband's ordeal.

Three days later, Mrs. Camp took the stand, her hair as platinum as Jean Harlow's, as ladylike as could be, and proclaimed the defendant a "philandering prevaricator" but probably not an embezzler.

Headlines screamed, "Der Romance Is Over."

On November 28, the assistant D.A. and the defense attorney gave their final arguments, Judge Wallace charged the jury, and deliberations commenced. On December 2, 1939, the jury found Kuhn guilty, and Judge Wallace sentenced him to two-and-a-half to five years in Sing Sing, eligible for parole after a minimum of twenty months served. Kuhn ended up serving forty-three months in prison. During that stretch, his US citizenship was revoked.

By this time, Germany and the United States were at war. Kuhn was rearrested on June 21, 1943, as an "enemy agent" and interned by the federal government. Now, instead of boldly goose-stepping American streets, Bund members had to worry about their homes being raided by feds, such as happened in Syracuse, where agents busted into two German Americans' homes, making arrests and seizing guns, ammunition, walkie-talkies, and cameras.

On September 15, 1945, the war over, Kuhn was deported to Germany. He sailed across the Atlantic aboard the SS *Winchester Victory* and worked as a free man for a small chemical factory in Munich before being arrested again under Germany's de-Nazification laws. He was again caged and released only shortly before his death on December 15, 1951.

One of his last acts was to write a letter to Walter Winchell: "Herr Winchell, I will lift to piss on your grafe."

But he didn't. Winchell outlived him by twenty years.

EPILOGUE

Hollywood usually kept their gangster movies and Nazi movies separate, and an unofficial survey revealed only one feature film, *All Through the Night*, made in 1942 by Warner Brothers, in which both groups were central to the plot.

The stars were Humphrey Bogart, William Demarest, Jackie Gleason, and Phil Silvers. It was a comedy. There was even a scene in which the gangsters infiltrated and busted up a meeting of American Nazis.

In a weird piece of slapstick, the hoods confused the assembled Nazis by shouting German-sounding double-talk. Studio bigwigs hated the scene and wanted it cut, but a test audience thought it was a riot, so it stayed in the picture.

At the end of World War II, Judge Nathan Perlman, the catalyst behind the gangsters versus Nazis war, became a consultant to Supreme Court Justice Robert H. Jackson, who'd been appointed by President Harry S Truman to prosecute Nazi war criminals.

Judge Perlman died at the age of sixty-four on June 29, 1952, of heart failure at Beth Israel Hospital in Manhattan. A small street outside Beth Israel was later renamed Nathan D. Perlman Place.

He was buried in Mount Hebron Cemetery in Flushing, Queens,

also the final resting place of Louis "Lepke" Buchalter and Emanuel "Mendy" Weiss from Murder, Inc.

Judge Perlman's gravestone reads:

> JURIST—LEGISLATOR—HUMANITARIAN
> HIS LIFE WAS FULL OF KIND WORDS
> AND GENTLE DEEDS

And as we now know, sometimes not-so-gentle deeds. The stone also features an incorrect birthdate—January 1, 1890—that chops three years off his age.

At the time of his death, he was best remembered as being instrumental in establishing a probationary system in federal courts for first offenders, thus relieving overcrowded jails.

Today, we remember him for so much more—for thinking outside of the box and teaching anti-Semites that Jews were tough and it could be dangerous to be a Nazi.

During World War II, Meyer Lansky, Bugsy Siegel, and Charles "Lucky" Luciano had a contract out on Hitler, but they couldn't get a hit man inside enough to do the job. American mobsters continued to show their patriotism, with Luciano himself helping the war effort by supplying geographic and social intelligence regarding Sicily and Italy, where US troops would eventually invade.

In the meantime, Jewish kids who grew up during that era would always have Jewish gangsters as their heroes, the tough guys who confronted evil head-on and kicked its ass—without a single fatality.

Meyer Lansky, the giver of giant gift baskets, lived to be old and was never convicted of anything more serious than illegal gambling. How did he stay out of trouble? Author Anthony Summers wrote that Lansky possessed compromising photos of J. Edgar Hoover and his close aide Clyde Tolson.

The closest Lansky came to prison came in the late 1960s, when he was investigated by the IRS for tax evasion. The probe must have had some substance because Lansky fled to Israel in 1970, was deported back to the United States in 1972, and was acquitted at a trial in 1974.

He spent his last years relaxing in Hallandale, Florida. Most of his money and property were in other people's names, but he had access to all of it when he was alive. The trouble was, his widow and three kids discovered his personal estate to be worth only fifty-three thousand dollars.

Lansky survived being a gangster but not a smoker, dead from lung cancer in 1983 at the age of eighty.

Louis "Lepke" Buchalter, on the lam during the Nazi-busting era, eventually found himself in the death house at Sing Sing. A fellow resident was Mendy Weiss, veteran of the Yorkville Casino riot. Both were scheduled to be executed on the same night. The executions were delayed four times, but finally, on March 4, 1941, no one called to save them.

One of the cruelest features of the Sing Sing death house was that when another prisoner was fried, the large draw of current for the electric chair caused the lights to dim and flicker in the cells. Even the toughest hoods winced at the sight of that flickering light.

As the final hours approached, the men, the former backbone of Murder, Inc., started their final countdown. Lepke was visited by his wife, Betty, and twenty-year-old son, Harold.

Another hood in the death house at that time was Louis Capone, of the Italian wing of Murder, Inc. All three veterans of Midnight Rose's back room would be executed together. That night, around eleven o'clock, they took the long walk.

Capone and Lepke were stoic, tight-lipped, and silent. Lepke glanced briefly at the gallery of thirty-four spectators when he entered, sat in the chair without assistance, and kept his eye on every movement as he was strapped in—right up until the moment they pulled the hood over his head.

Mendy, on the other hand was a mess. Chewing gum, accompanied by Rabbi Jacob Katz, he entered screaming, "I'm innocent. This was a frame up! I'm innocent and Governor Dewey knows it! The only reason I am going is because I am a Jew. I've been framed because I'm a Jew!" And then exhausted, he added, "Give my love to my family and everybody else. I am innocent."

Each hood got four jolts of juice, after which Dr. Charles Sweet opened their shirts, listened with a stethoscope, and said, "This man is dead." Capone, it was said, was the five hundredth person to be executed in Sing Sing's electric chair. Quite an honor.

Abraham "Kid Twist" Reles, Buggsy Goldstein, and Harry "Pittsburgh Phil" Strauss beat up Nazis together, performed hits together, and went to trial for murder together. The hit job in question was that of Irving "Puggy" Feinstein, who was running a gambling house in the wrong neighborhood.

The three men had a hard time killing Feinstein and created a messy crime scene that made veteran cops gag. The body was dumped in a vacant lot in the Flatlands section of Brooklyn.

It was Kid Twist who ratted them out. The trick was to keep Kid Twist alive long enough to testify, an impossible task as it turned out, as Twist fell, jumped or was pushed out of the sixth-floor window of Coney Island's Half Moon Hotel, leading to the line, "The canary who could sing but couldn't fly."

At the trial of Buggsy and Pittsburgh Phil, Blue Jaw Magoon turned state's evidence. Buggsy and Phil stayed together right to the end, executed at Sing Sing on June 12, 1941.

Blue Jaw Magoon's downfall was a femme fatale. Cops questioned his yakety-yak girlfriend, Evelyn Mittleman—a woman with a kiss-of-death reputation. The twenty-five-year-old Mittleman was reliably affectionate toward generous hoods. *Three* men had been murdered over her, it was said.

Soon after turning rat, Magoon disappeared, and no one knew where he was until 2003, when his skeleton was found partially buried in the desert sand outside Las Vegas.

Tic Toc Tannenbaum also vanished. Some say he lived under a new identity for a while in Georgia before being taken on a one-way boat ride on the Atlantic Ocean.

Jacob Drucker's gangster life didn't make it through the war years, either. He was arrested by feds in 1943, extradited to New York, and became a weenie at Thomas Dewey's racket-busting weenie roast.

Charles "Bug" Workman was arrested during the winter of 1940 in the Brighton Beach section of Brooklyn and charged with the murder of Dutch Schultz in New Jersey. Unlike his old Murder, Inc. pals Buggsy Goldstein and Pittsburgh Phil, the thirty-four-year-old Workman wasn't executed, but he was sentenced to a life of hard labor at Trenton State Prison.

Workman became a model prisoner and, after twenty-three years, was released on parole in 1964. He went straight, took a job in the garment district, and lived out the rest of his life without discussing his violent past. He died sometime in the mid-1970s. His proudest achievement, Bug said late in life, was keeping his son Chuck out of the mob. Chuck only whacked golf balls, touring as a PGA golf pro for ten years.

During the summer of 1939, "Midnight Rose" Gold was busted for racketeering and perjury. Cops said she ran a brothel upstairs from her candy store, kept a policy bank, gave out loans to suckers, and helped distribute the locations for a floating crap game.

The indictment for Mrs. Gold boasted seventeen counts, and the old lady was facing a prison sentence of eighty-five years and fines of eighty-five thousand dollars. Lucky for Mrs. Gold, she knew people.

Powerful legal aid rushed to her rescue, and she was quietly released. The official reason was that she was old and sick and the justice system had been unnecessarily harsh on her. In jail, her health grew worse, but once she was out, it improved dramatically.

Judd Teller, the journalist who supplied Murder, Inc. with the list of "Nazi scumbags," became an advisor to national Jewish groups and an assistant professor at Yeshiva University. He was the political secretary of the World Zionist Organization and a consultant to the Conference on Jewish Material Claims Against Germany. He died after a brief illness in 1972 at the age of fifty-nine. At the time, he lived on the East Side of Manhattan, in the Gramercy Park area.

Jake Guzik, the man Judge Perlman called in Chicago, the man who was called Greasy Thumb because he was always counting Al Capone's money, lived to age sixty-nine. In 1959, he dropped dead in a restaurant over his lamb chops. He was given a lavish funeral with a coffin that cost five grand.

Guzik was eulogized by Rabbi Noah Ganze of the Chicago Loop Synagogue as a generous man whose "vast contributions" to charities large and small over the years had greatly helped the community.

Herb Brin, the Chicago reporter who infiltrated the Bund, survived his undercover stint without ever being outed as Jewish. The biggest difficulty he had while spying on the anti-Semites was romantic, not political. There was a woman named Kathleen who attended the meetings, and he became expert at parrying and ducking her advances as she plied him with Rhine wine and seltzer. Maintaining his virtue proved to be more of a challenge than the task at hand.

Herb and his longtime girlfriend, Selma, were married on December 25, 1940, in the YMCA hall. "A complete Jewish move," laughed Herb's son Dan in a recent interview. "Christmas Day in a Christian organization hall. They knew it would be available for cheap!"

Brin was one of millions of American boys who enlisted in the US Army after Pearl Harbor. His dreams of fighting Nazis with a gun in his hand died when he badly injured his lower extremities in an accident during basic training.

Rather than discharging him, the army—aware of his journalistic skills—gave him a job writing for *Yank* magazine. He took the job but wasn't happy, later telling his son that interviewing celebrities on USO trips seemed weak when he knew his fellow Jews were being murdered by Hitler.

Brin returned to reporting after the war and became famous when he exposed Chicago Mayor Ed Kelly's corruption in what became known as the Consumer Coal Company scandal. When Kelly promptly wrote out his letter of resignation, he gave it to Brin.

In 1947, Brin moved to Los Angeles and took a reporting job for the *Glendale News-Press*, but he quit after the paper's exposé of L.A.'s Communist Party turned out to be no more than a gathering of local Democrats.

He moved to the *Los Angeles Times*, where he was the only reporter at Union Station to cover Charlie Chaplain's departure from L.A.

During the Cold War, he mortgaged his home to start up his own periodical, the *Heritage Jewish News*, and when America had its eyes on the so-called Red Menace, itself a movement that smacked of anti-Semitism, Brin continued to focus on the reactionary right, covering American Nazi leaders such as Wesley "Shifty Legs" Swift and George Lincoln Rockwell. He wrote scathing reviews of Willis Carto, whose Liberty Lobby proclaimed the Holocaust to be a myth. His scope became global, and he wrote about the Soviet Union's suppression of Jewish culture.

In 1968, he was in the Ambassador Hotel when Robert Kennedy was assassinated.

Brin continued his anti-Nazi work for his entire life. When he was close to eighty years old he drove to an Aryan nation camp, a place where White supremacy was preached and the Holocaust denied. He went into the camp's front office and talked to a lady there. He identified himself and asked nicely if he could have a tour of the place. She was cautious but said all right. When the tour was complete, they were back in the office and Brin noticed the "Aryan Nation" coffee cup that someone had left on a small table.

"Hey, that's a great mug. I'd love to have one. How much do they cost?"

"It will be complimentary, but I have to find one. Give me a moment?"

"Of course."

The lady left the room, and Brin worked quickly, especially for a man his age. He opened drawers, grabbed documents, and stuffed as much as he could in his pockets. The woman returned with the mug, he thanked her, and he left.

Brin made a series of exposés out of those stolen documents, and today the papers live in the Western States Jewish History Archives at UCLA.

He lived to be eighty-eight and died in 2003.

Boxing champ Barney Ross became a Marine after Pearl Harbor and was sent to the Pacific Theater, where he fought in the battle of Guadalcanal. He and two other Marines were on patrol one night when they were attacked by a squadron of Japanese with machine guns. His three buddies were seriously wounded.

Ross managed to pull them into a foxhole and single-handedly returned fire to keep the Japanese from advancing. When he had fired all four hundred bullets he had, he threw twenty-two hand grenades at the machine-gun positions and managed to keep the enemy at bay until dawn.

Ross later recalled that he forgot he'd renounced his religion that night and prayed all night long in that foxhole, "most of it in Hebrew." By that time, two of the Marines in his foxhole were dead.

Still at his fighting weight, 138 pounds, he picked up the 230-pound survivor and carried him to safety. He was shot twice during that process, once in the leg and once in the foot, and when help arrived, they found thirty pieces of shrapnel embedded in Ross's helmet.

Sadly for Ross, along with a Silver Star Medal for heroism, he also picked up a nasty morphine addiction during his recovery. He kicked the habit (a subject later turned into the 1957 United Artists movie *Monkey on My Back*, starring Cameron Mitchell as Ross) and continued living an exemplary life.

He died of throat cancer in 1967 in his hometown of Chicago at age fifty-seven.

Jacob "Sparky" Rubenstein missed the first two years of World War II, classified 1-H for being too old (thirty as of Pearl Harbor) and 3-A for financial hardship at home. But by 1943, it was all hands on deck, and he was drafted into the Army Air Force that May.

He never made it overseas. After five months of training in Farmingdale, Long Island, he spent the remainder of his military service down South, where he once got in trouble for breaking the teeth of a sergeant who called him a "Jew bastard."

He cried when FDR died, cheered on V-E and V-J Days, and was sent home to Chicago in 1946, where he spent a couple of years in business selling stuff with his brothers.

He was fired by his brothers—allegedly for selling items from other companies—and in 1947, he left Chicago forever and went to Dallas to help his sister Eva manage a couple of nightclubs.

Sparky enjoyed brawling just as much in 1950 as he had in 1938. He could fight with or without a cause. During one fight in 1950, his opponent bit his right forefinger off at the first knuckle—which was why when it came time for him to commit his most notorious act, he had to pull the trigger on his .38 snub with his middle finger.

By 1953, the man formerly known as Sparky was in the Dallas nightclub business himself, and in 1963, he operated two clubs, the most famous of which was a strip joint on Main Street called the Carousel Club. He'd changed his name to the less ethnic Jack Ruby and as part of his service as a strip-club operator, he supplied "girls" to parties thrown by the rich and powerful men of Dallas.

He became globally famous on Sunday morning November 24, 1963, when, on live TV, he shot and killed alleged presidential assassin Lee Harvey Oswald in the basement of the Dallas Police Station. He'd gained access to the heavily guarded area because of two rules of behavior he'd learned years before. He was friendly with the cops, and he knew the guy guarding the back door.

He told police he shot Oswald to prove that Jews were tough, a line that came right out of the Judge Nathan Perlman playbook. He was tried and convicted of murder despite an insanity defense conjured up by his flamboyant attorney, Melvin Belli.

Barney Ross, Sparky's friend to the end, paid his legal bills. While they were investigating the assassination, US Congressman (later president) Gerald Ford and US Supreme Court Chief Justice Earl Warren traveled on behalf of the Warren Commission to Dallas and interviewed him in jail.

Ruby told Ford and Warren that he was a true patriot at heart. He loved America. And to demonstrate that, he told his distinguished interrogators about Chicago in the old days when he and his pals would bust up Bund meetings. "I cracked a few Nazi heads," Ruby boasted.

He also told Ford and Warren that he believed the assassination had been carried out by the right-wing John Birch Society, a plot hatched by "Johnson and the others." That meant President Johnson, who became president the instant JFK's head exploded. Sparky's quote was not heavily publicized because LBJ was the leader of the free world at the time.

The last interview Ruby gave was with newspaper columnist and TV game-show panelist Dorothy Kilgallen—Barney Ross knew both Ruby and Kilgallen—who said she was going to "blow the lid off the assassination." However, she died suddenly before she had a chance to publish what he'd said.

Sparky himself died in prison not long after his conviction, killed by a historically aggressive cancer.

Chicago fight club operator Davey Miller remained a referee until December of 1949 at age sixty-one. His last fight featured a blubbery and balding Joe Louis taking out a "crude" opponent as a step toward a comeback that never happened. After the fight, Miller had nothing but nice things to say about the ex-champ and announced his own retirement, telling the boys from the press that thirty-five years in the ring was enough.

Davey wasn't a gangster, but gangsters usually surrounded him, and that was what eventually did him in. He went to a Chicago movie theater with his brother Max. Coming out of the theater, the brothers faced immediate incoming, just like Dillinger, from a gunman who was supposed to whack Max but shot and killed Davey instead. Max ended up dying of TB.

In 1939, not long after the campaign against the Nazis, Longie Zwillman married divorcee Mary Steinbach, who had a son. Important men—politicians, millionaires—came to the wedding, while outside, feds wrote down license plate numbers.

After the war, Zwillman partnered up with Willie Moretti and ran the Marine Room, a plush gambling parlor inside the Palisades Hotel. In 1956, the feds came after Zwillman for tax evasion, but Zwillman, an expert at bribing jurors, beat the rap.

Zwillman and Willie Moretti shared Newark's gambling rackets. Both came to bad ends years later. Moretti was shot to death on October 4, 1951, at Joe's Elbow Room on Palisades Avenue in Cliffsdale Park, New Jersey.

On the morning of February 26, 1959, Zwillman was found hanging from the rafters of his twenty-room mansion in West Orange, New Jersey. He was wearing a bathrobe, pajamas, slippers, and socks. He had a half-full bottle of tranquilizers in his pocket, and a half-drunk bottle of booze was nearby. His funeral was a great event in Newark, with a full synagogue and a crowd outside clogging traffic. He was interred in a concrete vault at B'nai Abraham Memorial Park in Union, New Jersey.

Zwillman's widow remarried in 1962 to Harry Wismer, owner of the New York Titans (now the Jets) of the then American Football League.

Puddy Hinkes went to jail soon after his days of busting up Bund meetings. He was sent to a minimum-security facility in Leesburg, New Jersey, where he had several guards in his hip pocket. He had food, drink, and women delivered to him, and he wined and dined in a "private room" above the barracks where the other prisoners were kept.

When he got out, he ran Longie Zwillman's policy bank and was in charge of bribing the politicians who ran Newark. As a cover and for added income, Puddy and his brothers operated the Hinkes Brothers Trucking Company.

Hinkes and Zwillman had dinner together at a restaurant in Westwood on the night before Longie died. After Zwillman's death, Puddy's days as a gangster were through. He lived to age seventy-four, dying in 1985.

In 1992, the Synagogue of the Suburban Torah Center in Livingston, New Jersey, held a dinner to honor Hinkes for the manner in which he "wrecked havoc" on those who would "do harm to Jews."

Boxer Nat Arno, leader of the Newark Minutemen, joined the army ten months before Pearl Harbor and eventually fought with the Twenty-ninth Infantry Division. He was a celebrity and even fought some exhibition bouts during his time in the service. But the great majority of his fighting was done with his gun. He crossed Europe the hard way, from D-Day to V-E Day, Normandy to Berlin. He was wounded five times but never out of action for long. Nobody fought more Nazis than Arno. Twice, he claimed, he recognized German POWs, and they recognized him, all veterans of the Newark war.

Arno retired as a pro boxer after the war and taught boxing for a while. Then he reverted to his gangster ways, shook guys down, and in 1947 was popped for extortion. Lucky for Arno, Zwillman was still his friend, and the trial was fixed in Arno's favor.

But his time in Newark was through. He spent his remaining years operating a liquor store in California and died in 1973 at age sixty-three. In 2002, he was inducted into the New Jersey Boxing Hall of Fame.

Hymie "the Weasel" Kugel, one of the best fighters among the Newark Minutemen, was inducted into that same hall of fame in 1986 as a referee. His final arbitration came on August 3, 1938, during the Newark war: Fritzie Zivic versus Joe Lemieux at the Meadowbrook Bowl in Newark. Kugel was born and lived and died in 1945 at the age of fifty-six—all of it in Newark. Officially, he refereed eighty-four bouts, all of them held in New Jersey.

Minuteman Abie Bain fought in World War II and afterward headed west to Hollywood, where he worked as an adviser on boxing movies, including the great *Requiem for a Heavyweight* (1962), in which actor Anthony Quinn patterned the voice and movements of his character Mountain Rivera on those of Bain, who had a small role in the movie as well.

"I talk this way because I been hit a million times," Bain explained in his urgent whisper.

Bain's daughter Babette Bain became a show-biz kid, her career highlighted by her roles as Miriam in the 1956 version of *The Ten Commandments* and as a teenager in *Bye Bye Birdie* (1963). Her dad was inducted into the New Jersey Boxing Hall of Fame in 1976. In 1984, he retired to Florida and died there in 1993 at the age of eighty-six.

*　*　*

Harry "the Dropper" Levine, the largest of Arno's crew, was drafted not long after Pearl Harbor and served as a member of the military police. After the war, he returned to Newark and became a Newark cop. According to his niece, he rarely spoke about his days as a Nazi buster.

Today, Camp Nordland is known as Hillside Park, its Nazi past all but unknown to the New Jerseyites who picnic there.

The Radio Priest, Father Charles E. Coughlin, was another pro-Nazi whose freedom of speech turned to sedition as soon as the Japanese bombed Hawaii. What was once called isolationism was now sympathizing with the enemy.

Coincidentally, in some cities, it was Coughlin's program that was interrupted on Sunday afternoon, December 7, 1941, for the bulletin that America was at war. After Pearl Harbor, FDR wasted no time shutting down Coughlin's radio program and forbade the distribution of his periodical, *Social Justice*.

Coughlin continued to preach hate until Bishop Edward Aloysius Mooney, later Cardinal Mooney, told Coughlin that only if he discontinued his politics would he remain pastor of the Church of the Little Flower. Coughlin took the deal and said mass in Royal Oak until 1966.

After a brief illness, Father Coughlin passed away in 1979 at the age of eighty-eight. He's buried in Holy Sepulchre Cemetery in Southfield, Michigan.

With America at war, William Dudley Pelley was convicted of sedition and thrown in the slammer. Released in 1950, Pelley returned to the world of publishing, with his new fixation being UFO stories.

He never stopped talking to the dead, however, and claimed that during séances he frequently had conversations with the prophet Nostradamus and through him had met George Washington and Mark Twain, great Americans who enthusiastically told him to keep up the "good" work, which he did right up until his death in 1965.

In 1939, "Davey the Jew" Berman married a professional dancer named Gladys Evans. After Pearl Harbor, Berman tried to enlist in the US military but was rejected because he was a convicted felon.

Undeterred, he crossed the border into Canada, enlisted in the Canadian army, and saw action in Europe with the Eighteenth Armoured Car Regiment, also known as the Twelfth Manitoba Dragoons.

After the war, he and Gladys had their only child, a daughter named Susan. Despite his active gangster life, he managed to keep his business separate from his home life. His wife and daughter knew he was a businessman but were unclear on the details.

He returned to his role as Minnesota's gambling czar until his operation was dismantled by the state's star gangbuster, future Vice President Hubert Humphrey. Berman then moved to Las Vegas, where he operated a series of casinos with Moe Sedway of the Genovese family, including the El Cortez hotel and the Flamingo.

Siegel, Sedway, Lansky, and "Ice Pick Willie" Alderman all owned pieces of the Vegas project with Berman. But the pie had been cut into too many pieces, and consolidation was achieved in the usual manner.

After Siegel was murdered, Sedway and Berman walked into the Flamingo and announced that they were now in control of the hotel and casino's operations. Berman later became involved with the Riviera Hotel as well.

Berman died on Father's Day 1957 during a colon operation. He's interred in a mausoleum along the Corridor of Eternal Life at the Home of Peace Memorial Park in East Los Angeles.

After Berman's sudden death, his daughter Susan came to live with her uncle, Chickie Berman, also a Nazi buster, in Lewiston,

Idaho—a bit of a culture shock after living in L.A. Her mother was ill and unable to care for her. She attended Lewiston Junior High School and was remembered as a smart girl who enjoyed writing. When Susan's mom died not long after Susan's dad, classmates remember buying flowers for her.

Susan was sent away to boarding school. In 1963, Uncle Chickie was sentenced to six years in Terminal Island federal prison and ordered to pay a thirty-five-thousand-dollar fine for a five-million-dollar stock swindle. Susan ended up earning a bachelor's degree at UCLA and then a master's at UC Berkeley. In the 1970s and 1980s, she worked as a print and electronic journalist and wrote two books, *Easy Street: The True Story of a Mob Family* (adapted into a movie) and *Lady Las Vegas*. One chapter of *Easy Street* involved her dad telling her what to do in case she was kidnapped. Another told of the year that Liberace played at her birthday party.

A sad and bizarre footnote: Susan Berman was murdered on Christmas Eve 2000 in her Benedict Canyon two-bedroom house at the age of fifty-five. After neighbors found her door open and one of her dogs loose, they investigated and found her dead with a single bullet wound to the head.

At first, of course, the suspicion was that Susan had been killed because she'd written about mobsters. Friends said that couldn't be true because everyone she wrote about was already dead. Still, she had been working at the time of her murder on a TV project about Vegas wiseguys.

As it turned out, the mob had nothing to do with it. Her murder was allegedly committed by alleged multiple murderer and millionaire Robert Durst. In theory, he killed her because she knew too much about the suspicious death of one of Durst's ex-wives. She'd known Durst since her days at UCLA, thought of him as the brother she never had, and he gave her away at her wedding, but he reportedly was a psycho and she allegedly knew too much.

The diminutive Moe Dalitz, the Jewish boss of Cleveland, enlisted in the Army after Pearl Harbor, rose to the rank of lieutenant, and was discharged after V-J Day. After the war, Dalitz invested in Nevada real estate as a charter member of the Vegas Club. He was one of the visionaries who saw a gambling parlor as big as a city, a humongous cash machine, cheaper and more lucrative than building your own mint, and legal!

He proved that he really was afraid of nothing in 1964 when he had a beef with the world heavyweight boxing champion, Sonny Liston, a bear of a man with a fearsome punch. It happened in the Beverly Rodeo Hotel in Hollywood. The men were not exactly nose to nose, as Moe's nose only came up to Liston's belly button, but Dalitz nonetheless reminded Liston that he might be able to fight, but that did not mean he was bulletproof.

"Touch me and you're dead in under twenty-four hours," Dalitz said, and the boxer, who had a reputation as a bad man, backed down.

By that time, Dalitz was among the four hundred richest men in America (according to *Forbes* magazine). He beat the odds and lived to be old, with failing eyes, kidneys, and heart. He died in 1989 at the age of eighty-nine.

In 1966, newspaper columnist Jack Anderson ran into Hyman "Pittsburgh Hymie" Martin, one of the fighters in the Great Lakes Bund busts. He was still doing his thing and apparently not missing any meals.

"These days they don't call him Pittsburgh Hymie anymore. They call him Fat Hymie," Anderson wrote.

Despite the obesity, Martin lived to be eighty-four and died in 1987.

Martin's partner in crime, Louis Rothkopf, was another Vegas investor. He liked to inspect the troops, if you will, at his gambling and show palaces, and was referred to as Uncle Louie by the showgirls.

He also owned a piece of a string of horse-racing tracks with Moe Dalitz, across the Midwest—River Downs and Thistledown Park were the first two.

He and his wife lived on a thirty-seven-acre estate, in a mansion that had once housed a country club. Somehow things went bad for him and his wife though, something money couldn't fix. During the mid-1950s, the missus shot herself, and Lou took the Big Nap in his garage, locked inside his running car.

Of all of our Nazi fighters, Shondor Birns's demise was the most violent. He even managed to die more violently than his own mother, who'd checked out after running through the street as a human fireball following a still explosion.

It was spring 1975, thirty-seven years since he'd punched his last Nazi. Shondor was sixty-nine years old and drinking in a Cleveland dive strip joint called Christy's Tavern at West Twenty-fifth Street and Detroit Avenue. Sometime after midnight, he'd had his fill of whiskey and tits, so he weaved his way out the door and got into his Lincoln Continental parked outside. As he turned the ignition key, the car exploded so violently that the entire block shook. Pimps hit the deck. A man in a nearby alley received a nasty bite wound to his junk.

Birns was blown to bits, although most of him remained in two large chunks, upper and lower, with the upper splattering on and through a nearby chain-link fence.

Mickey Cohen was not much for naming names, but he later admitted that he'd gone to war against the Nazis years before the United States did because he'd received a call from "some judge."

After that private war, he survived every assassination attempt from underworld competitors but couldn't outwit the feds. He was twice convicted of tax evasion, went away for four years the first time and ten the second.

While in prison, someone smashed him on the head with a lead pipe so hard that he was partially paralyzed. He was released in 1972 and died four years later, at age sixty-three.

* * *

During the summer of 1940, Bugsy Siegel was busted for the murder of mob rat Ralph Greenberg. He was moved from his luxurious home to the L.A. County Jail, where the accommodations were surprising. He was allowed to have his meals delivered from his favorite restaurants. He had two telephones with which to conduct business and received unlimited visitors twenty-four hours a day so the starlets of Hollywood didn't have to go unserviced. In case you were wondering about the price of a "Get Out of Jail" card in those days, Siegel donated fifty thousand dollars to John Dockweiler's successful campaign for county district attorney, and soon after the election, the charges against Siegel were dropped and he was allowed to go home.

Siegel became the man who opened up Las Vegas for the underworld and constructed the Flamingo Hotel. At 10:45 P.M. on June 20, 1947, Siegel was shot and killed while sitting on a couch in the Beverly Hills home of his girlfriend, Virginia Hill. His friend Allen Smiley was also there, and Virginia's brother was upstairs working out with his girlfriend.

The building was a pink Moorish mansion on North Linden Drive. Bugsy was reading a newspaper when he was hit, shot six times in the head and torso from a .30 caliber military carbine.

The killer had a clear target as Siegel's head was silhouetted in the window, drapes open, by a nearby lamp. The killer had rested the gun on the latticework of a rose-covered pagoda and shot through the living room window.

The bullets did terrible things to Siegel's handsome face. Police found one of his eyeballs on the floor in the next room. The other eye and Siegel's nose were also smashed. His cervical vertebrae were shattered to powder.

Robert Noble, the loudmouth L.A. Nazi who got his head bonked by Mickey Cohen, tried to continue his pro-fascist program after Pearl Harbor without considering the legal ramifications. On January 4, 1944, a federal grand jury returned an indictment for Noble and twenty-nine others—twenty-seven men and two women. The charges were that Noble had violated the Federal Espionage Act of 1917 by participating in a large plot to "incite mutiny in the armed forces, unseat the government, and set up a Nazi regime." The evidence consisted of pamphlets, books, and circulars that Noble had continued to publish even after Germany had declared war on the United States.

According to the federal indictment, the message Noble was spreading was that "democracy is decadent; a Nazi or fascist form of government should be established and a Nazi revolution was inevitable in the U.S."

The charges stuck, Noble went away, and he disappeared from public view.

Noble's compatriot Ellis O. Jones not only survived his attack at the hands of Mickey Cohen in a Los Angeles holding tank, but he also had a very successful life in the legitimate world and lived to be ninety-three years old. Jones was one of the founding editors of *Life* magazine and also edited the *Ladies Home Journal*. His participation in anti-war activities as head of the Copperheads was just a footnote in his obituary. By the time he died, in 1967, being "anti-war" had a very different connotation. Nowhere was there mention of the fact that Jones wasn't so much a dove as a guy who didn't think Hitler was so bad, so why go to war against him? He'd been anti-war before America's entry into the First World War as well, and in 1915 had accompanied fellow fascist Henry Ford on a "peace expedition" to Germany.

Isadore Greenbaum, the plumber who tried to single-handedly break up the Nazi rally at Madison Square Garden, enlisted in the US Army and fought the Nazis again in Europe, this time with a gun.

Greenbaum remained happily married to his beautiful Gertrude. They had three kids—Jerry, Barbara, and Hedy—and moved to Southern California. He lived to be eighty-four, dying in 1997. He's buried in Corona del Mar, Orange County, California.

(Voice over)

Eighty years have passed since America first
learned just how many of our neighbors are anti-
Semitic, racist, White supremacists. Eighty years
have passed; the lessons of the Holocaust and World
War II should still be vivid, yet we still hear echoes
from the horrible past—bullets inside a synagogue, a
swastika flag waved on American soil. Where is our
Captain America now? Where is our Meyer Lansky, our
Sparky Rubenstein, our Barney Ross, Mickey Cohen,
Mendy Weiss, and Longie Zwillman? Where's Herb Brin
to beat that guy on the bus's ass from one end of the
park to the other? When does our hero charge in and
sock the Nazi, with his philosophy of hate, right on
the jaw?

Fade out.

SOURCES

BOOKS

Berman, Hyman, and Linda Mack Schloff. *Jews in Minnesota*. The People of Minnesota. St. Paul, MN: Minnesota Historical Society Press, 2002.

Buntin, John. *L.A. Noir*. New York: Broadway Books, 2009.

Cohen, Mickey, and John Peer Nugent. *In My Own Words*. Englewood Cliffs, NJ: Prentice-Hall, Inc., 1975.

Cohen, Rich. *Tough Jews: Fathers, Sons, and Gangster Dreams*. New York: Vintage Books, 1999.

Donahue, Greg. *The Minuteman*. Grand Haven, MI: Brilliance Publishing, 2019.

Fleming, E. J. *The Fixers*. Jefferson, NC: McFarland & Company, Inc., 2005.

Fried, Albert. *The Rise and Fall of the Jewish Gangster in America*. New York: Columbia University Press, 1994.

Gordon, Albert I. *Jews in Transition*. Minneapolis, MN: University of Minnesota Press, 1949.

Grover, Warren. *Nazis in Newark*. Abington, UK: Taylor and Francis, 2017.

Hart, Bradley W. *Hitler's American Friends: The Third Reich's Supporters in the United States*. New York: St. Martin's Press, 2018.

Hoke, Travis. *Shirts! A Survey of the New 'Shirt' Organizations in the United States Seeking a Fascist Dictatorship*. New York: American Civil Liberties Union, 1934.

Mann, William J. *Tinseltown*. New York: Harper, 2014.

Platt, Ivan. *The League for Human Rights: Cleveland Jewry's Fight Against Naziism*. Cleveland, Ohio: Cleveland State

University Press, 1977. (Cleveland State University master's thesis.)

Rockaway, Robert. *But He Was Good to His Mother: The Lives and Crimes of Jewish Gangsters*. Lynbrook, NY: Gefen Publishing House, 2000.

Sevareid, Eric. *Not So Wild a Dream*. New York: Atheneum, 1976.

Strong, Donald S. *Organized Anti-Semitism in America: The Rise of Group Prejudice During the Decade 1930–40*. Washington, DC: American Council on Public Affairs, 1941.

The Warren Report: Report of the President's Commission on the Assassination of President John F. Kennedy. New York: St. Martin's Griffin, 1992.

Webb, Jack. *The Badge*. New York: Thunder's Mouth Press, 2005.

Whitman, James Q., *Hitler's American Model*. Princeton, NJ: Princeton University Press, 2018.

NEWSPAPERS AND PERIODICALS

American Jewish World

American Jewish Yearbook

The Atlantic

Baltimore Sun

News-Palladium (Benton Harbor, MI)

Bergen Evening Record (Hackensack, NJ)

Berkshire Evening Eagle (Pittsfield, MA)

Brooklyn Daily Eagle

Central New Jersey Home News (New Brunswick, NJ)

Chicago Tribune

Coshocton (OH) *Democrat*

Des Moines (IA) *Tribune*

Detroit (MI) *Jewish Chronicle*

Emporia (KS) *Gazette*

Fight Game (New York, NY)

Fortune

Irvington (NY) *Gazette*

Jewish Light (St. Louis, MO)

Journal of Criminal Law, Criminology, and Police Science

Meriden (CT) *Journal*

Meriden (CT) *Record*

Los Angeles Times

StarTribune (Minneapolis, MN)

Minnesota History Journal
(New Ulm, MN)
Daily News (New York, NY)
New York Post
New York Times
Oakland (CA) *Tribune*
Rochester (NY) *Democrat and
Chronicle*
Rocky Mount (NC) *Telegram*
St. Cloud (MN) *Times*
Modern View (St. Louis, MO)

Santa Cruz (CA) *Evening
News*
Shamokin (PA) *News-Dispatch*
Smithsonian Magazine
Spokesman-Review (Spokane,
WA)
Tampa Bay (FL) *Times*
Time
Washington Post
Wisconsin Jewish Chronicle
(Milwaukee, WI)

WEBSITES

ajwnews.com/hitlers-
american-friends
(American Jewish World
News)
bookpatrol.net
boxrec.com
chicagojewishhistory.org
chicagoreader.com
jewishvirtuallibrary.org
jta.org (Jewish Telegraphic
Agency)
MNopedia.org (Minnesota
history website)
newarkmemories.com
njjewishnews.timesofisrael.
com (New Jersey Jewish
News)

libbyhellmann.com/nazis-
america-meet-german-
american-bund (Libby
Fischer Hellmann website)
mosaicmagazine.com
npr.org
petalumahistorian.com
siouxlandproud.com
thehistoryreader.com
timesofisrael.com
tjpnews.com (Texas Jewish
Post)

ACKNOWLEDGMENTS

The author would like to thank the following people and organizations, without whose help the writing of this book would have been impossible: Rebecca Baker, program coordinator, University of Washington Libraries, Special Collections; Mitchell Bard, executive director of the American-Israeli Cooperative Enterprise; David Bogart, senior vice president of Talent Relations and associate publisher, Marvel Entertainment, LLC; Keith Brenner; David and Dan Brin, sons of Herb Brin; Nicolette Bromberg; Lia Brown; super-editor Gary Goldstein; my agent extraordinaire Doug Grad of the Doug Grad Literary Agency, Inc.; Lisa Grasso-Benson; Christine Green; Glenn Greenberg; Heidi Heller, Minnesota Historical Society; Gene Hyde, head of Special Collections, Ramsey Library, University of North Carolina Asheville; *Jewish Telegraphic Agency*; Melissa Lindberg, reference librarian, Prints and Photographs Division, Library of Congress; Minnesota Historical Society Collections; Mount Hebron Cemetery; Jenna Molster, National Public Radio; National Museum of Organized Crime & Law Enforcement (the Mob Museum), Las Vegas, Nevada; Vince Palamara, JFK assassination researcher and author; Danielle Quenelle, office administrator, Historic Seattle; Sarah Quick, reference archivist, Center for Brooklyn History, Brooklyn Public Library; Geoff Quinn, education director, Holocaust Awareness Museum and Education Center; Robert Rockaway, professor emeritus at Tel Aviv University; San Francisco Museum; Deb Sperling; Yaphank Historical Society.

ABOUT THE AUTHOR

MICHAEL BENSON was born in Rochester, NY, and raised in Chili, NY. Today, he is one of the world's most popular true-crime writers. On TV, Benson was recently seen on ABC's *20/20* and is a regular commentator on the Investigation Discovery (I.D.), Oxygen, and HLN channels. He has appeared on *Murder in the Family with Geraldo Rivera*, *Inside Evil with Chris Cuomo*, *People Magazine Investigates*, *Evil Twins*, and *Evil Kin*.

During his four decades as a professional writer, Benson has worked closely with a former gangster for biographies of Mafia dons Carmine Persico and Albert Anastasia, a retired Army Intelligence agent during the tense days after 9/11 for a book about the CIA, and a retired FBI agent for a book about National Security. He has co-written two books with a former New York Police Department "Cop of the Year," explored the Grassy Knoll in Dallas with a former KGB agent while researching his highly-acclaimed *Who's Who in the JFK Assassination*, collaborated efficiently with an astronaut, and covered the Stephen Hayes triple-murder trial in New Haven, CT, for the *New York Post*.

Benson has a B.A. with honors in Communication Arts from Hofstra University. He is the winner of an Academy of American Poets award, and was in 2016 named a Wheatland-Chili High School Graduate of Excellence.

TURN THE PAGE FOR AN EXCITING PREVIEW!
**The incredible true story of the most powerful brothers in
Hollywood history—a wildly entertaining saga studded with
glamorous stars, scandals, mobsters, murders, and one
legendary blond bombshell . . .**

They were the Godfathers of the Movies. Groundbreaking
pioneers of the Hollywood Dream Factory, Joseph and Nicholas
Schenck may not have been household names like the Warner
brothers or Louis B. Mayer, but they were infinitely more
powerful, influential—and ruthless. A pair of Russian
immigrants with giant ambitions, the Schencks turned their
small nickelodeon business in New York's Bowery into a
partnership with Loew's movie theaters and a controlling
interest in three major studios: MGM, 20th Century-Fox, and
United Artists. They painted the silver screen silver, laid the
foundations for the all-powerful studio system, and ruled a
global movie empire from their Gatsby-sized mansions on the
East and West coasts. The Schencks had become moguls.

Their story is the stuff of legends—and their scandals are among
the greatest stories Hollywood never told. This riveting, behind-
the-scenes account reveals the surprising truth about:

From the earliest days of silent films and the swinging era of the
Roaring Twenties, through the Golden Age of the studio system
and the patriotic call of WWII, to the Red Scare paranoia of the
McCarthy years, the history of the Schenck brothers is the story
of Hollywood itself—and the enduring power of the American
Dream. *Moguls* is a must-read for film fans, history buffs, and
anyone who loves the movies.

MOGULS

**The Lives and Times of Film Pioneers Nicholas
and Joseph Schenck**

Power, Scandal, Mob, Marilyn

MICHAEL BENSON and CRAIG SINGER

INTRODUCTION
Some Compelling Facts About the Schenck Brothers . . .

Joseph and Nicholas Schenck were the most powerful brothers in Hollywood history, more than twice as powerful as the Warner brothers. In fact, it has been estimated that the Schencks were the most powerful brothers in any industry. They held controlling interests in three major studios: Metro-Goldwyn-Mayer (MGM), Twentieth Century-Fox, and United Artists (UA). But chances are you've never heard of them because they preferred to run their global empire behind closed doors. Nick was Louis B. Mayer's *boss*.

  *They created the Motion Picture Academy and the Oscars.

  *They laid the cornerstone for the Hollywood studio system. They were the ones who painted the screen silver, creating a glorious world-changing product that is truly an American original. Like jazz.

  *Nick lived in a Gatsby-like mansion—thirty rooms, twenty acres—on Long Island's North Shore, was happily married to a former showgirl named Pansy, and took

a yacht to work each day, his office sitting atop the
Loew's State Theatre in Times Square. About Nick
Schenck, legendary director John Huston once said,
"Nick Schenck has been for decades the ruler of rulers.
He never gets his picture in the papers, and he doesn't go
to parties, and he avoids going out in public, but he is the
real king of the pack."

*Joe lived in a nine-bedroom, ten-bathroom Italian
Renaissance–style mansion known as Owlwood in the
enclave of Holmby Hills overlooking Sunset Boulevard.
It was there that, after a failed marriage to Norma
Talmadge, he lived the life of a swinging bachelor,
becoming in 1947 Marilyn Monroe's mentor and special
friend.

* For nineteenth-century Europeans, Joe and Nick were
large men. Joe grew to be five-nine, stocky and powerful, and Nick was five-ten, both looking down upon the
relatively diminutive men with whom they'd compete.

*While Joe was a genius at finding stars, Nick's forte was
location, location, location, and he oversaw real-estate
acquisition. Nick, as Marcus Loew's partner, helped create a mammoth theater chain, many of the venues extrav-
agant palaces like the Loew's Kings Theatre on Flatbush
Avenue in Brooklyn.

*Joe joined what is today known as the "mile-high club"
very early in aviation history. He and actress/singer Lili
Damita might not have been a mile up, but they were up.

*Joe did four months and five days in the fed pen for tax
evasion—one of his deductions involved a ménage à
trois—but was quickly released after allowing the USO
to use one of his houses in Palm Springs.

*Everyone thought MGM studio head Louis B. Mayer was a dictatorial leader, the boss of bosses, but those closest to him knew that he made no decisions without first "checking with New York," and that meant Nick.

*When silent-film star Roscoe "Fatty" Arbuckle was arrested for the alleged sex-crime death of a starlet, Joe paid his legal bills.

*Joe was silent-film legend Buster Keaton's first producer and best friend. If you took the star power of Adam Sandler, Will Ferrell, Seth Rogen, Kevin Hart, and Zach Galifianakis and put them into a blender, you still would not match the comic brilliance and influence of Buster Keaton. Not only was Keaton a major influence on the above-referenced celebrities, he completely changed physical comedy, and performed some of the most innovative and dangerous stunts all by himself—even more dangerous than many of the stunts Tom Cruise does with the benefit of modern rigging and technology. (Luckily for us, all of Keaton's feature films for Joe Schenck are on YouTube. Start with *The General*. You'll be amazed.) Keaton and Joe Schenck were lifelong friends. The men married sisters, film star Norma and her less-talented sister Natalie.

*Nick was a charter board member at Technicolor, Inc., a pioneer in color film.

*They helped turn back an attempted Nazi takeover of the industry during the mid-1930s and turned around an attempted shakedown by the Mob.

*While everyone else in Hollywood hired publicists to get their names in the papers, Nick hired a public relations specialist to keep his name out.

So, there you have it. Joe and Nick were great men. Flawed, of course, but great. This is a story about the early days of American cinema, with its heaping helpings of glamour and sleaze, stories of hungry immigrants who didn't just live the American Dream, they created a "dream factory." Joseph and Nicholas Schenck's story is a classic tale of rags to riches, arriving on the boat from Europe, surviving on the Lower East Side and then East Harlem, selling newspapers on a corner, working in a pharmacy, owning pharmacies, buying and operating amusement parks, booking vaudeville acts, managing theaters, producing pictures, running studios, and wielding incredible power.

Their story is also a history of the twentieth century in America: war, jazz, prohibition, sex, Great Depression, more war, organized crime, gambling, Red Scares, and blacklists. In its telling, you'll glimpse New York's Lower East Side at the turn of the twentieth century, Hollywood in its infancy, the swinging scandals of the 1920s, the lush fantasy of Hollywood's Depression period, the propaganda machine of the war years, and the paranoid malaise of the 1950s.

The Schencks were the Godfathers of the Moving Image. Their influence, and through them the influence of the cinema upon the twentieth century, cannot be overstated. From the earliest frantic days of flickering silents to the 1950s when TV invaded American living rooms, virtually every neighborhood in the country included its own picture show.

By the 1930s, there were only six major studios in Hollywood, all of which were integrated conglomerates that owned the talent and produced, distributed, and collected the tickets at their own theaters: MGM, Twentieth Century-Fox, Paramount, Columbia, Warner Brothers, and RKO. Disney and Universal were also players on a smaller scale. At one point the Schencks controlled about a third of the motion picture business, which was the fourth largest industry in America. Nick was the eighth richest man in the country and Joe wasn't far behind. Nick was head of more than one hundred corporations. (Nick was once asked, while under oath, to name every corporation he ran. He said, "Give me a break." He was the highest-paid theatrical manager in the world.)

Joe owned vast real estate in Arizona and California. With Jacob Paley, Joe owned the once gentile-only Del Mar Race Track and a resort in Lake Arrowhead. With Sid Grauman, he built and operated Hollywood Boulevard's plush Roosevelt Hotel. Joe controlled the Federal Trust and Savings Bank and was a major stockholder in the Bank of Italy, which became the Bank of America. Mega-publisher William Randolph Hearst liked to hang out with Joe because he felt Joe played in the same league. And Hearst knew few who did.

But the Brothers Schenck held power in a way not adequately measured in money or social prominence. They were Influential with a capital I. The *world* formulated its vision and opinion of the U.S. through their product. Joe wrote that Hollywood was twenty times more important than all the U.S. embassies around the world. American pictures globally dictated how people thought, what they did, how they dressed.

Even domestically their celluloid concoctions set a specific silvery social tone, a lifelike depiction of the America of our dreams, with strong nuclear families in which Father knew best, and a basic fairness to the world. Good guys won. Crime didn't pay.

And everyone did their best to fall in line. In 1941, a poll indicated that more than a third of Americans went to the picture shows at least once a week. Around the world, our collective imagination was taken by the hand and guided to a happy place by motion pictures.

Despite this A-list influence, the Schencks were largely unheralded outside of the industry. With so much power, they didn't require fame. As a young man, when he ran an amusement park, Nick had been a popular public figure—but as a film/theater mogul he became shy, living in luxury on Long Island with his faithful wife and talented kids. By all accounts domestic bliss. He succeeded in keeping his nest private. At work he was "The General," a man feared by an entire industry—at night he was Papa Bear.

Joe, through carelessness, became known in later years for his outrageous self-indulgences, in a gambling casino, with starlets on either arm. But a lot happened before Joe became Hollywood's number-one swinging bachelor mogul. He'd loved and married a woman who didn't love him back, an actress who married her producer for job security. Burned, Joe fell in love a second time, and again it was an actress using him. This one even had a "manager" who steered her from one powerful man to another. After that, Joe gave up on romance. That man with a starlet on either arm was heartbroken, occupied in an endless attempt to fill the inner void left by Norma Talmadge and Merle Oberon.

Like twin Citizens Kane with bookend Xanadus, the Schencks had the world of show business covered. Despite the physical distance between them, these giants remained close and were said to talk on the phone three times a day.

Though the Schencks worked as a team, they were not identical twins, and their differences came with entertaining ironies. Joe, the older, learned to speak English without an accent. Nick's Jewish-Russian accent hung on his entire life. Joe was a nonsmoker; Nick always had a Pall Mall between the fingers of his right hand. Nick, most agreed, was the good-looking one—yet he was the family man. Joe, to put it nicely, looked like he could be your tailor, stocky with heavy jowls, a blobby nose, and sparse hair—yet he was the "swinger." Joe was a people person and could spot star quality in a performer, yet it was Nick, who normally excelled in the dry world of real estate and board meetings, who had the penchant for show business and could even be a bit of a ham. If they bickered—and how could they not, being brothers?—they didn't do it in public, and everyone knew if you feared one, you'd better fear the other as well.

Acquaintance Howard Dietz once described Joe as "a philosopher who had a comic sense. He was not opinionated, and he gave good advice, such as, 'If four or five guys tell you that you're drunk, even though you know you haven't had anything to drink, the least you can do is lie down a little while.'"

Nick wanted others to see him as a simple man. He said his three greatest joys were being a dad, staying in shape, and going to the racetrack. Sam Marx, an MGM executive, told a story about Nick taking him on a walking tour of his waterfront Long Island estate on a Sunday morning. He showed Marx his chicken coop, where one chicken had been picked on by the others, bloodied and rendered featherless. Nick said, "Marx, you look at that and you realize that this is the way you must behave in the world . . . You must not let others pick you to pieces."

While Joe was generally beloved in Hollywood, Nick was feared and loathed (known as "Nick Skunk" behind his back). Stories of Nick's complete lack of sentimentality made the rounds. It was said Nick took out a million-dollar insurance policy on star Rudolph Valentino, and then, after Valentino died, refused to share the money with members of Valentino's family. Another story says that after the death of MGM executive Irving Thalberg, Nick made moves to limit compensation to Thalberg's widow, the MGM star Norma Shearer. Nick felt Thalberg already had too much money, a brilliant but whiny employee who against Nick's wishes had been given a piece of the pie.

Joe and Nick visited each other regularly. In later years, they flew, but back in the day they'd cross the country on the Chief, L.A. to Chicago, and the Twentieth Century Limited, Chicago to New York. Sometimes, at the train station, a small photo op was arranged. One time in 1932 Joe and Nick traveled west together and were met at the Pasadena train station by the boys from the press and a small gathering of UA and MGM top brass, which included Louis B. Mayer and Irving Thalberg appearing uncharacteristically subservient.

It is impossible to tell the story of Joe and Nick Schenck without excavating many of Hollywood's juiciest scandals and most important events, such as the:

lurid Fatty Arbuckle affair, in which the film star allegedly killed a woman in a hotel suite by puncturing her bladder, and Joe paid for his defense;

murder of Thelma Todd, mistress to both Joe's close friend director Roland West and alpha gangster Lucky Luciano;

formation of the Academy of Motion Picture Arts and Sciences and *invention* of the Oscars;

industry's panicky metamorphosis from silence to sound;

creation of the Agua Caliente Resort, Casino, and Racetrack (a stick in the eye of L.A.'s exclusive WASP-y country clubs);

Mob's attempted takeover of Hollywood;

plan of Hitler's to control Hollywood and transform it into a pro-Nazi propaganda machine;

prison sentence given to Joe Schenck for perjury;

birth of United Artists, MGM, and Twentieth Century-Fox;

Red Scare, commies in Hollywood, the Waldorf Conference, and the Schencks' role in the creation of the Hollywood blacklist;

warfare at MGM between Nick and Louis B. Mayer;

* of devil television; and the

strange "suicide" of TV's Superman, George Reeves.

This last item involved longtime Schenck enforcer Eddie Mannix, an iron-fisted Irishman who'd first faithfully worked for Nick as a youthful and enthusiastic bouncer during Nick's amusement-park days. Mannix and Howard Strickling (who'd been a publicist for Metro since 1919) became respectively general manager and publicity director at MGM. They were called "the fixers," and it was their job to smooth over anything that might put the studio in a bad light. They had, under their collective thumb, doctors, reporters, cops, DAs, judges, whatever it took. Gay performers were provided beards. In the case of untimely deaths, the fixers got to the scene before the police. Stars were kept out of jail, and names out of the paper. Among the suppressed scandals were the suspicious death of Jean Harlow's husband, Paul Bern; the murder of Ted Healy (creator of the Three Stooges) by actor Wallace Beery and others; the murder of comic actress Thelma Todd; Judy Garland's drug addiction; and Loretta Young's illegitimate baby fathered by a married Clark Gable.

Joe and Nick Schenck survived it all and, though "progress" stomped and kicked dirt on the fantasy worlds they created, they retired fabulously wealthy men. Theirs and the story of Hollywood are one and the same.

Looking at old-time Hollywood moguls, the first thing you notice is how similar they were. Such a small club with so much power. Jewish immigrants, driven out of Europe by anti-Semitism, who'd scraped their way up from poverty—not that they practiced their religion. In fact, their Jewishness was seldom discussed as they dedicated their energies to being all-Americans (i.e., Christian/secular) and no longer identified with their European birthplaces.

Nicholas Schenck was born in Russia but after he came over on the boat, he seldom returned to Europe. New York, and later Miami Beach, were all he needed. (Brother Joe was more adventurous, once sailing his own yacht from California to New York through the Panama Canal and regularly hitting European hot spots.)

Carl Laemmle, head of Universal Pictures, was born in Laupheim, Germany, and came to America when he was seventeen. In 1906 he purchased his first nickelodeon (a coin-operated machine that showed moving pictures). He invested in theaters, distribution, and production until his business became Universal Pictures. Universal City, opened in 1915, was at that time Hollywood's largest studio, and Laemmle is generally credited with being the first to use the "star system"—that is, recognize that customers were more apt to watch a picture if they already knew and liked the players.

William Fox (born Wilhelm Fuchs), who was the Fox in Joe Schenck's conglomerate Twentieth Century-Fox, was born in 1879 in Tulchva, Austria-Hungary. He started with one penny arcade, expanded to fifteen theaters, and eventually formed the Fox Film Corporation.

Adolph Zukor was born in 1873 in Ricse, Hungary. An orphan who spent his childhood unloved, a fact that left a void that could never be filled no matter how much power Zukor accrued. He came over on the boat at sixteen with $47 sewn inside his vest. As a kid, when he wasn't boxing or playing baseball, he had his nose in a dime novel, and those simple adventures with their strong sense of right and wrong, and clear delineation between hero and villain, became the basis for Zukor's contribution to motion pictures. A boyhood friend of Marcus Loew's, they met as cutting-and-sewing co-workers for a furrier. Zukor started his own furrier business, became wealthy quickly, and invested that money in nickelodeons, calling his flickers "Automatic Vaudeville." (Early films were called flickers because of primitive projection systems and the rapid alternation of light and dark frames in the film.) Zukor never lost his thick European accent or mastered English. He bought into a 125th Street arcade in Harlem to show flickers, and then built an arcade of his own downtown on 14th Street. This evolved into film production: *The Prisoner of Zenda*, and *Tess of the D'Urbervilles*. In 1914 he merged his company with that of theater producer Jesse L. Lasky to form Famous Players, which used a distribution company called Paramount. Zukor didn't like the terms he had with Paramount and by 1915 took over that company so that he was both making and distributing his own pictures—Paramount Pictures. His early partner was Cecil B. DeMille.

Samuel Goldwyn was born Shmuel Gelbfisz (Goldfish) in Warsaw, Poland. He married Jesse Lasky's sister, formed a series of smaller studios, one of which was Goldwyn Pictures, later to become the G in MGM. Goldwyn was known for his malaprops, a mangling of the English language worthy of Bowery Boy Slip Mahoney: "I'll give you a definite maybe." "I never liked you and I always will." "We're overpaying him, but he's worth it." "A verbal agreement isn't worth the paper it's written on."

Harry Cohn was born in 1891 in New York City—his parents came over on the boat—and started in the picture business as Carl Laemmle's secretary. In 1924 he formed Columbia Pictures.

Louis B. Mayer was born in 1885 in Minsk, Russia, and grew up in Canada. He worked for a brief period as a scrap metal dealer before switching to film exhibition and distribution. In 1924, when the big merger came, he became the second M in MGM, and managed the largest studio in history.

Lewis Selznick was born in Europe, in what is now Lithuania, although he later claimed to be from Ukraine. A former jewelry dealer, he came over on the boat at eighteen, and in 1914 organized the World Film Corporation to distribute independent pictures. He got along with Marcus Loew, hated Nick Schenck, and agreed to distribute, through his Select Pictures, Joe Schenck's first picture with Norma Talmadge. He wasn't well liked by anyone. By 1925, he'd gone out of business, stomped out by the big guys who liked his kid David but weren't sorry to see Lewis go.

The Warner brothers (Harry, born 1881; Albert 1884; Sam 1887 and Jack 1892) were very poor and came over from Poland in 1895. They started with one projector and a traveling tent show. By 1918 they were making their own pictures. Harry and Albert stayed in New York and handled finances; Jack and Sam moved to Burbank and supervised production.

So, demographically, the Schencks fit right in with this tiny group of ambitious men who would give birth to and control a world-changing industry.

Could we lower the lights please . . .